DOCUMENTS

CHIEFLY UNPUBLISHED,

RELATING TO THE

Huguenot Emigration

TO VIRGINIA

AND TO THE

SETTLEMENT AT MANAKIN-TOWN,

WITH AN

APPENDIX OF GENEALOGIES,

PRESENTING DATA OF THE

FONTAINE, MAURY, DUPUY, TRABUE, MARYE, CHASTAIN, COCKE, AND OTHER FAMILIES,

EDITED AND COMPILED FOR THE

Virginia Historical Society

BY

R. A. BROCK,

To Which is Added

Communication from Governor Francis Nicholson Concerning the Huguenot Settlements with "List of Refugees," 1700.

Southern Historical Press, Inc.
Greenville, South Carolina

This volume was reproduced
from a personal copy located in
the Publishers private library

Please direct all correspondence and book orders to:
SOUTHERN HISTORICAL PRESS, Inc.
PO Box 1267
Greenville, SC 29602-1267

Originally printed: Richmond, VA. 1886
ISBN #978-1-63914-148-7
Printed in the United States of America

INTRODUCTION.

The history of the religious persecution of the Huguenots in France, from the massacre of St. Bartholomew to the infamous outrages which preceded and followed the Revocation of the Edict of Nantes, is so familiar, through frequent graphic narrative, that any attempt at repetition here would be quite unnecessary, were the means to be employed adequate. But recently this topic has been ably considered, and a comprehensive narrative of the establishment of the fugitive Protestants in the New World presented as well.[a] An unpretentious assembling of scattered data relating to the Huguenot settlement in Virginia, and of families of the lineage, happily to serve as material in abler hands in the future, may only be essayed by the present editor.

Desultory Walloon emigration to Virginia early in the seventeenth century is indicated by names of record in the State Land Registry; and the Walloons of Leyden, planning to follow the example of their Puritan neighbors, the Pilgrim Fathers of New England, presented, July 21, 1621, to Sir Dudley Carleton, the British Ambassador at the Hague, a petition signed by fifty-six heads of families, Walloon and French, all of the Reformed Religion, who desired to come to Virginia. The answer of the Council of the Virginia Company, though not

---

a The excellent works of two learned brothers: *History of the Rise of the Huguenots in France*, by Professor Henry M. Baird, 2 vols., 8vo., (to be followed by two uniform volumes on *The Huguenots and Henry IV*, and it is hoped by others, covering the period of struggle and suffering down to the Edict of Toleration), and *History of the Huguenot Emigration to America*, by Charles W. Baird, D. D., 2 vols., 8vo.

altogether adverse, appears to have been not sufficiently encouraging, as the correspondence went no further. Eight years later, in June, 1629, a similar application was made to the English Government, by Antoine de Ridouet, Baron de Seance, in behalf of a body of French Protestants, asking for encouragement to settle in Virginia. His proposal was favorably entertained. The emigrants destined for Carolina, landed in Virginia, but the colony maintained a languid existence for a few years only.[b] An act styled "Concerning Denizations," giving encouragement to foreign settlers, was passed by the Colonial Assembly in March, 1657 [1658]. It provides that "all aliens and strangers who have inhabited the country the space of ffower yeeres, and have a firme resolution to make this country their place of residence, shall be free denisons of this collony." etc.[c]

In March, 1659 [1660], and October, 1660, acts of naturalization in favor of John Johnson, millwright, being a Dutchman; and of Nicholas Boate, severally, were passed.[d] An act passed September, 1671, allowed "any stranger * * upon petition to the grand Assembly, and taking the oaths of allegiance and supremacy to his Majesty" to be naturalized, and "be capable of office, traffique, and trading, of taking up, purchasing, conveying, devising and inheriting of lands," etc.[e] Under this act, patents of naturalization were granted by the Assembly, in September, 1673, to Joshua Mulder, Henry Weedick, Christopher Regault, Henry ffayson Vandoverage, John Mattoone, Dominick Theriate, Jeremy Packquitt, Nicholas Cock, Henry Waggamore, and Thomas Harmenson, aliens; in October, 1673, to John Peterson, Rowland Anderson, Michaell Valandigam, Minor Doodes, Doodes Minor,[f] and Herman Kelderman, aliens; in March, 1675 [1676], to Christian Peterson; in February, 1676 [1677], to Garratt Johnson, and in April, 1679, to Abraham

---

b Baird, C. W., I, pp. 163-5.

c Hening's Statutes at Large, I, p. 486.

d Ibid., I, p. 545; II, p. 16.

e Ibid., II, 289-90.

f Said to have been born in Holland in 1644; *m.* in Virginia —— Garrett, and had issue, four sons: William, Minor, Peter and Garrett: progenitors of the Minors of Virginia, and the Southern and Western States.

Vincler, John Michaell, Jacob Johnson, John Pimmitt and John Keeton.[g]

Refuge in Great Britain was sought by the Huguenots early in the sixteenth century, and in the latter decades of that cycle, emigration thither steadily increasing, had contributed immensely to the constituent population and useful citizenry of England, Scotland, Ireland and Wales, comprising all ranks, from the peasant to the noble—artisans, cloth-makers, lace-makers, silk-weavers, glass-makers, printers and manufacturers. Their skill, industry, and worth speedily secured recognition and consequent prosperity, and there is scarce a branch of literature, science and art in which they have not distinguished themselves. Their descendants may still, at this day, be numerously, and in honorable station, identified by name, though the family designations of by far the greater number have long since been completely Anglicized and ceased to be thus traceable. Between the years 1599 and 1753, there were established in the city of London alone no less than twenty-eight French churches.[h]

Following the Revocation of the Edict of Nantes, which was signed on the 18th and published on the 22d of October, 1685, the exodus thither was immense. "It was reserved," pungently remarked President John Jay, in his Introductory Address before the Huguenot Society of America at New York, October 22, 1885 (having previously referred to the Massacre of St. Bartholomew in 1572), "for that most Christian and grand monarch, Louis XIV, more than a century later, to renew the persecution of the Huguenots by a crime of similar magnitude; and with folly without a parallel, to lose for France, by means similarly atrocious, hundreds of thousands of those same heretics, who carried industry, intelligence and prosperity, light, truth and happiness to other lands, including our own. Of the number lost to France, Sismondi computes the total number of emigrants at from 300,000 to 400,000; and thinks that an equal number perished in prison, on the scaffold, at the galleys, or in their attempts to escape.

"So far as a moral estimate of the act is concerned, it has been well remarked that the revocation stands at so indefinite a height

---

g Hening's Statutes at Large, pp. 302, 308, 339, 400, 447.

h Smiles' Huguenots, pp. 368–9.

among the follies of statesmen that no exaggeration of facts can aggravate it.''[i] The significant fact in requital, has been published that eighty-nine descendants of the Huguenots, who were banished from France by the Revocation, returned in 1870 as officers of the invading German army.

Of the army of William of Orange, numbering eleven thousand, which sailed from Holland, and by whose aid he obtained the Crown of England, three regiments, each containing seven hundred and fifty effective men, were Huguenots. To these were added a squadron of horse. There were also about seven hundred officers distributed among the other battalions of the army. In gratitude to these zealous and effective supporters, and in sympathy with the great multitude of their suffering brethren driven violently from their homes and native country simply for their religion, the king invited them to make their home in his new dominions.

Many of such refugees soon turned their eyes to America and sought a home in Virginia. Many families took their residence along the Potomac, Rappahannock and James rivers.[j]

The expenses of transportation to America was usually borne by the Relief Committee in London. In fact, no small part of the Royal bounty—the English people's bounty—went to pay for the passage of the refugees across the ocean.

In the year 1700, as enumerated in the documents herewith presented, more than five hundred emigrants, at the head of whom was the Marquis de la Muce, were landed in Virginia by four successive debarkations.[k] Three ministers of the Gospel, and two physicians were among the number. The ministers are Claude Phillipe de Richebourg, Benjamin de Joux,[l] and Louis Latané. The physicians were Castaing [Chastain ?] and La Sosee.

---

i Commemoration of the Bi-Centenary of the Revocation of the Edict of Nantes, October 22, 1885, at New York, p. 9.

j Foote's Huguenots, p. 521.

k The number is stated by other authorities to have been more than 700. *Beverley's History of Virginia*, edition of 1722, p. 244. *Baird, C. W.*, II, p. 177.

l He died prior to April 1, 1703 [1704], as an inventory of his effects is of record of that date in Henrico County Court.

Preparations for this important movement had long been on foot, and more than once its destination had been changed. Two years before the date of the embarkation, negotiations were opened by the leaders of the body with Dr. Daniel Coxe, "proprietary of Carolana and Florida," for the purchase of half a million acres of land in the latter territory. The tract in question was situated near Appalachee Bay, and the purchasers were to have the privilege of an additional half million of acres at the nominal rent of "a ripe Ear of Indian Corne in the season" for the first seven years. At another time Carolina was the objective point of the expedition. A third site suggested for the settlement was in Norfolk county, Virginia, on the Nansemond river, in the neighborhood of the Dismal Swamp.[m] They appear to have settled at different points; a portion about Jamestown, some in Norfolk county, others in Surry, and two hundred or more at a spot some twenty miles above Richmond, on the south side of James river (now in Powhatan county), where ten thousand acres of land, which had been occupied by the extinct Manakin[n] tribe of Indians, were given them. They were also exempted from the payment of all taxes for seven years, and were allowed to support their minister in their own way. Accordingly, in dividing the grant into farms, all running down to the river in narrow slips, a portion of the most valuable was set apart for the minister, and was thus possessed and used whilst one resided in the parish. It was afterwards rented out, and the proceeds paid for such occasional services as were rendered by neighboring ministers. Bishop Meade[o] states, 1857, that services were then regularly held in the old church at Manakin-Town settlement.

According to Beverley, the emigrants, in 1702, "began an Essay of Wine, which they made of the wild grapes gathered in the woods; the effect of which was a strong-bodied Claret, of good flavour."[p] The interesting fact is exhibited in the docu-

---

m *Baird, C. W.*, II, pages 176–8.

n Monacan, in the Indian dialect—a warlike tribe, who resided from the Falls of James river to "Monocan-Town," and whom Powhatan in vain attempted to subdue.

o *Old Churches and Families*, I, page 466.

p *History of Virginia*, edition of 1722, page 245.

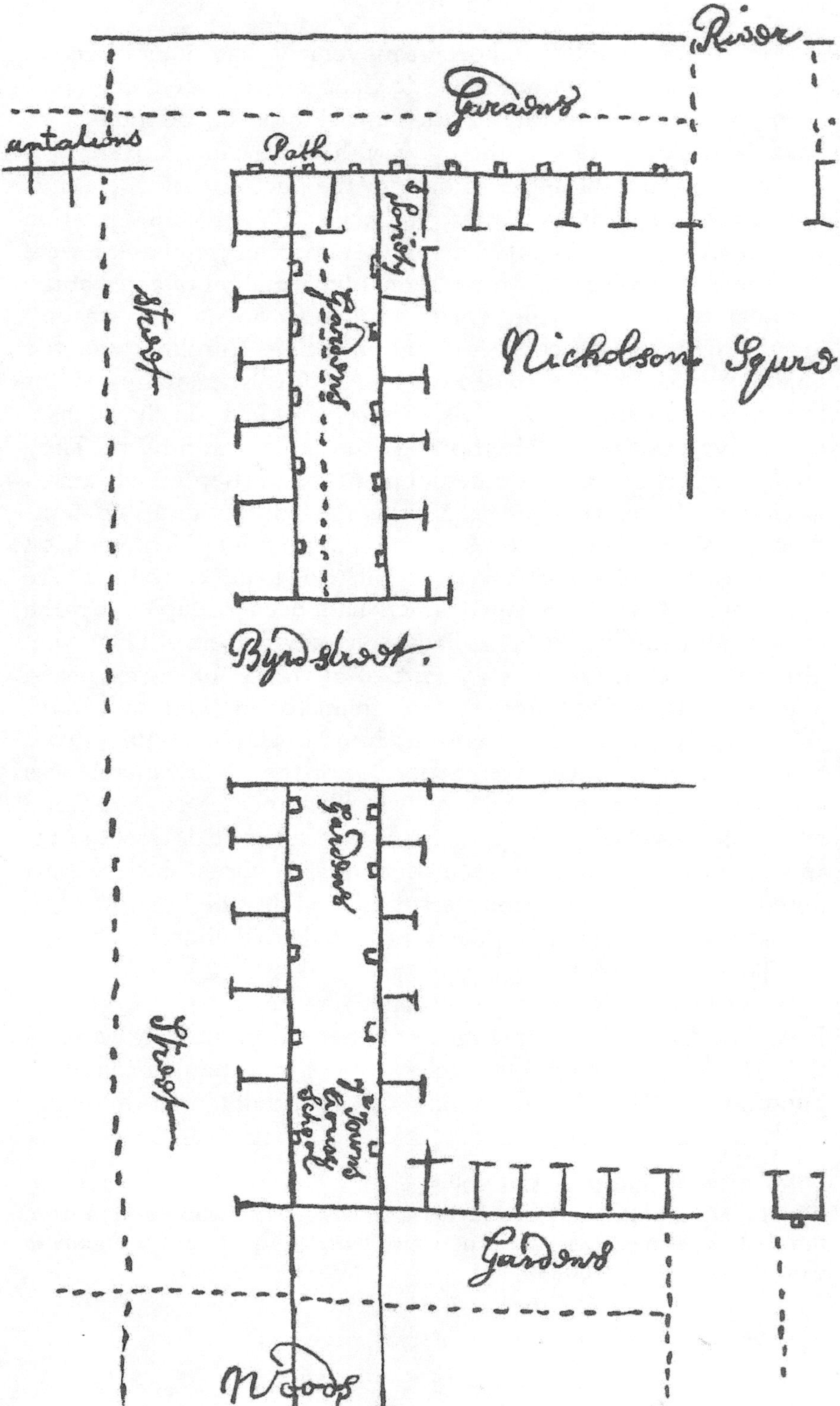
River
Gardens
Path
Gardens
Street
Nicholson Square
Byrd street.
Gardens
Street
Gardens
Woods

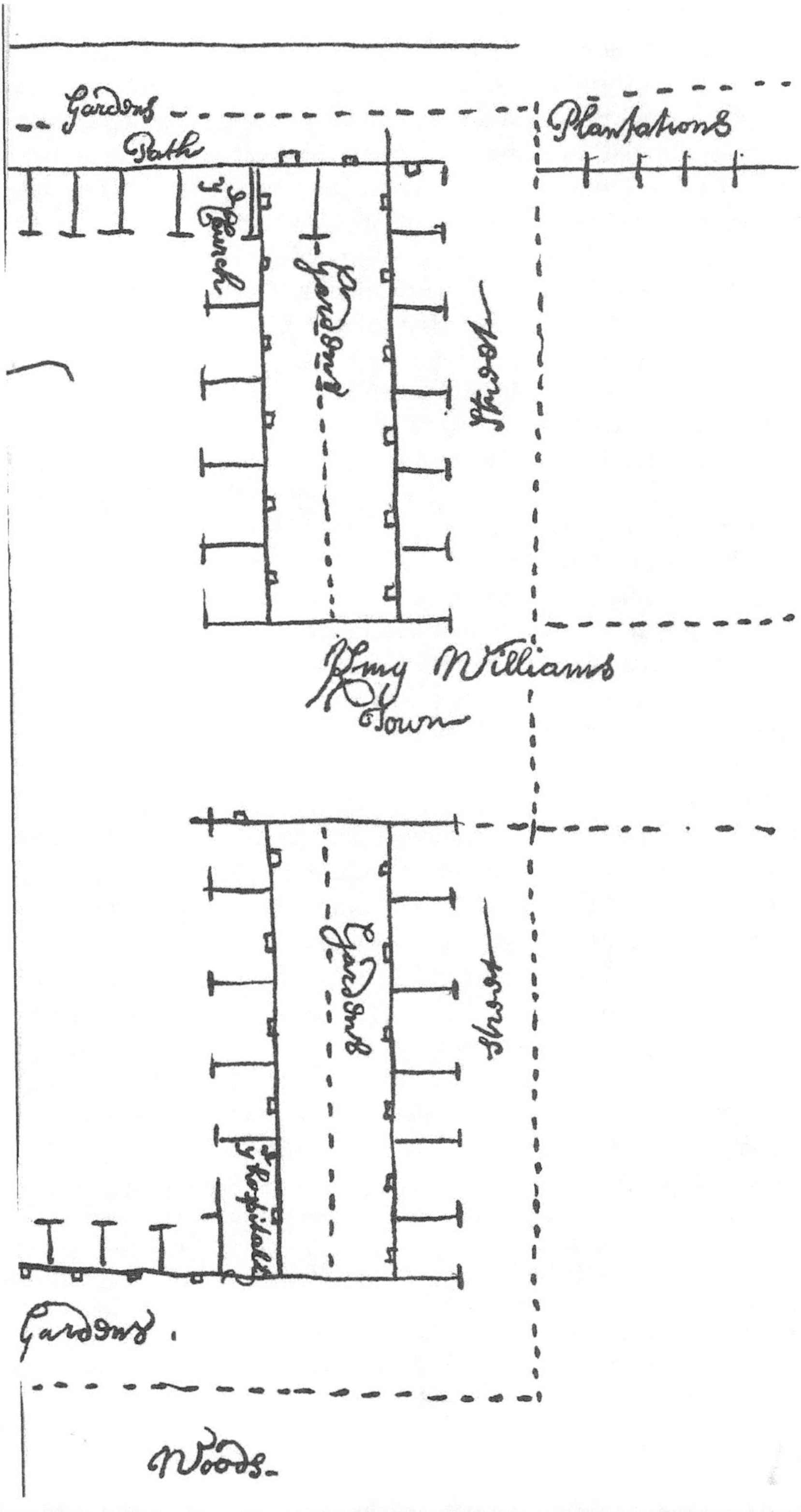

Gardens
Path
Plantations
y^e Church
Gardens
Street
King Williams Town
Gardens
Street
y^e Hospitall
Gardens.
Woods.

ments presented herewith (page 43), that the discovery of bituminous coal in Virginia was near the Manakin-Town settlement early in 1701. This deposit, subsequently known as the Dover Mines, it is alleged, was the first mined in Virginia. It is believed that bituminous coal was not to any extent used as a fuel in the State until after the Revolution, and then for a considerable period only for the heating of residences.[q] The Dover Mines were last operated in 1870 under the management of General Charles P. Stone, formerly of the United States Army, and late of the staff of the Khedive of Egypt.

Among the names which have been preserved of the ministers who served the parish of King William regularly, or occasionally, were the following: Benjamin de Joux, until his death in 1704; Claude Phillipe de Richbourg, removed to Carolina in 1707; Jean Cairon, died in 1716; Peter Fontaine, 1720, 1721; Francis Fontaine, 1722–24; William Finney, 1722, and probably later; William Murdaugh, of St. James'-Northam, Goochland, and Zachariah Brooke, of Hanover county, in 1727; Mr. Nearne, or Neirn, 1727, 1728; David Mossom, of St. Peter's parish, New Kent county, 1727; Mr. Swift and Daniel Taylor, of Blissland parish, New Kent county, in 1728 and 1729; James Marye, 1731–1735; Anthony Gavain, 1739. From 1750 to 1780, the Rev. William Douglass,[r] of Goochland; and other neighboring ministers occasionally served it. Subsequently the Rev. Mr. Hopkins, of Goochland, was the minister.

It is exhibited that there were numerous instances of individual settlement of French Huguenots in Virginia prior and subsequent to the influx of 1700. The names of Barraud, Bertrand,[s] Boisseau[t], Bowdoin,[u] Cazenove, Contesse, Cottrell,[v] For-

---

q It has been asserted that there were shipments to Philadelphia, Pennsylvania, for manufacturing purposes, prior to the Revolution.

r An early tutor of Thomas Jefferson.

s "John and Paul Bertrand, brothers, fled from France during the persecutions of Louis XIV; came over to England, and from thence to America. They were both clerks in the Church of England. John Bertrand, the eldest, settled in Rappahannock county, Virginia, having married in London, 29th September, 1686, Charlotte Jolié, the daughter of a French nobleman, with whom he had escaped from France. John Bertrand left issue two children. William, the elder, who died in 1760, left issue an only daughter, Mary Anne, the wife of Leroy Griffin, of

loines, Flournoy,[w] Fuqua, Ghiselin, Jacquelin, Jouet,[x] Lacy, Mauzy, Michie, Micou, Moncure, Seay,[y] Trezevant[z] and others, have been most estimably represented.

Rappahannock county. They were the parents of Thomas Bertrand, Dr. Corbin, Cyrus and William Griffin. [There was a daughter, also, Elizabeth, who married Colonel Richard Adams, the elder, of Richmond, Virginia.]

"Paul Bertrand settled in Calvert county, Maryland, on a farm purchased by him called 'Cox Hayes,' west of Patuxent river. He died soon after his marriage, leaving a widow and one son—Paul. They went to London, where the son married Mary, daughter of one Dearling, a very eminent Toyman of London; settled at Bath, and died without issue about 1755. This widow was alive in 1766."

The tradition in the Griffin family is, that it is of Welsh extraction. There are grants of 1,155 and 1,046 acres of land to Samuel Griffin, in Rappahannock county, in 1660, and of 1,000 acres to William Griffin, in Northampton county, in 1662, of record in the Virginia Land Registry.

As the names Samuel and William have been transmitted by the descendants of Leroy Griffin for generations, it may be presumed that one of the brothers, grantees of land as named, was his ancestor.

His son, Cyrus, born 1749, was educated in England. Returning to Virginia, he became a member of the Legislature, delegate to the Continental Congress—1778, 1781, and in 1787, 1788—and was its President in 1788; President of the Supreme Court of Admiralty; a Commissioner, in 1789, to the Creek Nation of Indians; Judge of the United States District Court for Virginia from 1789 till his death at Yorktown, Virginia, 14th December, 1840. He married Lady Christine Stuart, daughter of John, sixth Earl of Traquar, Baron Stuart of Traquar, Baron Linton and Cubarston in the peerage of Scotland. Mary, the daughter of Judge Cyrus and Lady Christine (Stuart) Griffin, married her cousin, Dr. Samuel Stuart Griffin. Their son, Dr. James Lewis Corbin Griffin, who died 22d October, 1878, in his 64th year, at "Lansdowne," Gloucester county, claimed to be the rightful representative of the Barony of Traquar, etc.

t The progenitor of the family, Rev. James Boisseau, served as a minister in the Colony prior to 1697. *Perry's Church Papers of Virginia*, 34.

u Pierre Bowdoin first settled in Ireland; then, with his wife and four children, emigrated to Casco, Maine. He was godfather to Peter Fanueil, the donor of Fanueil Hall, Boston. A daughter married a Temple, and was thus an ancestress of Hon. Robert C. Winthrop. A son, James Bowdoin, was the friend and compatriot of Washington and Franklin. Another son, John Bowdoin, removed to the Eastern shore

The family, De Cazenove (or De Castionovo, which is the original orthography of the name), was an old and respectable one in the south of France. The name and history began with a knight, who, in the year 993, added the name to his baptismal appellation, adopted a "new castle" as his coat-of-arms and styled himself Sieur Cazenove. Several knights of the name engaged in the crusades. During the reign of Henry IV, Guilliame De Cazenove was entitled Admiral. But during the reli-

---

of Virginia about 1700. His granddaughter was the wife of Professor George Tucker, of the University of Virginia. Pierre Bowdoin was a Burgess from Northumberland county in 1736, and John Bowdoin, in 1774 and 1775; died 1775. Preeson Bowdoin was a member of the Phi-Beta-Kappa Society of William and Mary College in 1776. John Bowdoin was a member of the House of Delegates from Northumberland county in 1778.

v Charles Cottrell patented 123 acres of land in Goochland county, August 28, 1748. Susanna Cottrell and Howard Cash, Executors of Thomas Cottrell, deceased, patented 700 acres in Amherst county, August 30th, 1763. *Virginia Land Registry.*

w There are various grants of land of record in the Virginia Land Registry to Jacob, John James, and Francis Flournoy. Thomas Stanhope Flournoy was a member of Congress from Virginia, 1847–1849; Whig candidate for Governor in 1860, and member of the Virginia Convention, 1860–'1. Hon. Henry W. Flournoy is the present Secretary of the Commonwealth of Virginia.

x Matthew Jouett patented large tracts of land in Hanover in 1732. Thomas Jouett patented lands in Albemarle in 1752. Captain Jack Jouet, by hard riding in May, 1781, apprised the fugitive Legislature, then sitting at Charlottesville, Virginia, of the approach of the British under Tarleton, and thus prevented their capture. The service was acknowledged by a resolution of thanks, passed June 12, 1781, and the presentation of an elegant sword and a pair of pistols. Captain Matthew Jouett, of the State Line in the Revolution, fell in the service, and his representative received 4,000 acres of bounty land. A son of Captain Jack Jouett, the late Matthew Jouett, of Louisville, Kentucky, is said to have rivalled in ability Gilbert Stuart as a portrait painter. It is claimed that the name was originally De Jouet.

y Originally Saye.

z James Trezevant was member of Congress from Virginia, 1825–1831, and a member of the Virginia Convention of 1829–30. The Trezevants were from the northern part of the province of Maine. *Baird,* II, pages 97, 98.

gious troubles, from the time of the Reformation to the Revocation of the Edict of Nantes, the Cazenoves became impoverished. Some of them fled to Switzerland. Paul Cazenove married Marie Plantamore, of Noyons, and his three sons were admitted citizens of Geneva. Jean, the eldest son of Pierre Cazenove, married Elizabeth, daughter of Jacob Bressonnet, Doctor of Theology and president of the Consistory. Paul Cazenove, the son of Jean, was so unfortunate as to live in the days of the French Revolution, and he and his two sons, Jean Antoine and Antoine Charles, were imprisoned with several of the Genevese aristocracy, and his wife was kept under guard at Mont Brilliant, a beautiful country seat on the banks of lake Geneva. They were tried before the Revolutionary tribunal and were condemned to death. But, fortunately, just at this time Robespierre was overthrown and the work of death was stayed. Being obnoxious to the Jacobins (both having been educated at the military school of Calmar, in Germany), the two brothers, in company with Albert Gallatin, sailed to this country to await more quiet times, for Jean had been a military instructor and leader of the aristocracy, and Charles had once held a commission in the unfortunate Swiss body-guard of Louis XVI. The brothers married in this country, sisters, the daughters of Edmond Hagan, a political refugee from Ireland. When the troubles in Europe were stilled, Jean returned to Geneva and died, leaving no male issue. Antoine Charles took up his residence about the year 1799 in Alexandria, Virginia, where, as a commission merchant and a polished Christian gentleman, he passed a long life, highly respected. His descendents are numerous and widely scattered from Massachusetts to Georgia. Another branch of the family settled in Holland. A descendant, Theophile Cazenove, Dutch minister to the United States, led over a colony of Hollanders to Central New York, which settled in and around the town, Cazenove. Still another branch of the family returned from Geneva to France and its representatives now reside in Lyons. Raoul De Cazenove is the head.[aa]

Dr. Louis Contesse lived and practiced his profession in Williamsburg, Virginia, during the first quarter of the eighteenth century. Neither the date of his emigration, nor the definite

---

aa Foote, pp, 574, 577.

place of his birth in France have been transmitted.[bb] He patented, August 12, 1725, two tracts of land of 400 acres each on the south side of James river in Henrico county. The first is described as lying near the land of John Lavillain, and the second as being bounded by the lands of Francis and John James fflorenoy (Flournoy).[cc]

His only daughter, Anne Contesse, married John Tyler, Marshall of the Court of Vice-Admiralty of Virginia. Her son, John Tyler, the father of President John Tyler, was born February 28, 1747, and died January 6, 1813. He was successively Speaker of the House of Delegates, Judge of the General Court, Governor of the State, and Judge of the United States District Court for Virginia. The name, Contesse, survives only as a Christian appellation in Virginia, but the lineage is represented in the names of Tyler, Seawell, Bouldin, Greenhow, and others similarly esteemed.

Edward Jaquelin or Jacquelin, son of John and Elizabeth (Craddock) Jaquelin, of county Kent, England, and a descendant of a Protestant refugee from La Vendee, France, during the reign of Charles IX, of the same lineage as the noble family of La Roche Jaqueline, came to Virginia in 1697, settled at Jamestown, married Miss Cary, of Warwick county, and died in 1730, leaving issue three sons (Edward, the eldest)—neither of whom married—and three daughters : Elizabeth, who married Richard Ambler ; Mary, who married John Smith, who is believed to have been a member of the House of Burgesses, of the Council, and of the Board of Visitors of William and Mary College; Martha, who died unmarried in 1804, aged 93 years. Edward Jaquelin " died as he had lived, one of the most wealthy men in the colony."

Richard Ambler, son of John Ambler, sheriff of county York, England, in 1721, migrated to Virginia early in the eighteenth

---

bb Marie Contesse married, March 10th, 1705, in the French Church in New York, Jacques Rezian de St. Martin en Ré. *Baird, C. W.*, II, p. 305. Jean Contesse, of Rouen, in Champagne, was received into the French Church in London, September 10, 1699. He had a wife, Judith, and three children. Jean Moyse Contesse was in New York in 1705 and in New Rochelle, New York, in 1709.

cc Virginia Land Registry, Book No. 12, pp. 323, 324.

century, settled at Yorktown, married Elizabeth Jaquelin and had issue nine children, all of whom died at early age, except three sons: Edward, collector of the port of York, married and left issue. He was a man of consideration in the colony, and when Lord Botetourt came over as Governor, he brought a letter of introduction to him from Samuel Athawes, merchant, London.[dd] John, born December 31st, 1735, Burgess from Jamestown, and Collector of the District of York River, died May 27, 1766, in Barbadoes. Jaquelin, born August 9, 1742; married Rebecca, daughter of Lewis Burwell, of "White Marsh," Gloucester county, member of the Virginia Council during the Revolution and long State Treasurer. He left issue: Eliza, married first, William Brent of Stafford county, and secondly, Colonel Edward Carrington, of the Revolution, and member of Congress (no issue). Mary Willis married Chief Justice John Marshall. Anne married George Fisher, of Richmond. Lucy married Daniel Call, lawyer and legal reporter, Richmond. Upon the tomb of John Ambler, of Jamestown, Virginia (born September 25th, 1762, died September 8th, 1836), in Shockoe Hill Cemetery, Richmond, Virginia, the Ambler and Jaquelin arms are quartered. Ambler—*Sa. on a fesse, or. between three pheons, ar. a lion passant guardant, gu.* Jaquelin—*On a bend, three roses.* Crest—*Two dexter hands conjoined sustaining a mural crown.* The descendants of Edward Jaquelin and Richard Ambler have intermarried with the families of Baylor, Byrd, Carter, Nicholas, Norton, Randolph, Wickham, and others of prominence.[ee]

William Lacy, a grandson of the emigrant ancestor of the family in Virginia, with his wife, Elizabeth, appear to have been residents of King William parish in 1741. In that year a son, David, was born to them, and in 1743, another son, Henry. According to Foote (p. 582), William Lacy and his wife, "Catherine Rice," removed to Chesterfield county, where their son Drury, with a twin sister, was born October 5th, 1758. An acci-

---

dd See *Virginia Historical Register*, III, 1850, pp. 25, 26.

ee Meade's Old Churches and Families of Virginia, I, p. 97, *et seq*, gives much information regarding the Amblers and Jaquelins of Virginia.

dent in childhood, the explosion of a musket, by which he lost his left hand decided the future course of the life of Drury Lacy, and induced him to strive to obtain an education to fit himself for a teacher or some profession. While engaged in teaching in a private family, he came under the notice of Rev. John B. Smith, President of Hampden Sydney College, by whom he was encouraged and assisted in completing a classical education. He became a minister of the Gospel; and was for years Vice-President of the college at which he had been educated. He possessed marked powers of oratory. He could lift up his voice like a trumpet, and its silvery notes fell sweetly upon the ears of the most distant auditors in large congregations, wherever assembled, in houses or in the open air. A silver finger affixed to the wrist of his shattered hand gave him the name of the "silver hand."

The Church remembers him as Lacy of the "silver hand and silver voice." He married a Miss Smith, and reared three sons and two daughters. Two of the sons became ministers of the Gospel. The eldest, William Smith Lacy, preached for a time as a missionary, and then became pioneer of the Church in Arkansas. The youngest, Drury, was pastor for some time in Raleigh, North Carolina; then served as President of Davidson College; and subsequently as chaplain in the State hospitals. The third son became a physician. Each of the sons reared a son for the ministry. Of these, one, the Rev. B. T. Lacy, was the chosen chaplain of General T. J. Jackson, Confederate States Army, and another was a chaplain in the Army of Northern Virginia. Two grandsons entered the army; one died in Petersburg from disease brought on by exposure; and the other, Major J. Horace Lacy, saw much active service.

The two daughters each married Presbyterian ministers. The elder became the wife of Samuel Davies Hoge. the son of Rev. Moses Hoge, D. D., Professor of Theology of the Virginia Synod. Her two sons entered the ministry. The elder is the distinguished pulpit orator, Rev. Moses Drury Hoge, D. D., pastor of the second Presbyterian Church, Richmond, Virginia. The younger son, Rev. William James Hoge. D. D., died in 1864, pastor of the Tabb Street Church, Petersburg, Virginia. The youngest daughter married Rev. James H. Brookes, and reared one son for the ministry, who is now pastor of a church in St. Louis, Missouri.

Henry Mauzy fled from France in 1685, emigrated to Virginia and settled in Fauquier county. He married, probably in England, a daughter of a Dr. Conyers. Their son, John Mauzy, married Hester Foote, grand-aunt of Hon. Henry S. Foote, of the United States and Confederate States Congresses and Governor of Mississippi. Another son, Henry Mauzy, born 1721, married Elizabeth Taylor, born 1735. He died in 1804, and she in 1829. They left issue, among other children, the following sons and daughters: John, Thomas, Richard, Michael, and the late Colonel Joseph Mauzy, of Rockingham county, whose son Richard is the editor of the *Staunton Spectator*. Susannah, one of the daughters, born 1765, married Charles Kemper, born 1756. She died in 1843; and he in 1841.[ff]

Paul Micou was a fugitive from Nantes. After some years of exile, probably in England, he emigrated to Virginia, and settled in Essex county. He had been educated for the bar, and was a man of great and acknowledged worth. He served as a justice of the peace from 1700 to 1720. He died May 23, 1736; aged seventy-eight years. A son, Paul Micou, Jr., served also as justice of the peace for Essex, 1740-1760, and a grandson of the same name, for the period 1780–1800. One of his daughters married Rev. J. W. Giborne, of Lunenburgh parish, Richmond county.

Another daughter, Judith Micou, married Lunsford Lomax. His son, Major Thomas Lomax, was the father of Judge John Tayloe Lomax, so long and favorably known in the Virginia courts. Another daughter married Moore Fauntleroy, whose ancestor, Lieutenant-Colonel Moore Fauntleroy, was a patentee of lands in New Norfolk county in 1643. A descendant in the present generation of Paul Micou, the venerable James Roy Micou, has served as clerk of Essex for quite a half century. Another descendant, Mr. A. R. Micou, formerly editor of the *Tidewater Index*, is the present State Superintendent of Public Printing. Rev. John Moncure, the progenitor of the worthy family of the name, was of Huguenot descent. One of his

---

ff *Foote*, pp. 578, 579.

daughters, Jean, who possessed the poetic gift, was a highly intelligent lady, zealously pious, and abounding in philanthropy; was the wife of General James Wood, Governor of Virginia. Another honored descendant was the late learned and guileless Judge, Richard C. L. Moncure, of the Court of Appeals of Virginia.

TABLE OF CONTENTS.

APPENDIX OF GENEALOGIES.

ERRATA AND CORRIGENDA.

Page 129. For Confederary read Confederacy.

" 52. " Charles V " Charles I.

" 152. " Louis IV " Louis XIV.

" 155. "*Saunders*" should be Saunders.

' 165. For Issue of Mary and —— (Dupuy) Dickinson read Issue of L. and Mary (Dupuy) Dickinson.

" 176. For Issue of —— and Sallie (Dupuy) Thomason read Issue of Poindexter and Sallie (Dupuy) Thomason.

" 187. John Lawrence Marye is stated to have "graduated A. B. and B. L. University of Virginia,' an error into which the editor was led by genealogic data supplied him, prepared by James Theodosius Marye in 1858. Hon. J. L. Marye graduated in 1840–'42 in the schools equivalent to those now required for the degree A. B., but at that period such degree was not awarded by the University of Virginia. The law studies of Mr. Marye were pursued in Fredericksburg, Va.

DOCUMENTS

RELATING TO THE

Huguenot Emigration

TO VIRGINIA.

A DECLARATION OF THE OPINION OF THE FRENCH MINISTERS, WHO ARE NOW REFUGEES IN ENGLAND, ABOUT SOME POINTS OF RELIGION, IN OPPOSITION TO THE SOCINIANS.[1]

We under written, the Refugees, *French* Ministers in England, having understood by a Letter which my Lord, the Bishop of *London*, who at present is in *Holland*, hath writ to Monsieur le Coq, Counsellor in the Parliament of Paris, and an Illustrious Confessor of the Truth, the strange Reports that have been spread, as if we were not found in the Faith, and particularly with relation to the Doctrine of the Holy *Trinity*, and Grace, and the need there is to dissipate the same; and being moreover perswaded that by this Explication of our Belief we shall perform a thing that will serve for the Edification and Consolation of our Brethren, and will have its fruit, if the Lord please, especially in the Land of our Nativity, after some Amicable and Brotherly Conferences we have had upon this matter, in the

---

[1] Appended to *Two Discourses on the Divinity of our Saviour*, small 4to; London, 1693, (a copy of which, bound with other religious tracts of the period, is in the possession of the Editor), by Charles G. Lamothe, who was the author also of *Inspiration of the New Testament Asserted and Explained*. 8vo; London, 1694.

presence of Monsieur le Coq, we have all of us agreed to declare, as we do in the Sincerity of our Hearts:

I. That we Believe the whole Scripture Divinely Inspir'd, so that all Men are obliged to receive everything therein Revealed with an entire Submission of Faith.

II. That we receive with Reverence and Submission whatsoever the Scripture teacheth concerning the *Nature of God* and his *Attributes*, of his *Spirituality*, *Infinitiveness*, *Incomprehensibility*, *Prescience*, even of *Future Contingencies*, and of all others, the said Scripture attributes to him.

III. That we Believe also what it delivers concerning the *Trinity of Persons* in one only *Divine Essence*, and concerning the *Incarnation of the Son*, according as the said Articles are set down in the VI, XIV, and XV of the Confession of Faith of the Reformed Churches of *France*.

IV. That we hold also as an Article of our Faith, That *Jesus Christ, by dying on the Cross*, hath not only left us an Example that we should follow his Footsteps, but moreover, that his Principal Design therein was to satisfie the Divine Justice for us in bearing the Punishment of our Sins, as he actually did.

V. That we detest the Opinions of Socinus, and of all others that are contrary to the forementioned Truths; not considering them as Innocent Opinions, or Tolerable Errors, but as Heresies which absolutely overturn the Foundations of the Christian Faith, and that consequently we can have no Religious Communion with those that follow them or teach them.

VI. That we do also condemn their Opinion, who deny the inward and immediate Operation of the *Holy Ghost* in the Conversion of Man to God, and who pretend that the Holy Ghost doth not so open the Hearts as to make Men believe the Word, incline them to love God, and to obey his Commandments.

We trust that God will give us his Grace to preserve the Doctrine pure and entire to our last Breath, and to evidence it as well in our publick Sermons as in our private Conversations.

London, the 30th of *March*, 1691.

T. Satur, formerly Minister of *Montauban*, Moderator.
A. Piozet, formerly Minister of *Mans*, Joint-Moderator.
C. G. Lamothe, formerly Minister of *Rouen*, Secretary.
Du Bourdieu, formerly Minister of *Montpelier*.

Le Chenevix, formerly Minister at *Mante*.

P. Charles, formerly Minister at *Mauvesin*.

L. Rival, formerly Minister at *Saliêz*.

O. Champion, formerly Minister at *Mougon*.

Benjamin de Daillòn, formerly Pastor of the Church of *Rochefaucault*.

Sers, formerly Minister in the Church of *Montredon*.

La Caux, formerly Minister at *Castres*.

De Guilhem, formerly Minister at *Brebyeres*, in *Peregord*.

J Lovis Malide, formerly Minister at *Casteljaloux*.

De Primerose, Minister of the *French* Church of *London*.

Mitault, formerly Minister at *Chef Boutonne*.

Samuel Metayer, Minister of *St. Quentin*.

De Joux, formerly Pastor of the Reformed Church of *Lyon*.

P. Testas, formerly Minister of the Reformed Church of *Milhan* in *Guienne*.

Marc Vernoux, formerly Minister of the Church of *Mazemet*, in *Languedoc*.

Fauleon, formerly Minister at *Fecamp*, in *Normandy*.

Betoule, formerly Minister of *Duras*.

J. Campredon, formerly Minister of the Church of *St. Aignan* upon the *Maine*, in *France*.

Jean Farcy, Minister of the Church of *Mouchamp*, in *Low Poicton*.

Jacques Severin, formerly Minister at *Chery ley Rosais*, in *Forache*.

F. Testas, formerly Minister at *Poitiers*.

Jacques Tirel, formerly Minister at *St. Vaast*.

Canolle, Minister of *Gontauld*.

Pont, formerly Minister of *Mazeres*.

Jean Gommarc, Minister of *Mussidan*, in the *Dutchy of La Force*.

Baignoux, formerly Minister at *Poitiers*.

David Grimaudet, formerly Minister of the Church of *Desaigne*.

Jacques Doulês, formerly Minister at *Angles*.

Pierre Fontaine, formerly Minister of *Royan*.

Daniel du Tens, formerly Minister of the Reformed Church of *Angers*.

J. Solinhac, formerly Minister at *Realville*.

Pierre Souchet, formerly Minister at *Rochouard*.

Jacob de Roussignac, formerly Minister at *Puycasque.*

J. Bardon, formerly Minister of *Bruinquel.*

Jean Baron, formerly Minister of *Mazemet.*

Jean Molles, formerly Minister of *Cardalhac.*

Daniel Chais la Place, formerly Minister of *la Grave*, in *Dauphint.*

Le Sauvage, formerly Minister at *Aleason.*

Jean Cabibal, formerly Minister of *Brassac.*

Etienne Molenèr, formerly Minister *de Lisle*, in *Jordain.*

Philippa la Loe, formerly Minister at *Orbec.*

Jean Couyer, formerly Pastor of *Linieres*, in *Angoumars.*

Jacob Asselin, formerly Minister at *Dieppe.*

Jean Forent, formerly Minister of the Church of *Syon*, in *Brètagne.*

C. Pegorier, formerly Minister of *Havre.*

Charles Bertheau, formerly Minister of *Paris.*

P. Roussilion, formerly Minister of the Baronny of *Montreden*, in the *Lower Languedoc.*

P. Pezé Degalimere, formerly Minister at *Mans.*

Barthelomy Balaguier, formerly of the Church of *Aiguefonde*, in the *High Languedoc.*

Paul Gravisset, formerly Minister at *Ardenay*, in the Country of *Maine.*

Jean Boudet, formerly Minister at *Genebrieres.*

Joseph de la Moihe, formerly Minister of the Reformed Church of *Puymiral.*

Jouneau, formerly Minister at *Barbesieux.*

J. Lions, formerly Minister at *Montelimart.*

Gabriel Barbier, Minister at *Greenwich.*

Pierre Blanc, Minister.

Rival, Minister.

J. Lombard, formerly Minister at *Angers.*

J. Majou, formerly Minister at Ciré.

Durand Raoux, formerly Minister of *St. Privat.*

J. Graverol, formerly Minister at *Lyons.*

Jacques Laborie, Minister.

Barthelomy Basset, Minister.

J. M. Verchiere, Minister.

Abraham Gilbert, formerly Minister at *Melle.*

Jean Charpentier, Minister.

Charles Contet, Minister.
Antoine Review, Minister.
H. de Rocheblave, Minister.
Jean le Febre, Minister.
A. Lombard, Minister.
Jean Bernard, Minister.
Eliscé Gerauld, Minister.
Brocus de Hondesplens, formerly Minister of *Casteljaloux*.
Mote, formerly Minister of the Place *de Barre*, in *Cevennes*.
Jacques Misson, formerly Minister at *Niort*.
Pierre Bossatran, formerly Minister at *Niort*, in *Poitou*.
Michel David, formerly Minister of my Lady Dutchess *de la Force*.
Pierre Ticier, formerly Minister of *Mauvesin*.
Jean la Motthe Minister of the Church of *la Bastide Rouaisouse*.
Michel Cordier, formerly Minister of *Fieux*.
Bertheau the Elder, Minister of the Church of *Montpelier*.
La Riviere, formerly Minister at *Toulouse*.
Brevet, formerly Minister of the Church of *Dompierre* and *Bourumf*.
A. Forues, Minister.
A. Richard, formerly Minister of *Esperausses*, in *Languedoc*.
P. Astrac, Minister of the Church of *la Gazelle*, in *Auvergne*.
Jean Chabbert, Minister.
La Porte, formerly Minister of the Church of *Agen*, in Low *Guienne*.
J. Dejoux, Junior, Chaplain in their Majesty's Ship the *Northumberland*.
A. de St. Denys, formerly Minister at *Sancourt*, in *Normandy*.

PROPOSALLS HUMBLY SUBMITTED TO THE L'DS OF YE COUNCILL OF TRADE AND PLANTATIONS FOR SENDING YE FRENCH PROTESTANTS TO VIRGINA.

(Presented in the year 1698.)

Whereas, His Majesty has been pleas'd to refer to your L'ps the care and Disposal of a Considerable number of French and

Vaudois Refugees that have had ye hard fortune to be driven out of their Country on account of their Religion, and some Proposals have been offered to your L'ps for ye sending 'em to a small Tract of Land lying betwixt Virginia and Carolina, which the Proprietors of Carolina call, and order to Settle a New Colony there; Upon a full enquiry into ye matter, and a due examination of all Circumstances, I humbly conceive it will appear that Territory is upon no account so fit a Place for this small Colony as ye upper Parts of James River in Virg'a, and that for these several Reasons:

1. Because that part of lower Norfolk claim'd by No. Carolina, to the Southward of Corotuck, is, according to its name, for ye most part, low Swampy ground, unfit for planting and Improvement, and ye air of it very moist and unhealthy, so that to send Frenchmen thither that came from a dry and Serene Clymate were to send 'em to their Graves, and that wou'd very ill answer his Maj'ty's charitable Intention, and prove as unsuccessfull as ye late expedition to Darien, whereas, on ye contrary, ye upper part of James River affords as good land and as wholesome Air as any Place in America, and here is room enough for 'em to live Comfortably altogether under a very easy Governm't, tho' perhaps it were better that they were to be disperst in small numbers all over ye Country, for then they would be less Capable of raising any disturbance and wou'd be much more easily Supply'd w'th necessarys towards their first Settlement.

2. In that part of Virginia they will not be put to so many difficultys and distress'd at their first Settlem't as of necessity they must in that dismal part of Carolina, Provisions being there much Cheaper and Assistances of all kinds nearer at hand, and then ye Expence of settling them will be much more reasonable, for if these poor wretches be sent recommended to Collo. Nicholson, Gove'r of Virg'a, he will be exceedingly active in an undertaking of so great Charity, and will place them in such a part of ye Country as may be most happy for them, and by his generous Example will encourage other People of Substance to contribute their assistance.

3. There is a Dispute betwixt the Government of Virginia and ye Proprietors of Carolina about this Tract of Land which they

call Lower Norfolk, for Carolina pretends, by virtue of its Patent, to extend its bounds as far as 36 Degrees and an half, w'ch takes in no more than part of this Territory, So that if these poor People shou'd go to settle there they wou'd be under a perpetual Vexation, both from these Proprietors and from Virginia, and in a Little time wou'd grow so uneasy under these and a hundred other hardships that those who surviv'd wou'd be forct [*sic*] to disperse themselves into Virg'a and Carolina, for which reason 'twill save them a great deal of Inconvenience to send 'em directly to Virginia.

4. 'Twill be more for ye Interest of His Majesty and of the Kingdom of England to send them to Virg'a, for 'tis well known how usefull such Subject there is to this Nation, Whereas in a New Colony 'twill be long before they'll be able to Supply their own necessitys, and much longer before they can possibly yield any advantage to England.

5. In a competition betwixt a Plantation belonging to ye King and another belonging to Proprietors, the first ought always, in duty and by Virtue of ye Prerogative, to be prefer'd.

6. If these People shou'd be settled in that Fog end of N. Carolina under the Proprietors, all our Criminals and Servants wou'd run away thither for protection, as those of Maryland do to Pensilvania, and those of New York to ye Jerseys, and they'll be sure to receive 'em upon good Terms for ye Service and advancement of their new Colony, and I humbly Submit it to your L'd'ps' Consideration whether it were not necessary to injoin all Governors, under Severe penaltys, to cause diligent Search to be made after all Such Fugitives, and to send 'em back to ye Province from whence they made their Escape, for hitherto the Governor of Proprietys have been particularly deaf to all Such Complaints, to the great prejudice of his Maj't's more usefull Plantations; and, indeed, if the illegal Trade, Entertainment and Protection of Pyrates and other foul Practices of those lawless Governments were fully understood, the King wou'd be so far from establishing of New Proprietys that He wou'd have good Reason, as well as legal Title, to seize the old ones. So that I hope your L'ps, upon Consideration of all these particulars, will please to determine this matter in favour of Virginia, which prides it self on being ye

most advantageous to ye Crown of England of all its Dominions on the Continent.

W. BYRD.[2]

[2] Colonel William Byrd, the first of his name and family in Virginia; son of John and Grace (Stegge or Stagg) Byrd, London, (of the family of Brexton, Cheshire, England), was born in 1652, and came to Virginia, a youth, as the legatee of his uncle, Captain Thomas Stegge, merchant, landed proprietor and member of the Council. Colonel Byrd patented large tracts of land including the site of the city of Richmond; was a man of enterprise and influence; married Mary, daughter of Colonel Warham Horsemanden, of "Purley, in Essex, England;" member of the Virginia Council; Receiver General of the Colony by appointment from December 24, 1687 until his death December 4, 1704, when he was succeeded by his son William (the more distinguished of the family), born at "Westover," the family seat, March 10th, 1674; died August 26, 1744, and was buried there. The last was educated in England; "called to the bar in the Middle Temple, studied for some time in the Low Countries, visited the Court of France, and was chosen Fellow of the Royal Society, * * was thrice appointed public agent to the court and ministry of England, and being thirty-seven years a member, at last became President of the Council." His genius is embalmed in our national literature as the author of the *Westover Manuscripts*, which contain with other papers, the "History of the Dividing Line between Virginia and North Carolina as run in 1728-29;" Colonel Byrd being one of the Commissioners on the part of Virginia. He was the founder of Richmond, Virginia, which was laid off by Major William Mayo in April, 1737. He too, like his father, was much interested in the settlement of Virginia by the immigration of European Protestants. Drafts of letters of his written during the period 1735-1740, preserved at the hospitable seat, "Lower Brandon," James River (copies of which are in the possession of the editor) establish his frequent earnest efforts to secure the emigration of Swiss and German settlers, to whom he offered land, both in Virginia and North Carolina, on favorable terms. He was deeply interested in the development of the mineral resources of Virginia, and planted an extensive vineyard in 1735. He married twice. First, Lucy, daughter of Colonel Daniel Parke, Governor of the Leeward Islands; secondly, May 9, 1724, "Mrs. Maria Taylor, eldest daughter and co-heiress of Thomas Taylor, of Kensington, England," born November 10th, 1698; died August 25, 1771.

William, the eldest son by the second marriage, born September 6th, 1728; died January 1, 1777, was a member of the Virginia Council; and in 1756 served as Colonel of the Second Virginia regiment in the French and Indian war. He was married twice—first, April 10, 1748, to Elizabeth (born October 13, 1731; died July 14, 1760), daughter of John Car-

RECORDS RELATING TO THE HUGUENOT EMIGRATION TO VIRGINIA IN 1700.[3]

An acc't of what Contributions ye ffrench Refugees have rec'd.

	£	s.	d.
Of Mr. Devest, - - - - -	25	0	0
Of Mr. John Sehult, 5s. in snuff-boxes.			
Of Mr. Jaquean, 6£ 5s. in one ffusil.			
Of Mr. Perodin, 8£ 15s. in Taffety Caps.			
Of Mr. Deguerin, - - - -	1	5	0
Of Mr. Nicholay & Hamilton, 25£ in 3 watches and 3 paires of Pistols.			
Of Mr. de Lafontode, - - - -	1	5	0
Of Mr. Rozier, 1£ 5s. in powder.			

---

ter, of "Shirley," James River; secondly, January 29, 1761, to Mary, daughter of Charles and Anne (daughter of Joseph Shippen) Willing, of Philadelphia, Pa., who survived him. Charles Willing was the son of Thomas and Anne Willing, of Bristol, England.

[3] These records, relating to the emigration to Virginia in 1700 of the Huguenot refugees, have been kindly furnished by G. D. Scull, Esq., Oxford, England, who writes that they "were copied from a vellum-bound volume of manuscripts endorsed 'Original Papers relating to the French Plantation in the West Indies,' and found in the Bodleian Library. They are undoubtedly the original documents emanating from the Provincial Government of Virginia under Francis Nicholson, as they have the official signature of Dionisius Wright, who, it would appear, was the Secretary to the Council. When the emigration of the French was completed and the necessary papers connected with it collected, they were no doubt sent over to England for the inspection of Dr. Daniel Coxe, who had been the principal promoter of the enterprise. He was one of the Court Physicians to Queen Anne, and also in the preceding reign, and had some influence with royalty in directing the exodus of the French towards Virginia, where he had large grants of territory. He was a zealous churchman and a supporter of Christian missions, and sought to promote the spiritual and temporal welfare of the Huguenot refugees at the same time that he colonized his own lands. At his death his manuscripts were dispersed, and some of them fell into the hands of Rawlinson, the ardent and indefatigable collector, and were by him bequeathed to the Bodleian Library." Dr. Coxe was the author of Discourses and Papers in *Philosophical Transactions*, 1674; Alkaline Seeds; Sea Sand; Volatile Salt from Vegetables. His son, Daniel Coxe, resided in America fourteen years. He

	£	s.	d.
Of Mr. Brebant, - - - - -	2	10	0
Of Mr. Stringer, 10£ in fusils.			
Of Mr. Laurent, 3£ 15s. in Shotts and powder,			
Of Mr. Sehult and Maille, 65£,—vizt: 22£ 10s. to Doctor Coxe, and 42£ 10s. in tooles and other goods taken with them to fflorida and Carolina.			
Of Mr. Bachelier, - - - -	1	5	0
Of Mr. Hardoüin, - - - -	1	5	0
Of Mrs. de Laurancy and her daughter, -	2	10	0
Of Mr. Tutet, - - - - -	6	2	6
Of Mr. Dupont, - - - - -	9	15	0
Of Mr. De la Porte, - - - -	1	5	0
Of Mr. De Lorn, - - - -	25	0	0
Of Mrs. Perodin, her daughter and 2 Sons, -	5	0	0
Of Mrs. Perodin and her daughter, yet in fringe, gloves, Masks and 8£ 15s. carried to Carolina.			
Of Mr. Morand, - - - - -	1	5	0
Of Mr. Bonvet, - - - - -	2	10	0
Of Mr. Giborne, - - - -	2	10	0
Of Mr. Ducles Payen, - - - -	2	10	0
Of Mr. Perrodin, 2£ 10s. in a little watch carried to Carolina.			

---

claimed the territory originally comprised in Georgia, Florida, and Louisiana under the purchase of his father from the Earl of Arundel of the grant conveyed to the latter, which had been made by Charles I in the beginning of his reign to Sir Robert Heath, then Attorney General. He prepared: "A Description of the English Province of Carolana, by the Spaniards call'd Florida, and the French La Louisane; as also of the Great and Famous River Mischacebe or Mississippi; The Five Vast Navigable Lakes of Fresh Water, and the Parts Adjacent: Together with an Account of the Commodities, of the Growth and Production of the said Province; And a Preface containing some Considerations on the Consequences of the French making Settlements there, by Daniel Coxe, Esq. (Non minor est virtus quam quærere partu tueri.) [8vo., with folding map of 'Carolana and the River Mischacebe.'] London: Printed for Edward Symon, against the Royal Exchange in Cornhill, 1727." It was republished in 1741. Allibone, (*Dict. of Authors,*) says that there was an edition of 1722, but that of 1727 presents no evidence of any other having preceded it.

	£	s.	d.
Of Mr. Maille, 2£ 10s. in Gloves and hat bands carried to Carolina.			
Of Mr. ffrallon, - - - - -	1	5	0
Of Mr. Valoüe, - - - - -	1	5	0
Of Mr. Rambonnet, £25—vizt: 18£ 10s. to Doctor Coxe, in Canary wine, and ye rest in other goods taken away by him to Carolina.			
Of Mr. Harvey and Mr. Syms, - - -	50	0	0
Of Mr. Roger, - - - - -	30	0	0
Of Mrs. D'Heruart and Bodan, - - -	2	10	0
Of Mr. St. Germane, - - - -	1	5	0
Of Mr. Poher de Bretigny, - - -	1	5	0
Of Mr. and Mrs. de Lange, - - -	2	10	0
Of Mrs. Brunn and Ianthiall, - - -	2	10	0
Of Mr. Sarasin, Minister, - - -	2	10	0
Of Mr. de Mirmand, - - - -	1	5	0
Of Mr. Dumarest d' Antoguy, - - -	1	5	0
Of Mr. Benuerige, - - - -	1	5	0
Of Mrs. Perrodin, yet 5£ in Linnen Cloth.			
Of Mrs. Daversey and Le Bas, - - -	1	5	0
Of Mrs. Crassin, 2£ 10s. in Silk Caps.			
Of Mr. Saye, 3£ 15s.; returned unto him, -	1	5	0
Of Mr. fferrier, 6£ 5s.; returned unto him 3£ 15s. and so, - - - - -	2	10	0
Of Mr. Oger, 3£ 15s. returned unto him.			
Of Mrs. Perrodin, yet 1£ 5s. in butter.			
Of Mr. Billot, 5£ in shoes.			
Of Mr. Dejoux, 2£ 10s. in a note of 30s. upon a man in Ireland, who is not to be found, and 20 shillings, so, - - - - -	1	0	0
	£195	12	6

An Acc't of ye money lay'd out of the Contributions.

	£	s.	d.
To Mr. Lucas for printing 3000 projects and 1500 Tickets, - - - - -	4	10	0
ffor 40 Quires of Paper carried to fflorida, -		14	0

	£	s.	d.
for one Distiller and one Kettle, - .	3	2	0
To Mr. Stringer for fusils, coutlas, bayonetts, blunderbushes, flints, &c. 41£ 1s. of which abateing 10£ for his contributions remains paid, - - - - - - -	31	1	0
To the custome house, porters, cart, boats, &c., -	6	17	0
To De France for himselfe and to buy shoemaker's tools for John Breton, - - -	1	15	0
To Mr. Grimault for ye said Breton, - -		5	0
To Mr. Rosier for 2 candlesticks, spades, hoes, sithes, axes, grindstones, &c., - -	1	14	6
To Doctor Coxe in part of ye passage of our people 71£, of which Mr. Sehult has paid 22£ 10s. and Mr. Rambonnet 18£ 10s. and so remains paid, . - - - -	30	0	0
To Mr. Buckly, publick notary, for our Charter party, - - - - -	1	2	0
for ye charges and Expenses of yt day and of many other meetings, - - -	11	10	3
for ye Charges of Mr. Borel, Minister, and of his horse, from the 7th March, 1699, to ye 3d of Aprill, and for all ye Copys and Maps, left in severall Citys of Holland, Germany and Switzerland, and in Geneva, and of Severall bookes, and printing 2000 projects in Geneva,	18	1	0
For above 100 Charges, going and comeing, in all those parts, during 7 or 8 months, nothing.			
For ye Print of sixty Ticketts in English, -		5	0
For one piece of Druggett, - - -	1	14	0
For 14 Quires of Paper, - - -		6	0
For one great Trunck, cisers, Knives, thread, wool, &c., - - - - -	5	0	0
To Mr. Willette for severall pieces of Linnen Cloth, - - - - -	16	0	0
To Mr. Horard for hats, stockings and other goods, and for ye custome house pack, emballage, porterage, &c., - - - -	14	10	0
To Mr. Lees for printing 1000 projects in Englishe, - - - - - -	1	4	0

	£	s.	d.
To Mr. Compte for Garden seeds, flax and hemp, - - - - - -		7	10
To Captain Hawes for Bread, - -	16	17	6
For 30 Bags and one Lock, - - -	1	15	0
To Mr. Sparks, for saws, axes, spades and other tools, - - - - - -	26	0	0
To Mr. Bellet for several Coates, waist coates, briches, &c., - - - - -	10	0	0
To Mr. Degiac for one allarme watch and a great bell watch, - - - - -	15	0	0
To Mr. Clavis for blew Cloth handkerchieffs, cravats, &c., - - - - -	26	0	0
For a greate Black Trunck to put ye goods in, -		10	0
ffor netts, thread, Leather for Shoes, &c., -	1	11	0
for Charriers Sword and Belt, - - -		1	6
To Capt. Cooke for 3 tin pans, one Cullinder, one Sifter, one tin bale, one brass kettle, 2 hatchetts, 12 yds. of blew Duffles, 50 yards of red, 3 files and 2 Rosts, - - -	9	1	6
To Mr. Joyeux for 2 augurs, 2 hoes, 1 hand-saw, 2 fine tin candlesticks, - - -		17	0
To Capt. Webb for 53 Ells Canvass and 11 yards Kersey, - - - - - -	3	15	0
To Mr. Edward for 56 Ells Canvas, 15 yards of halfe thick, one Cross-cut saw and one large augur, - - - - - - -	4	4	0
	£265	11	1
	£195	12	6
	£69	19	7

There have been severall other extraordinary Charges not mentioned here, and some loss upon ye money, as Guineas, Severall other Spanish pistoles and German Crownes leight and other, who remaines something, having not paid wholly their Contributions.

A true Copie,

Test:

(Signed) DIONISIUS WRIGHT.

LIST OF ALL YE PASSINGERS FROM LONDON TO JAMES RIVER, IN VIRGINIA, BEING FFRENCH REFUGEES IMBARQUED IN THE SHIP YE PETER AND ANTHONY, GALLEY OF LONDON, DANIEL PERREAU COMMANDER (VIZ'T):

Monsieur de Joux, minister,	1
Jean Bossard, sa femme and 3 enfans,	5
Jean Morroe,[4]	1
Pierre Masset,	1
Solomon Jourdan,	1
Estienne Chabran, sa femme,	2
Susanne Soblet and 3 Enfans,	4
Jean Hugon,	1
Michel Michel,	1
Theodore de Rousseau,	1
Pierre Cavalier, sa femme and un garcon,	3
Pierre Anthonie Eupins,	1
Isaac Le ffeure,[5]	1
Jean Martain,	1
Jean Combelle,	1
Pierre Renaud,	1
Marthien Roussel,	1
Augustin Coullard,	1
Jean Coullard,	1
Jacques du Crow, sa femme and une ffille,	3
Paul Laurion,	1
Moise Broc,	1
Jean Pierre Bondurand,	1
Pierre La Badie,	1
Guilleaume Rullet,	1
Anthony Gioudar,	1
Anne Carbonnet and un enfans,	2
Guillemme Guervot, sa femme and un garcon,	3
Louis Robert and un fille,	2
Estienne Tauvin, sa femme and 2 enfans,	4
Paul Castiche,	1

[4] A corruption probably of Moreau.

[5] Now rendered Lefew in Virginia.

Jean Mazeris, - - - - - -	I
Noel Delamarre, sa femme and un fille - - -	3
Jean Le Vilain, - - - - - -	I
Jean Marisset, - - - - - -	I
Jean Maillard and 3 enfans, - - - -	4
Thimotthee Roux, - - - - - -	I
Gaspart Guamondet and sa femme, - - -	2
Jean Pilard, - - - - - -	I
Estienne Ocosand, - - - - - -	I
Abraham Remis, sa femme, - - - -	2
Jean Le Franc Vudurand, - - - - -	I
Daniel Maison Dieu, - - - - -	I
Pierre Baudry, - - - - - -	I
David Menestrier, - - - - - -	I
Jacob Fleurnoir, sa femme, 2 garcons and 2 fille, - -	6
David Blevet, sa femme and 6 enfans, - - -	8
Elizabeth Lemat, - - - - - -	I
Abraham Le Foix, sa femme and 4 enfans, - -	6
Jean Aunant, sa femme and un fille, - - -	3
Jean Genge de Melvis, - - - - -	I
ffrancois de Launay and un enfans; - - -	2
Gaspart, sa femme and 7 enfans, - - - -	9
Samuel Mountier, sa femme and deux enfans, - -	4
Jacques Corbell, - - - - - -	I
Jacob Capen, - - - - - -	I
Isaac Troc, - - - - - - -	I
Elié Gastand, - - - - - -	I
Anthonie Boignard, - - - - -	I
Nicholas Mare, sa femme and 2 enfans, - - -	4
Jacques Feuillet and sa femme, - - - -	2
Pierre Sarazin, - - - - - -	I
Jean Perrachou, - - - - - -	I
Phillippe Claude, - - - - - -	I
Simon Hugault, - - - - - -	I
Samuel Barrel, - - - - - -	I
Gaspar Gueruer, sa femme and 3 enfans, - - -	5
Jean Soulegre, - - - - - -	I
Louis Desfontaine, and sa femme, - - -	2
Daniel Rogier, - - - - - -	I
Pierre Gosfand, - - - - - -	I

Solomon Ormund,	1
Louis Geoffray,	1
Maize Verneuil, sa femme and 5 enfans,	7
Joseph Olivier,[6]	1
Jaques Faucher,	1
Pierre La Grand, sa femme and 5 enfans,	7
Pierre Prevol,	1
Daniel Riches,	1
ffrancis Clapie,	1
Jacob Riché, sa femme and un enfans,	3
Mathieu Passedoit,	1
Pierre Hiuert,	1
Michel Fournet, sa femme and deux enfans,	4
Jean Monnicat,	1
Simon Faucher,	1
	169

I, Daniel Perreau, Commander of ye above said Vessel, Certified that ye above one hundred and seventy Passengers—French Refugees—were Embarqued in London in my said Ship, men, women and children of several ages, for which said Passengers I have received full freight for their passage in London to Virginia the sum of seven hundred and seventy-five pounds sterling, and have given receipt in England for the same.

James Towne, in Virginia,

ye 20th of Sept'r, 1700.

DANIEL PERREAU.

5£ Sterling for each man and woman; 50 Shillings for children under 12 years of age. Males in all 155, at 5£ a head, 775£.

A true copy,

Test:

DIONISIUS WRIGHT.

[6] Probably from Niort, in Poitou. See *Baird's Huguenot Emigration to America*, II, 213.

AN ACC'T OF WHAT MONEY REC'D FOR YE TRANSPORT AND SUPPLIES OF THE FFRENCH REFUGEES.

	£.	s.	d.
Of Mr. Devest, - - - - -	0	5	0
Of Mr. de la Barthe, - - - -		2	6
Of Mr. Praivmaux, - - - -	1	2	6
Of Mr. Lantier, - - - -		4	6
Of Mr. Des Esserts, - - - -		5	6
Of Mr. de Bettens, - - - -		11	0
Of Mr. Ysuard Du Terrier, - - -	2	0	6
Of Mr. Kilchberger, - - - -		11	0
Of Mr. and Mrs. de Saumaise, - -		10	0
Of Mr. Chamberlaine, - - - -	1430	0	0
Of Coll. Harrison, - - - -	5	0	0
Of Mr. ffowler, - - - -	1	0	0
Of Mr. Edward, - - - -	2	0	0
In all, - -	1443	12	6

Besides 20£ given in London by Mr. Moor's Executors to assist Several who had been there along while waiting for the Imbarkation, and which have been distributed accordingly, and 20£ given by Mr. Harvey which we caused to be put into the hands of Mr. Dejoux, who distributed them, and 4£ given by Mr. ffoüace at James Towne to be distributed, one £ to Mr. Nan, one £ to Badoüet, 10s. to Mr. Delorn for a lame woman and a fatherlesse boy living with him, 2s. 6d. to Troüillard which occasioning severall others to complain wee gave yet of our owne money 20s. to Mr. Brouse saying that was also in want and could not relieve his Son and his Cosin who were very sick.

AN ACC'T OF YE MONEY LAY'D OUT FOR THE TRANSPORT AND SUPPLIES OF YE FRENCH REFUGEES.

	£.	s.	d.
In Rotterdam for ye Charges of 2 days of 75 come from Switzerland, - - -	7	12	0

	£.	s.	d.
To a man who made 2 peticons in English for the King, - - - - - -		5	0
To Capt. Yeoman, with whom we had agreed first at 6£ a head, 32£; but because he could not fitt out his vessell—and Capt. Hawes promising to transport y'm for 5£ if we would advance 100£ and hold one-4th part of the Ship—we thought it more advantageous to loose 32£, and to venture £100 to spare 5 or £6, as we have done, and so, - -	32	0	0
ffor all ye Charges of Letters of ye Committees of Sollicitations and Expeditions of ye officers of Councill of the Lords Commissioners for trade and plantations of ye Treasury, and of ye two Secretaries, and of ye Committee for disposall of the money and to fetch it, -	29	14	0
for all ye Charges of Courteers and voyages to look for Ships to make ye bargaines and treatys to pay the tradesmen and of ye Imbarkation, - - - - - -	15	16	0
To Capt. Hawes for one 4th part of ye Shipp, -	100	0	0
To the Custome-house for Cooks, Warrants, dutys of beddings and other goods, and to the Surveyors and Clerks, &c., - - -	18	4	0
To Capt. Hawes for ye passage, - -	945	0	0
To Mr. Roger for books, - - -	30	0	0
for Brandy, Sugar, figgs, raisons and sugar, biscuits for the sick, - - - -	5	0	0
ffor the six pence a head to ye custom of Gravesend, - - - - - -	5	2	6
To ye ship's crew for brandy, - - -		15	0
To three of our men, one to serve in ye kitchen and 2 to cleane ye shipp for 14 weekes, -	2	7	0
To the Marriners in James River, - -	1	2	0
To ye Cooke, - - - - -		5	0
To Ompton[7] to make ye Declaration, and to York to give his Excellency the King's Letter,		9	0

[7] Hampton.

	£.	s.	d.
To 2 men of Mr. Servant, who brought fruite, sider and milke to our people, - -		2	6
To Mr. Servant for 4 bусshels of Salt, - -		11	0
For a boat to put some people ashoare, and to goe to Mr. Servant for a Certificate how he saw Capt. Hawes abuse us and our goods, and to bring ye salt, - - - -		3	0
To Capt. Hawes for Hamacks, brandy, and other extraordinarys according to his note, -	21	8	0
for bread and baggs given to the people of James Town, upon ye Road, - - -	17	18	0
at ye falls and in Manikin Towne for a barrell of Butter, - - - - -	1	10	0
for 2s. 6d. a head given to one hundred goeing by land, - - - - -	12	10	0
To those who have loaden ye 2 first Sloops, -		6	0
for a great pewter dish lent to ye people and lost, - - - - - -		10	0
for 2 Muttons Killed at ye falls for ye people, -		17	0
To Champayne for dressing ye meat 2 dayes in the Towne, - - - - -		2	0
To the Troops who went up with us to Manikin Towne, - - - - -		15	0
for Smelt and Price Sloops, - - -	10	12	0
for a boat to load the last sloope, - -		7	0
To the men who set some of our people over James River, - - - -		5	0
for 3 great baggs, - - - -		12	6
for 3 horses, one Collar, Saddle, for Cart, the pasture, fferrys, &c., &c., - - -	16	18	0
for one Bullock at ye falls, - - -	2	10	0
To Capt. Weebb for 3 beefs, Corne, onions, tobacco, one Saddle, 4 Pannells and furnitures, &c., &c., - - - - - -	17	6	8
for 6 bundles of bed ropes, 3 of lines, 3 Cows' bells, two Lanthornes, 24 Girtes, one Leather halter, four paires of leather Stirrups, one Estrille, &c., &c., - - - -	2	9	0
for 2 Sithes and furnitures, - - -		11	0

	£.	s.	d.
for 10 pounds of Shoe thread, 12 Knives, one other cutting-Knife and awl blades, men's and woman's Lasts, tacks, punch, blades, &c., &c.,	2	3	9
for Joiners' tooles, - - - -	1	11	0
To Morel and Marche for 13 dayes to ye mill, -		13	0
To Boff and Moriset, - - - -		6	6
To Sugre and Orange for baking, - -		15	0
To Richard de Pré and Gacory, Senior, for marking and clearing the Cart road and ye streets of the Towne, - - - -		19	0
To Mr. Hatcher for carrying up Meale and goods, - - - - -	3	10	0
for one Grindstone and hands, - - -		17	0
for ye Charges of ye second Journey to James Towne, the first having been returned, -		18	0
To Mattory, Sugre and Cuper for bringing a barrell of fish from ye River, and for clearing the Cart road, - - - -		10	6
To Cuper for his Sabre broken by ye sentry upon the Shipp, - - - -		2	6
To Voyer and Panetier to dig a little store in ye ground, - - - - -		5	0
To Mr. Verry for seven dayes to the mill and to fetch the cart, - - - -		7	0
for ye Journey to Apomatox and ye ferryes, -		12	6
To Mr. Ascough for peas, and ye carrying y'm up w'th some meale and goods, - -	2	0	0
To Bouchet, Panetier, and Gaury, Junior, for 12 days in the woods, - - - -		12	0
To Gaury, Senior, for the subsistance of his child remaining of his passage, - -	1	7	6
To Du Tartre and Sassin for 33 dayes worke in the Kitchin to ye Mill, marking and clearing the Cart Road, - - - -	1	13	0
for great Nailes for the Pares doors, - -			9
To ye Miller to suffer our people by his fire and to dispatch them. - - - -		2	6
To Capt. Hebbs for one Cart and 6 busshells of Onions, - - - - -	3	11	6

	£.	s.	d.	
To Mr. Dejoux at Williamsburgh, - -		10	3	
To Capt. Cocke and his brother for 10 Cowes and a Calfe, - - -	23	11	0	
for ye Journey to Capt. Hebbe and Williamsburgh, and ye fferrys going and comeing, - - - -	1	9	9	
To Mrs. Ascough and Druly for carrying up meal and goods, - - -	3	2	6	
To Morel for the subsistance of his child remaining of his passage, - -	1	7	6	
To Mr. Ascough for carrying 600 meal, -		18	0	
To Joüany for 2 bushells of peas, carryed up,		11	0	
for one wheat mill and wheele, - -	3	10	0	
To Mr. Chastain for ye subsistance of his 4 chilldren remaining of their passage,	5	10	0	
To Saum for his child, - - -	1	7	6	
To ye widow ffaure for her child, - -	1	7	6	
To the new Miller, - - - -		2	6	
To Mr. Ascough for Corne, - -	1	7	0	
for Corne for ye Horse, - - -		1	0	
for severall presents in Snuff boxes and money to people kind and helpfull to us,	4	10	0	
To Mr. Phillipe, Minister, and others in money to assist them in their distemper, and tooles to put them to work above, -	42	17	3	9
To the carpenter and workmen who have cut downe, sawne and prepared timbers for ye Church and minister's house, -	5	8	0	
ffor the Charges of this Journey and severall others to the Mill, to ye falls, to Capt. Weebb, &c., &c., - - -	0	0	0	
	£1,422	03	11	9

Money received,	£1,443	12	06	
Money disburst,	1,422	03	11	9
Remaïnes,	£21	08	7	9

LISTE DES PERSONNES DU SECOND CONVOY QUI SERENT TOUTE L'ANNÈE A MANICANTON.

Pierre Labadie,	1
Samuel Aulegues, sa femme et deux enfans,	4
Estienne Asseau,	1
Pierre Baudry,	1
Anthoine Boignaut,	1
Jean Pierre Bondurant,	1
Jean Bossart, sa femme et trois enfans,	5
Daniel Bloüet, sa femme et sept enfans,	9
Jean Brand,	1
Moyle Broc,	1
Jacob Capon,	1
Paul Castiche,	1
Pierre Cavalier, sa femme et un enfant,	3
Estienne Chabran, et sa femme,	2
Anne Charboneau et 2 enfans,	3
ffrancois Clapier,	1
Jean Combel,	1
Jaques Corbet,	1
Augustin Coliart,	1
Anthoyne Dupuy,[8]	1

---

[8] An interesting "Memorandum" (from a copy of the original kindly furnished by Hon. L. C. Draper, LL.D., Madison, Wisconsin,) of the escape of Anthony Trabue, and of the settlement at Manakin-town, prepared by his grandson, Daniel Trabue, son of John James and Olymphia (Dupuy) Trabue, was published by the present writer in the *Richmond Standard*, May 10–17, 1879. Daniel Trabue writes: "My grandfather, Anthony Trabue, fled from France in the year of our Lord, 1687, at the time of a bloody persecution against the dissenters by the Roman Catholics. The law against the dissenters was very rigid at that time. Whoever was known to be one, or even suspected, if he would not swear to visit the priest, his life and estate were forfeited, and [he was] put to the most shameful and cruel torture and death. And worse than all, they would not let any move from the kingdom. Guards and troops were stationed all over the kingdom to stop and catch any that might run away. At every place where they would expect those persons might pass, there were guards fixed and companies of inquisitors, and patrols going on every road, and every other place, hunting for those heretics, as they called them; and where there was one who made his

Jean Burraud, - - - - - -	1
Isaac le Feme, - - - - - -	1
Jacob Fleminoie, sa femme et trois enfans, - -	5
Louis de Fontaines, et sa femme, - - - -	2
Abram Le Foy, sa femme et quatre enfans, - -	6
Elie Castral, - - - - - -	1
Anthoyne Guiodan, - - - - -	1
Jean George de Melez, - - - - -	1
Pierre le Grand,[9] sa femme et cinq enfans, - -	7
Simon Hugaut, - - - - - -	1
Salomen Jourdan, - - - - - -	1
Gaspard Kernent, sa femme et trois enfans, - -	5

---

escape, perhaps there were hundreds put to the most shameful torture and death. * * When the decree was first passed, a number of the people thought it would not be put in execution so very hastily; but the priests, friars and inquisitors were very intent for their estates, and they rushed quick. * * I understand that my grandfather, Anthony Trabue, had an estate, but concluded he would leave it if he could possibly make his escape. He was a very young man, and he and another young man took a cart and loaded it with wine, and went on to sell it to the farthermost guard; and when night came they left their horses and cart, and made their escape to an English ship, which took them on board, and they went over to England, leaving their estates, native country, relations, and everything for the sake of Jesus who died for them."

Mr. A. E. Trabue, Hannibal, Missouri, is in possession of the original certificate on vellum given his ancestor by the ministers and civil officers of Lausanne. He communicates the following extract: "We commend him to the care of Divine Providence, and to a cordial reception from our Brethren. Done at Lausanne this 15th day of the seventh month, A. D. 1687."

Anthony Trabue died in Manakin-town, Virginia, January, 1724, aged 56 or 57 years, leaving three sons: Anthony, Jacob and John James Trabue, who married Olymphia, daughter of John James and Susanna (Lavillon) Dupuy. Their issue, as given in the "Memorandum" of Daniel Trabue, differs somewhat in order and name from the Dupuy "trees." He gives: James, John, William, Daniel, Edward, Stephen, Samuel, Magdalene, Phœbe, Jane, Mary, Martha, Eliza, Judith, Susan.

[9] His descendants in several generations followed the calling of Land Surveyor. They embrace many highly respected names, including that of Dibrell, formerly Du'Breuil. Peter Le Grand was the Burgess from Prince Edward county, 1758-1765.

Lavfue de Launay (alias francoise de Monine),	1
Elizabet Leurat,	1
Jean Hugon,	1
Jeane Malard, ve fue a trois enfans,	4
Nicholas Mare, sa femme et 2 enfans,	4
Noé de la Mare, sa femme et un enfant,	3
Jean Maricet,	1
Jean Marot,	1
Pierre Massot,	1
Jean Mautin,	1
Jean Maseres,	1
David Menetrie,	1
Michel Michel,	1
Joseph Olivier,	1
Jean Onan, sa femme et un enfant,	3
Pierre Prevot,	1
Abram Remy, et sa femme,	2
Josue Petit, sa femme et 2 enfans,	4
Loüys Robert, et sa fille,	2
Jaques Riche, sa femme et 2 enfans,	4
Theodore Rousseau,	1
Mathieu Roussel,	1
Timothié Roux,	1
Guillaum Rullean,	1
Susanne Soblet, et trois enfans,	4
Jean Soulegre,	1
Estienne Tanin, et sa femme,	2
Isaac Troe,	1
Jean Vilain,	1
Moyre Verrüeil, sa femme et cinq enfans,	7
Gaspard Sobry, sa femme et sept enfans,	9

ffait ce 1. Xbre 1700.

B. De Joux, Ministre.

3me Convoy.

Jean Reniol,	1
Anthoyne Rambæye,	1
ffrancois Agnast,	1
Pierre Rondere,	1

Jaques Giraut,	1
Jaques Roux,	1
	145

fait ce 1, Xbre 1700.
B. De Joux, ministre.

Copia,
Test : DIONISIUS WRIGHT.

S'r,—Here enclosed is a copy of ye List of ye Refugees given to ye Miller, as it has been sent unto mee by Messrs. de Joux and Philipe under their hands; but there is no corn, and Mr. de Saillee lying here sick since he came from Westopher, and having already provided all what he could, cannot supply them any longer; so I don't know what to do unless some care be taken to send some corn up. I heard that y'r Excellency hath our Indenture of the Lands we have purchased in fflorida; so I desire y'r Exc'y to send it up to mee, keeping a copie if you please, because it cost us a great deal of money, which we expect to recover, or part of it. I wish also that ye Factious and scandalous Petition presented by Mr. de joux be delivered unto me if you please, or burnt, to pacifie all what is past, avoid complaints and disputes, and to procure Peace and Love.

Mr. Philipe haveing no allowance in England is not able to subsist with his wife unless your Exc'y grant him some money out of the gratifications made to the refugees which shall be a Charity very great and necessary. I desire Coll. Byrd to lett me know if I can have accommodations to go to England in one of ye Ships Lying by Westopher; after his answer I shall endeavor to go to Williamsburgh to take my leave, and to assure your Excellency that I will ever be,

S'r, y'r Exc'y's most humble and most obed't serv't,

OLIVIER DE LA MUCE.[10]

ye 15th of ffeb., 1700 [1701].

To his Exc'y ffrancis Nicholson, Esq., his Maj'y's L't and Gov'r Gen'l of Virginia at Williamsburgh.

---

[10] Bonaventure Chauvin Seigneur de la Muce Ponthus, whose seat was near the city of Nantes, in Southern Bretagne, was one of the first to

A LIST OF THE REFUGEES WHO ARE TO RECEIVE OF YE MILLER OF FALLING CREEK MILL ONE BUSHEL A HEAD OF INDIAN MEALE MONTHLY AS SETTLED AT OR ABOUT KING WILLIAMS TOWN TO BEGIN IN FFEB. 1700 [1701].

Mr. De Joux, Philipe and his wife, - - - -	3
Mallett and his wife, - - - - -	2
Moulin and his wife, - - - - -	2
Jonthier, Farcy, and Chastain, - - - -	3
Nicod, Duloy, and Minot, - - - - -	3
Joüany and his wife, - - - - -	2
Gaury, his wife and one child, - - - -	3
Tho. Constantine, - - - - -	1
ffaure, his brother, and 2 Sisters, - - - -	4
Tillou, Tignaw, and Bilboa, - - - -	3

embrace the new faith in the early days of the French Reformation. He became its most earnest supporter, "consumed with zeal for the cause of religion," and his descendants inherited the same devotion. His three sons fought in the Huguenot armies under Henry IV, and his grandson, David, Marquis de la Muce, presided over the political assembly of the Protestants held in La Rochelle in the year 1621. For his attendance upon that assembly, contrary to the King's commands, he was condemned to be drawn and quartered, a sentence which was executed upon him in effigy, whilst his beautiful castle was actually demolished and razed to the ground. Cæsar, his son, and Olivier, his grandson, were elders in the Reformed Church of Nantes. Under the provisions of the Edict of Nantes the Seigneurs de la Muce claimed the right of holding religious services in their own house, and besides supporting this worship they contributed generously to the funds of the "temple" in the adjoining village of Sucé. Soon after the Revocation Olivier de la Muce fled from his home and was arrested on the island of Ré, while waiting for an opportunity to make his escape to England. Imprisoned for two years, first in La Rochelle, and afterwards in the Castle of Nantes, he resisted every effort to persuade him to deny his faith. At length an order was given for the expulsion of the Marquis de la Muce from the kingdom as an obstinate heretic. Accordingly, he was placed on board a foreign ship, the captain of which received orders to land him in England, but carefully to conceal from him the fact that he was about to be set free.

Twelve years later, he headed the expedition to Virginia and became the founder of the Manakin-town settlement. He was a man of recognized excellence of character. *Baird's Huguenot Emigration to America*, II, 87-89.

Laureau, Parontes, and his sister,	3
Bazoil, Voyer, and his wife,	3
the two Gourdonnes,	2
Gowry and his wife,	2
Guichet and Panetier,[11]	2
Savin and his Mother,	2
Chambor, his wife, and Peru,	3
Malver his wife and her father,	3
Brousse, his son and Corine,	3
Arnaud and his wife,[12]	2
Chalaine and 5 children,	6
Godriet, Lavigne[13] and Sayè	3
Chenas and Augustin Symend,	2
Verau and his wife,	2
Soblet, his wife and 5 children,	7
Verry and Gigon,	2
Katharine Billet,	1
Guerin and Sassin,	2
Chalanier, his wife and one child,	3
Tonin and his wife,	2
Du Tartre and Cupper,	2
Bernard,[14] his wife and Caboine,	3
Richard and his wife,	2
Morell, his wife and one child,	3
Cantepie and Castra,	2
Le Febvre, Martin and Robert,	3
Onan, his wife and one child,	3
Michel and his wife,	2
La Vilain and Remy,	2
ffoix, his wife and four children,	6
Sobriche, his wife and seven children,	9
hugon and le Roux,	2
Bossard, his wife and 3 chil'n,	5
Durand and his wife,	2

---

[11] "Jacques Panetier, fugitif de Soubise," (Arch. Nat.), John Pantrier, naturalized in England, March 8, 1682. *Baird*, II, 18.

[12] Probably from la Tremblade in 1683. See *Baird*, II, 33.

[13] A fugitive from Royan in 1684.

[14] Joseph Bernard, fugitive from Ré in 1685. *Baird*, I, 308.

Clapier, Du Puy, Joseph and Brooke,	4
Chabran and his wife,	2
Chinandan, his wife and 2 chil'n,	4
Des Rousseau and Morisset,	2
Labadie, Castige, Rounel, de Logny, and Mazel,	5
Legrand, his wife and 6 chil'n,	8
Malarde and 3 children,	4
Richet, his wife and 2 children,	4
Corbet and Bonduran,	2
Mare, his wife and 2 children,	4
Des fontaine and his wife,	2
Baudry, hugo, and Prevost,	3
Trion, his wife and one child,	3
Riviole, Rambrey and De Launay,	3
fflemnois, his wife and 3 children,	5
Jourdan and his wife,	2
Verdüil, his wife and 5 children,	7
Bloüet, his wife and seven children,	9
La Maro, his wife and Petit,	3
Cavalier, his wife and one child,	3
Gerner, his wife and 3 children,	5
Samuel, his wife and two children,	4
Durand, Boignan, Morizet,	3
In all,	218

If any of the above named don't settle above, or leave their settlement, or dye, their names are to be blotted out upon ye advices of Mr. de Joux or Philipe, given every month to ye said Miller, who is desired to distribute unto them by turne such meale as he shall have for them without partiality, and so doing he shall oblige his servant at Capt. Webb's[15] house.

OLIVIER DE LA MUCE.

This 4th of ffeb'r, 1700 [1701.]

[15] Captain Giles Webb, who died June, 1713. He married the widow of Henry Randolph, Jr., Clerk of Henrico county. In his will, which is of record in Henrico county, he mentions a brother, Thomas, and his step-son, Henry Randolph. The name Webb has been prominent in the annals of Virginia. John Webb was a patentee of land in 1624. Stephen Webb was a Burgess from James City county in October, 1644.

ROLLE DES FRANCOIS, SUISSES, GENEVOIS, ALEMANS, ET FLAMANS EMBARQUES DAM LE NAVIRE NEMMÉ LE NASSEAU POUR ALLER A LA VIRGINIE.

Mons'r Latane,[16] Ministre, Madame sa femme un Enfan unne Servante, - - - - - -	4
Mr. Daniel Braban, sa femme, 3 enfans, 1 garcon, -	6
Jean Pierre Gargean, sa femme, 3 enfans, - - -	5
Jacob Amonet,[17] sa femme, 4 enfans, - - -	6
Paul Papin, - - - - - -	1

Giles Webb was commander of a body of rangers in Henrico county in October, 1692. *Calendar of State Papers of Virginia*, I, 43. George Webb was elected, December 17, 1776, by the Virgiina Assembly, Treasurer of Virginia, to succeed Robert Carter Nicholas, resigned.

[16] Rev. Lewis Latané was rector of South Farnham parish, Essex county, from 1700 until his death, which is mentioned by Commissary Blair in a letter to the Bishop of London, dated March 24, 1734 [1735]. *Perry's Virginia Church Papers*, 257. He was the joint patentee with Bartholomew Yates, Christopher and John Robinson, Jeremiah Clowder, Harry Beverley, William Stanard and Edwin Thacker of 24,000 acres of land on the south side of the Rapid Anne in Spotsylvania county, July 20, 1722. *Virginia Land Registry*, Book No. 11, page 147. Rev. Lewis Latané was twice married before he came to Virginia, and afterwards married, thirdly, Mary Deane, (died 1732) by whom he had issue five daughters and one son, William, who married Ann Waring, of Essex county, and had issue: i. Lucy married Payne Waring; ii. Henry, born 1777; married ——; iii. Daughter, married John Temple, and others. A descendant of Rev. Lewis Latané, the gallant Captain Latané, fell near Old Church, Hanover county, Virginia, on the second of the famed four days' raid of General J. E. B. Stuart, Confederate States Cavalry (June 12-15, 1862), around the lines of General George B. McClellan, and found romantic burial at the hands of Virginia ladies, assisted by their servants. He was buried at "Summer Hill," the seat of Captain Willoughby Newton, Confederate States Army (who also, a little later, sealed with his life his devotion to his country), near Hanover Town, Virginia, the burial service of the Episcopal Church, being read by the venerable mother of Captain Newton. The scene was perpetuated on canvass by Washington, a Virginia artist, and the engraving from the painting is a favored decoration in Virginia households. Another descendant is Rev. James A. Latané, Bishop of the Reformed Episcopal Church of the United States.

[17] "Jacob Pierre et Matthieu Ammonet, chefs de famille a Loudun, 1634," (La France Protestante, *s. v.*) *Baird*, II, 51.

Jean Leroy, - - - - - -	I
Jacques Lacaze, - - - - - -	I
Jean Dubroq, - - - - - -	I
Catharine Basel, une fille, - - - -	2
Ester Lefebre, - - - - - -	I
Ester Martin, un enfan, - - - - -	2
ffrancois Ribot, - - - - - -	I
Joseph Molinie, sa femme, - - - -	2
Leon Auguste Charéitiè sa femme, - - -	2
Jean Barachin, sa femme, - - - -	2
Joseph Caillau, and sa femme, - - - -	2
Jean Dauphin, - - - - - -	I
Jeane Bellin, - - - - - -	I
Margueritte Gautie, - - - - -	I
Marie Mallet, - - - - - -	I
Thomas Deneille,[18] - - - - - -	I
Jacques Macan, et sa femme, - - - -	2
Jean Thomas[19] and sa femme, - - - -	2
Jean Robert, sa femme and une fille, - - -	3
Alexandre Madouy, - - - - -	I
Noel Richemon and sa femme, - - - -	2
Jean ffonnielle and sa femme, - - - -	2
Estienne Bocar, sa femme and 2 enfans, - - -	4
Jaques ffradot, - - - - - -	I
Gabriel Maupain,[20] sa femme and 3 enfans, - - -	5
Jacob Sponge and sa femme, - - - -	2

[18] Deneale, a well-known Fairfax county, Virginia, name, is probably a corruption of Deneille.

[19] *Baird*, II, 41, states that Jean Thomas settled in South Carolina, and gives from *Liste des Francois et Suisses Refugiez in Caroline* this extract: "Jean Thomas, né à St. Jean d'Angely in Saintonge, fils de Jean Thomas et d'Anne Dupon.

[20] The name is now rendered Maupin in Virginia. An estimable representative was the late Socrates Maupin, Professor of Chemistry in the University of Virginia (1853–1871), and chairman of its faculty (1854–1868); killed by a fall from his horse October 19, 1871. Daniel Maupin, doubtless a son of the refugee, was granted 1,188 acres of land in Albemarle county September 20, 1745. (*Virginia Land Registry*, Book No. 31, page 652.) Gabriel Maupin was keeper of the public magazine at Williamsburg in 1791.

Ester Duncan	1
Jaques Hernon,	1
Jean Chaperon,[21]	1
ffrancois Felsau,	1
Jean Prain,	1
Salomon Taniere and sa femme,	2
Pierre Odias,	1
Jean ffaouton,	1
Pierre fferré,[22] sa femme and un enfant,	3
francois Gonfan, sa femme and sa fille,	3
Lazare Lataniere and sa femme,	2
Jean Belloe,	1
Jacques Delinet,	1
Salomon Bricou and sa femme,	2
Glaude Barbie and sa femme,	2
Estienne Dehon,	1
Henry Corneau,	1
Daniel fferran,	1
Jean Gomar, sa femme and 5 enfans,	7
Jean Rousset,	1
Pierre Montgut,	1
Alexander Vaillan,	1
Salomon Gondemay and sa femme,	2
Louis Girardeau,	1
Daniel Dousseau,	1
Michel Cahaigne,	1
Daniel Duval,[23]	1
Corneille Prampain,	1
Paul Coustillat,	1

[21] Probably from Rouen. See *Baird*, II, 74.

[22] Probably from St. Sévère, in the Province of Berré. See *Baird*, II, 105.

[23] A descendant was Major William Duval, of the Revolutionary War, and subsequently a prominent member of the Richmond (Virginia) bar. His son, William Pope Duval, born 1784, lawyer and statesman, served as Captain of the Mounted Rangers in the war of 1812; member of Congress, 1812–15; Governor of Florida Territory, 1822–34; died at Washington, D. C., March 19, 1854. He was the original of "Ralph Ringwood," of Washington Irving, and "Nimrod Wildfire," of J. K. Paulding.

Pierre des maizeaux,	1
Jean Velas Lorange,[24] sa femme and un enfan,	3
Jean Egarnae,	1
Pierre Gueraux,	1
Anthoine Lalorie,	1
Matthieu Bonsergent et sa femme,	2
Paul Leroy and sa femme,	2
Bernard Lanusse and sa femme,	2
ffrancois Charpentier and sa femme,	2
Jean Surin,	1
Jacques Lemarchand,	1
Isaac Bonviller,	1
Melkier de Vallons,	1
Isaac de'Hay,	1
Abraham Cury,	1
Joseph Berrard and sa femme,	2
Charles Parmantie,	1
Emanuel Langlade,	1
Jean Olmier,	1
Charles Charier,	1
Sebastian Prevoteau,	1
ffrancis Delpus,	1
Henry Collie, sa femme et un enfan,	3
Estienne Cheneau and sa femme,	2
Daniel Duchemin[25] and sa femme,	2
Daniel Gueran,[26] sa femme and 4 enfans,	6
Jean Soulié, sa femme and 3 enfans,	5

[24] "La Veure des Sr. Lorange, paroisse St. Sauvier, La Rochelle, fled to England in 1682, leaving 'quelque bien en Poitou,'" (Arch. Nat.) *Baird*, I, 296. The name is also rendered L'Orange.

[25] *Baird*, II, 71, states that "Daniel Du Chemin (born at Caen, in Normandy) was naturalized in New York, September 27, 1687, with his son, Daniel, and his daughter, Catharine, born at the Isle of St. Christopps. * * * The name does not reappear until eighty years later when another Daniel Duchemin obtains a marriage license in the city of New York, July 7, 1767, and receives letters of naturalization May 20, 1769.

[26] Probably from St. Nazaire, in Saintonge, (see *Baird*, II, 16). The name is now rendered Guerrant in Virginia. John Guerrant was a member of the Virginia Convention of 1788, and the name has been often prominently represented in Virginia.

Nicholas Ducré and sa femme,	2
Jean Noel Levasseur and sa femme,	2
Rebecá Poitevin,[27]	I
Louis Losane, sa femme and 2 enfans,	4
Elizabet Curien,	I
Jean Boyé Surgan,	I
Marie Catherine Lecoin,	I
Jean ffauquaran[28] and sa femme,	2
Elizabet Morel,	I
Pierre Balaros,	I
Paul Legover,	I

(*Suisses.*)

Jean Jacques Faizant,	I
Jacob Aigle,	I
Pierre Shriflit,	I
Ouly Cumery,	I
Madame Herbert, 4 demoiselles, sa filles,	5

Genevois.

Jean Pasteur,	I
——— Dupuy,	I
Charles Pasteur and sa femme,[29]	2

[27] Probably of Orsemont. See *Baird*, II, 97.

[28] Now rendered in Virginia Fourqurean.

[29] The name Pasteur is now invested with world-wide special interest through the recent scientific discoveries of the eminent French chemist in alleviation of the dread malady, hydrophobia. A curiosity as to his descent may be pardonable. It may be that he springs from the same conscientious strain as the refugee of the text. Rev. James Pasteur appears as "lecturer" for Norfolk parish, Norfolk county, in 1754.—(*Perry's Church Papers of Virginia*, page 413.) William Pasteur, a descendant in the second generation, probably of the refugee, was, in 1752, an apprentice with Dr. George Gilmer (surgeon, physician and apothecary in Williamsburg, Virginia, and the ancestor of the distinguished Virginia family of the name), and served as a surgeon in the Virginia line during the Revolutionary war.

Elizabet Hayer, alemande, - - - - - -	1
Marie Hehns, yanwelle flamande, - - - -	1
Total, - - - -	191

VIRGINIA—*ss:*

Delivered to the ffrench Refugees on the Charitable subscription of severall persons:

At ffalling Creek[30] 256 Bushells of Indian Corn, besides private donation. Quantity not Known, whether of Corn nor Wheate. Capt. Webb for Beeves and Corn to Monsieur de Joux Company, and Corn delivered Mons. de Joux Company from Mrs. Kennon's mill (10 Busshells by Capt. Webb's note), and ever since their arrivall by mine. Quantity not knowne.

---

[30] Falling Creek flows into James river on the south side, about seven miles below the city of Manchester, and twenty below the site of Manakin-town settlement. Upon this creek, in 1619, was erected the first iron-furnace in America, the operations of which were suspended by the Indian massacre of March 22, 1622. Colonel William Byrd obtained, April 20, 1687, a grant of 1,800 acres, within the limits of which was included the site of the ill fated iron-works. October 29, 1696, he obtained a grant of 5,644 acres lying contiguous thereto, giving as a reason therefor, in a note prefixed to a record of his landed possessions, that "there having been iron-works on Falling Creek in the time of the Company, and Colonel Byrd having an intention to carry them on, and foreseeing that abundance of wood might be necessary for so great a work, he took up a large tract," &c. It is not known that either he or his son ever revived the iron-works. A grist mill now owned by Mr. H. Carrington Watkins, located opposite to the site of the iron-works of 1619, in all probability occupies the site of the mill of William Byrd referred to in the text. The Falling Creek tract was purchased by Colonel Archibald Cary some time prior to the Revolutionary war. Upon it he erected his well-known seat, the name of which became in the records of the period part and parcel of his personal designation as "Archibald Cary, of Ampthill." He erected new iron-works on Falling Creek, but abandoned his forge, and converted his pond to the use of a grist-mill about 1760. The editor visited Ampthill and Falling Creek in May, 1876, and definitely identified, through bits of cinder remaining, the sites of both the iron works of 1619 and of 1760.

Two horses for their use,	- - - -	£10
Two Beeves, of 7 and 8 yeares old,	- - -	6
At my store at Arahettox for nailes about	- -	£11

besides money, meat, ffish, Corne and wheat given by severall charitable persons. Quantity not Knowne to

WM. BYRD.

MEMORANDUM, CASH PAID BY SEVERALL FOR YE USE OF YE FFRENCH REFUGEES.

	£.	s.
By his Excellency,[31] - - - - -	50	0
By Mr. Comissary Blair,[32] - - - -	5	0
By Mr. Benjamin Harrison,[33] - - -	5	0
By Colonel Randolph,[34] - - - -	5	0
By Mr. ffowler, - - - - -	2	10

[31] Governor Nicholson.

[32] Rev. James Blair, D. D., born in Scotland, 1660, died at Williamsburg, Virginia, August 1, 1743; appointed commissary, 1689; raised a subscription of £2,500, and procured the charter of William and Mary College. February 19, 1693; was its president until his death. Also president of the Council of Virginia. He assisted in compiling "The State of His Majesty's Colony in Virginia," by Hartwell, Blair, and Chilton, and published "Sermons and Discourses," four volumes, 8vo. London, 1742. He left his library and £500 to the College.

[33] Benjamin Harrison was clerk of Virginia Council in 1630. The name appears as a patentee of lands in "Warrosquoracke," and James City counties, 1635–43. Benjamin Harrison—doubtless him of the text—was assistant revisor of the laws of the Colony, 1700; Speaker of the House of Burgesses and Treasurer in 1706. He appears to have died in 1710, as Peter Beverley was ele ted Speaker and Treasurer in October, 1710, and at the same session of the Burgesses, Elizabeth, widow and administratrix of Benjamin Harrison, the younger, of Charles City county, gentleman, deceased, was empowered to sell land and slaves for the payment of his debts. *Hening's Statutes of Virginia*, III.

[34] Colonel William Randolph, of "Turkey Island," the alleged founder of the distinguished Virginia family of the name, "of Yorkshire, England," born, 1651, died, April 11, 1711.

	£.	s.
By Mr. Jno. Herbert,[35] - - - -	10	0
By Mr. Miles Cary,[36] - - - -	1	0
	78	10

Besides several summes given in to be collected at my stores, where they are to have credit for ye same.

W. BYRD.

	£.	s.
More given by his Excellency to Mons'r de Joux company that came in with him, - - -	25	0

More given for ye use of the Refugees (vizt.):

By Stephen Fouace[37] to Mr. Sailly, - - -	4	0
To one Badoüit, - - - - -	1	0
To another, - - - - - -		10

To those that were left at James Towne, 4 Barrells of Corne.

---

[35] John Herbert was granted 1,227 acres of land on the southward branch of Elizabeth river, July 21, 1669 (John Howard, a head-right), and 1,215 acres in Charles City county, April 21, 1690. Books Nos. 6, page 220, and 8, page 74, *Virginia Land Registry*.

[36] Colonel Miles Cary (fifth in descent from William Cary, Mayor of Bristol, England in 1546, born in Bristol, 1620, and son of Colonel Myles Cary, emigrated to Virginia, 1650; first collector of James river; burgess from Warwick county, 1659; member of the Council; Colonel in time of the Dutch incursions, 1665-7; died June 10, 1667), was born about 1655; married twice, first, Mary, daughter of Thomas Milner (born August 6, 1667, died October 27, 1700); second, Mary, daughter of Colonel William Wilson (died, 1708); died, 1708; clerk of the Assembly.

[37] Rev. Stephen Fouace was one of the trustees in the first charter of William and Mary College, February 8, 1692 [February 19, 1693, New Style]. He and the Rev. James Blair, as the only survivors of the original trustees, February 27, 1729, transferred the corporate rights invested in them to the faculty of the College.

By Mr. Lewis Burwil,[38] 12 Bushels of wheat.
Item, by the same, 5 Bushels of Corne.

Copia,

Test,

DIONISIUS WRIGHT.

VIRGINIA—*ss:*

At a Councill held at his Maj'tie's Royall Colledge of William and Mary, December 27, 1700—

Present: his Excellency in Council.

It is the opinion and advice of the Council that it is for his majestie's service, and the Interest of this, his Maj'tie's Colony and Dominion, that his Excellency do represent to his Majesty the present state of ye ffrench protestant Refugees, and the poverty and disability of the Country, and to address his Majesty that no more of them may be sent in.

At a Councill held at the hon'ble Mr. Auditor Byrd's, March 9th, 1700—

Present: his Excellency in Council.

Ordered, that a proclamation issue to the severall countyes of this, his Maj'tie's Colony and Dominion of Virginia, requireing ye Burgesses of each respective County to call in the Briefs, with the Subscriptions and Donations given to the reliefe of the French Protestant Refugees, and that they returne an account thereof to the hon'ble Mr. Auditor Byrd and Benjamin Harrison, Esquire, who are appointed to distribute the same for the support of the aforesaid ffrench Refugees.

Whereas, severall ffrench Protestant Refugees are lately arrived in York River in the Nassau, Capt. —— Tragian Comm'r, concerning whom his Excellency hath received no

---

[38] He was the second of the name in Virginia and son of Major Lewis Burwell, of the family of Bedford and Northamton-shire, England, who settled on Carter's Creek, in Gloucester county, Virginia, in 1640, and married Lucy, daughter of Captain Robert Higginson. A deduction of the Burwell family of Virginia was contributed by the present writer to the *Richmond Standard*, June 18–25, 1881.

perticular intelligence or Commands from his most Sacred Majesty, save only a Letter from the Lord Bishop of London concerning one Mr. Latiné, who comes in the Quality of a minister, and one other Letter from Mr. Blaithwayte concerning one John Boyer, a french Gentleman; and the aforesaid ffrench Refugees making no application nor proposalls to the Government in their owne behalfe, his Excellency and his Majestie's hon'ble Council, comisserating their poor and low condition, and willing as much as in them lies to find meanes for their present support—

Do thereupon Order that such and so many of them as are willing to go and inhabit at the Manakin Towne, where severall ffrench are already settled, may and shall receive reliefe from the Contributions given or hereafter to be given towards the support and maintenance of such as shall there Inhabit; and that such and so many of them as are not willing to go thither be Lycenced and permitted to disperse themselves amongst the Inhabitants of this country, to provide for their necessary support untill further order shall be therein taken. And it is further ordered, that a copy of the last Briefe be sent to Capt. Tragian and ye ffrench Minister, to be published amongst them.

March 10th, 1700.

His Excellency and the Hon'ble Council do recommend to Lt.-Colonel William Randolph and Captain Giles Webb, from time to time, to make enquiry into the state and condition of the ffrench Refugees Inhabiting at the Manakin Towne and parts adjacent, and communicate the same to his Excellency, and alwayes to Exhort the aforesaid french Refugees to live in unity, peace and concord.

DIONISIUS WRIGHT.

This Chart party, Indented—made the third day of December, anno Domini, 1700, and in the Twelfth yeare of the reign of our Sovereign Lord, William the third, King of England, &c.—Between Sir William Phipard, of the Town of Pool, in the county of Dorset, Knight, owner of the Ship called the Nassau of Pool, of the burthen of ffive hundred Tuns or thereabouts, now in the River of Thames, of the one part, and Moses Jaquean, Isaac Bellet, Matthew Perodin, Abraham Perodin, Peter

Bouvot, and John Hamilton, all of London, Merchants of the other part, Witnesseth, that (for the consideration hereunder mentioned) the said owner doth hereby for himself, his Executors and administrators, covenant, grant, and agree to, and with, the said Moses Jaquean, Isaac Bellet, Matthew Perodin, Abraham Perodin, Peter Bouvot and John Hamilton, their Executors, administrators and assigns, as followeth (vizt): That by the fifth day of this Instant, month of December, the said ship shall, at the said owner's charge, be fitted and Equipped with all Stores requisite for the voyage hereunder mentioned; and also at the like costs and charges be victualled for carrying the passengers hereunder mentioned to James Towne, in Virginia, with the same sort of provision as those for the ship's company, and that the said ship shall, by the said fifth day of this Instant, December, at the costs and charges of the said Owner, be fitted, and have fitted, and made ready, convenient Lodgings or Cabbins for the said passengers, for two in an appartment, or with hammocks to hold and carry at least 150 in number, and shall stay at or near Blackwall 3 days after the said 5th day of this instant, December, to receive and take in all such french Passengers, with their apparell and household goods, as the said Moses Jaquean, Isaac Bellet, Matthew Perodin, Abraham Perodin, Peter Bouvot and John Hamilton, or their assigns, shall please to send on board her, so many as she can conveniently carry, and with them, or as many of them as shall be willing to goe, shall then, as wind and weather permit, saile and make the best of her way directly unto James Towne, in Virginia, to the usuall place of Ships unlading there, and then sett and carry on Shoar all the said passengers with their said goods brought thither, and so end her said employment, the dangers of the seas and Enemyes alwayes excepted; and that the Master of the said Ship shall daily, from the time of the passengers coming on board at Blackwall as aforesaid, and during all their said passage to James Towne aforesaid, allow and give them, the said Passengers, the like or customary daily allowance as is and shall be given and allowed to the Ship's company in Messes, and deliver in the presence of the said master and overseers of the said Passengers every Munday morning weekly, during the said passage, to the said passengers their said full allowance in bread, butter and Cheese for that week, the rest of their provisions being to be distributed amongst them daily, as the Ship's Company shall be and in the same manner ; and that if the said Ship shall put into any Port or place by contrary wind in her said passage, and that any of the said passengers shall be on shoar, then the said Ship shall stay for their returneing on board 24 houres in the whole after the wind shall be fair to saile forward, if so required by the Overseers of the said Passengers, and send the Ship's boats on Shoar to bring them off, after which 4 and 20 hours the Ship to have liberty to proceed; and if any of the said passengers shall be so on shoar, shall not be willing to returne on board, the said master shall protest against them, if so required by the said overseers ; and the said Moses Jaquean, Isaac Bellet, Matthew Perodin, Abraham Perodin, Peter Bouvot and John Hamilton, for the considerations aforesaid, do hereby, for themselves, their executors and administrators, covenant and agree to and with the said owner, his executors and administrators, and assignes, that they, the said Moses Jaquean, Isaac Bellet, Matthew Perodin, Abraham Perodin, Peter Bouvot and John Hamilton, or their assignes, shall, and will, within 3 days after the said 5th day of this Instant, December, send on board the said ship at Blackwall aforesaid, at least the number of 150 french passengers, if not more, and upon shipping such passengers shall and will truly pay, or cause to be paid, unto the said owner, his executors or assignes, freight for their said passage, and provision to James Towne aforesaid, and for other the promises to be perform'd by the said owner to and for them, as aforesaid, at and after ye rate of 5 pounds sterling per head for each passenger so shipped, and at least for the number of 150 certain, always reckoning and accounting 2 passengers under the age of 12 years each to go and be paid freight for as but one passenger. Lastly, it is provided and agreed that after ye 3 days above mentioned for taking in the said passengers at London shall be expired, it shall be lawfull for the said Ship to proceed on her voyage with what number of them as shall be then on board without staying longer, and if the number then on board shall not amount to 150, the said Moses Jaquean, Isaac Bellet, Matthew Perodin, Abraham Perodin, Peter Bouvot and John Hamilton, or their assignes, shall pay the said owner, or his assignes, before the Ship's departure, freight for the passage of 150 passengers—750 Pounds. And to the performance of all and singular the clauses, covenants and Agreements herein contained, which on ye part and behalf of ye s'd owner, his exec'rs, adm'rs and assigns, are and ought to be done, kept and perform'd. The s'd owner bindeth himselfe, his ex'rs and adm'rs, and Especially ye s'd ship, her freight, Tackles, apparel, and furniture unto the s'd Moses Jaquean, Isaac Bellet, Matthew Perodin, Abraham Perodin, Peter Bouvot and John Hamilton, their Ex'rs, Adm'rs and assigns, in ye summe or penalty of 1,500 pounds of lawfull money of England, firmly by these presents. And to the performance of all and singular the clauses, covenants, payments and agreements herein contained, which on the parts and behalfes of the s'd Moses Jaquean, Isaac Bellet, Matthew Perodin, Abraham Perodin, Peter Bouvot, and John Hamilton, their Ex'rs and adm'rs, are and ought to be done, kept, paid and performed, the s'd Moses Jaquean, Isaac Bellet, Matthew Perodin, Abraham Perodin, Peter Bouvot and John Hamilton, bind themselves, their Ex'rs and adm'rs and every of them, joyntley and severally, unto the s'd owner, his ex'rs, adm'rs and assignes, in the summe or penalty of 1,500 pounds of lawfull money of England, firmly by these presents. In witnesse whereof, the s'd parties have hereunto interchangeably put their hands and seales in London the day, month and year first above written.

Memorandum.—It is agreed, That, although it is mentioned that the Passengers shall have the same allowance of provisions as the Ship's company, It is the intent and meaning of the s'd parties y't they shall have the allowance as followeth (vizt): to every passenger above the age of 6 yeares, to have 7 pounds of Bread every weeke, and to a mess, 8 passengers in a mess, and to have 2 peeces of Porke, at 2 pounds each peece, 5 dayes in a weeke, with pease; and 2 days in a week to have 2 four pound peeces of Beefe a day and pease, or one four pound peece of Beefe with a Pudding with pease; and at any time if it shall happen that they are not willing the Kettle should be boyled, or by bad weather cannot, In such case every passenger shall have 1 pound of cheese every such day; and such children as are under 6 yeares of age to have such allowances in flower, oatmeal, Fruit, Sugar and Butter as the overseers of them shall Judge Convenient.

Sealed and Del'v'd, being first duly Stamped in ye presence of John Clarke, George Wharton, W. Boteler, Notaries.

M. JAQUEAN. [s]
I. BELLET. [s]
M. PERODIN. [s]
PETER BOUVOT. [s]
JOHN HAMILTON. [s]

This is a true copy of ye originall, which, after comparing, I attest.

London, the 4th December, 1700.

W. BOTELER, *Not. Pub.*
Dec. 4, 1700.

December ye 3d, 1700. Received of Messrs. Moses Jaquean, Isaac Bellet, Matthew Perodin, Abraham Perodin, Peter Bouvot, and John Hamilton ye summe of 892 Pounds, 10 Shillings, in full, for the passages of 197 French Passengers to James Towne, in Virginia. Rec'd: WILL. PHIPPARD.

Witnesses:

John Clarke,
Wm. Boteler, } Not's.
George Marton,

DIONISIUS WRIGHT.

THE STATE OF THE FFRENCH REFUGEES.

10 and 11th May, 1701.

The 10th of May, last, I with Coll. Randolph, Capt. Epes,[39] Capt. Webb, &c., went up to the new settlements of ye ffrench Refugees at ye Manakan Town. Wee visited about seventy of their hutts, being, most of them, very mean; there being upwards of fourty of y'm betwixt ye two Creeks, w'ch is about

---

[39] Captain Francis Eppes, grandson of Colonel Francis Eppes, County Lieutenant, who settled at City Point, Prince George county, Virginia, (then forming a portion of Charles City county), about the year 1635. A brief deduction of the Eppes family is given in *Slaughter's History of Bristol Parish*, pages 172-3.

four miles along on ye River, and have cleared all ye old Manacan ffields for near three miles together, as also some others (who came thither last ffeb'ry, as Blackman told us) have cleared new grounds toward the Lower Creeke, and done more worke than they y't went thither first. They have, all of y'm, some Garden trade and have planted corne, but few of y'm had broke up their ground or wed the same, whereupon I sent for most of y'm and told y'm they must not expect to enjoy ye land unless they would endeavour to improve it, and if they make no corne for their subsistance next yeare they could not expect any further relief from the Country. Mon'r de Joux promised at their next meeting to acquaint them all w'th w't I said, and to endeavour to stirr y'm up to be diligent in weeding and secureing their corne and wheat, of w'ch latter there are many small patches, but some is overrun w'th woods, and the horses (of w'ch they have severall, w'th some Cows) have spoiled more; most of y'm promise faire. Indeed, they are very poor, and I am not able to supply y'm w'th Corne (they being about 250 last month), having bought up all in these two counties, and not haveing received one month's provision from all ye other Countyes, there being some in the Isle of Wight, but cannot hire any to fetch it. There are above 20 families seated for 4 or 5 miles below the Lower Creeke and have cleared small plantations, but few of y'm had broke up their grounds. Wee went up to ye Cole, w'ch is not above a mile and a-half from their settlement on the great upper Creeke, w'ch, riseing very high in great Raines, hath washed away the Banke that the Coal lyes bare, otherwise it's very deep in the Earth, the land being very high and near the surface is plenty of Slate[40]. Tho' these people are very poor,

---

[40] Lawson, the Surveyor-General and historian of North Carolina, ascribes the discovery of the coal to a Huguenot settler at Manakin-Town, "who having shot a fowl, which fell into the river near where the bank was precipitous, went down to the assistance of his dog, who, going for the fowl, had difficulty in regaining the summit of the bank. The Frenchman, in his efforts to climb back, dislocated some earth at the foot of a shrub of which he had taken hold. and revealed the outcropping coal. Making known his discovery, the land was surveyed and patented by one of the gentry." The patentee appears to have been William Byrd, "who understanding that there was a coal mine upon some land lying near Monacan town, which had not been granted

yet they seem very cheerful and are (as farr as wee could learne) very healthy, all they seem to desire is y't they might have Bread enough. Wee lodged there that night and returned the new Road I caused to be marked, which is extraordinary Levell and dry way and leads either to the ffalls or the mill, a very good well beaten path for carts.

W. BYRD.

THE CLAUSE OF A LETTER TO HIS EXC'Y FROM GOV'R MASON,[41] COL'L AND COMMANDER AND CHIEF OF ALL YE MILITIA, HORSE AND FOOT, IN YE COUNTY OF STAFFORD, DATED OCTOBER 28TH, 1701.

Sir,—Wee have no news in these parts, only that ye ffrench Refugees is, most of them, gone to Maryland, and have left an ill distemper behind them, ye bloody flux, which has affected some of our neighbours. Ye ffrench Refugees' great ffriend, Col'l Fitzhugh,[42] dyed tuesday, ye 21st, at night, Nov'r 6th, 1701.

---

to the French, took out a patent for 344 acres, including the same, which patent was dated October 20, 1704."

MS. Book of the Titles of the Landed Possessions of William Byrd, in the Collections of the Virginia Historical Society.

[41] Colonel George Mason (son of Colonel George Mason, a native of Staffordshire, England, an adherent of Charles I, who fled after the Royalist defeat at Worcester, landed at Norfolk, Virginia, in 1651, and settled on the Potomac river at Accokeek,) married Sarah, daughter of Colonel Gerard Fowke. The wills of both himself and wife were admitted to probate in Stafford county in November, 1676. His son married the daughter of Stevens Thomson, Attorney-General of Virginia (died 1713), and they were the parents of the patriots, George Mason, of "Gunston," and Thomson Mason.

[42] Colonel William Fitzhugh, lawyer, planter, merchant and shipper, the ancestor of the excellent Virginia family of the name, was born in Bedford, England, January 9th, 1651. He settled in that portion of Stafford which now comprises King George county, calling his seat "Bedford." He married, May 1, 1674, Mary Tucker. He was the counsel for Major Robert Beverley (the father of the historian) in the trial of the latter for "plant-cutting" and other misdemeanors, in 1682. A MS. copy of his letters, written during the period May 15, 1679—April 26, 1699, is among the MS. collections of the Virginia Historical Society.

A LIST OF YE FRENCH REFUGEES THAT ARE SETTLED ATT YE MANNACHIN TOWN ARE AS FOLLOWS:

In ye first Shipp.

Mr. Phillip[43] and his wife,	2
Mr. Peter Chalin, his wife and 3 chil'n,	5
Mr. Abrah. Nicod,	1
Mr. Char. Saillee,	1
Theph. Mallott and his wife,	2
Gulte,	1
Mullin,	1
John ffarcy and his wife,	2
Steph. Chastaine and his wife,	2
Peter Tuly and his wife,	2
John Joacmi and his wife,	2
Minst and his wife,	2
Gawey and his wife,	2
Bilbun and his wife,	2
ffaur, his brother and sister,	3
Parcule and his wife,	2
Leverre,	1
Gillan,	1
Voyer and his wife,	2
Peter Gaway and his wife,	2
John Saye,	1
Pantier,	1
Chambures and his wife,	2
Morret and his wife,	2
Peter Perry,	1
Mallon, his wife and father,	3
Brouse and one child,	2
Corun,	1

[43] The full name of the minister thus modestly designated was Claude Phillipe de Richebourg. He was a relative of Isaac Porcher de Richebourg, the ancestor of a prominent Huguenot family of South Carolina, both being descended from the Counts of Richebourg, of St. Sévère. Owing to disputes in his parish, which were referred to the Council of Virginia, September 2, 1707, M. Phillippe, with numerous followers, left Virginia soon after this date and settled in the Carolinas.

Cabarnis[44] and his wife,	2
Imbart and his wife,	2
Sasin,	1
Vigne,	1
Garrén,	1
Chalagenie, his wife and one child,	3
Debart,	1
Bernard and his wife,	2
Cath. Billet,	1
Sublet, his wife and four children,	6
Moroll and his wife and one child,	3
Cocuelguie,	1
Veras and his wife,	2
Isaac Verey,	1
John Buffe, Du Clue, La Cadon,	3
	81

The names of such as came in the second ship:

Mr. Benj'n De Joux,	1
Barel, his wife and one child,	3
Govin, and his wife and Joshua Pettit,	3
Alocastres, John Gunn and Timothy Russ,	3
Isaac Lefavour and his wife and John Martin,	3
John Owner and his wife and Meshall,	3
Remy and his wife, Gavand and his wife,	4
Villam, and his wife and Shabron,	3
Abrate Befour, his wife and 4 children,	6
Jasper Subus, his wife and 4 children,	6
	35

All and every ye persons herein before mentioned are seated between ye creeks (excepted Duclow and Sneadow) who came also in ye first ship and are settled on ye other side ye said creek.

[44] Now rendered Cabaniss in Virginia.

And these that follow are likewise seated between ye said creeks but came in the third ship, (vizt.):

Rapine, his wife and 2 children, - - - -	4
ffran Benon and Gillaum, - - - - -	2
Treyon, his wife and 1 child below ye creek, - -	3
	9

The names of those y't came in ye fourth ship and are also settled between ye creeks:

Buffo, Shulu, and his wife and 3 children, - - -	6
Tumar and his wife, Chevas and 2 children, - -	5
Vallant, ffasant, John Pastour, - - - -	3
Mary Legraund, - - - - -	1
Robert, his wife and one child, - - - -	3
Mocks, his wife and one child, - - - -	3
Lamas, - - - - - - -	1
	23

A List of such as came in ye second and fourth shipps, and that are seated below ye creeks are as follows:

Greordocaso, - - - - - -	1
Jno. Boshard, his wife and 3 children, - - -	5
Dan'l Bluet and 2 children, - - - -	3
Pet'r Musset and his wife, and Misar Brock, - -	3
Jos. Oliver, Po. Leaseo, and Jno. Marsarae, - -	3
ffr'a Clapy and Legraund and 3 children, - - -	5
Nicti Mar, his wife and 2 children, - - -	4
Sam'l Huntteeker, his wife and 2 children, - -	4
ffra Duacon, Anth. Bonion, and Provo, - - -	3
Muller and 1 child, - - - - -	2
Dufontaine, his wife and one child, - - -	3
Jasper Gardner, his wife and 3 children, - - -	5
	41

In ye fourth Shipp:

John Leroy, booker, and his wife and one child, - -	4
Coullon and his wife, - - - - -	2
	6

below ye Creek:

Merchant Suillee, his wife and 2 children and one negro woman, - - - - - - -	5
Anthony Obray between ye Creeks, - - -	1
	6

These two persons last mentioned came from New York.

David Ministres and his wife not gone up falling creek, -	2
	6
	6
	41
Nov. 10, 1701,	23
WM. BYRD,	9
Copia,	35
Testa,	81
DIONISIUS WRIGHT.	
Total,	203

A COLLECTION OF ALL MATTERS RELATING TO THE FFRENCH PROTESTANT REFUGEES—1700.

At a Councill held at his Maj'tie's Royall Colledge of William and Mary, the 25th October, 1700—

Present—his Excell'y in Councill.

Whereas, several ffrench Refugees have lately, (vizt.) on or about the 20th Instant, arrived at James City, in this Colony, with designe to goe up to Manikin Towne in the upper parts of James River, whither severall ffrench are already gone to make Settlement; his Excellency and the Hon'ble Councill taking the same into their serious consideration, are of opinion, that (considering the poverty and disability of the said Refugees, their ignorance in the Customes and affaires of this Colony, their wants and necessities, being destitute of all meanes of support and sustinence at present), It will be most for their advantage and interest to disperse themselves, and do accordingly Order, License and permitt the aforesaid ffrench Refugees to disperse themselves into severall parts of this country that they may thereby the better provide for the future support of themselves and ffamilies untill the next fall, at which time further care may be taken therein

At a Council held at the Hon'ble Mr. Auditor Byrd's, 14th day of November, 1700—

Present: his Excellency in Councill.

Whereas, severall ffrench Protestant Refugees have been by his most sacred Majesty sent into this Colony with particular Instructions from his Majesty to his Excellency, the Gover'r, to incourage and protect them in their settling here;

And whereas, by former Order in Councill the place of their settlement was appointed at the Manikin Towne, above the falls of James River, to the end that all due observance and obedience may be paid to his Maj'tie's aforesaid Royall instructions in that behalfe, and the Government be the better enabled to render unto his most sacred Maj'tie a full and briefe acc't of the particular proceedings therein:

It is ye opinion of ye Councill, and accordingly ordered, that Monsieur De Sailly render an acc't (to the next Councill to be held at his Maj'tie's Royall Colledge of William and Mary ye Third of December next) what French were carried up to the aforesaid place, in what state and condition they now are, w't money he hath received in England for their use, and how it hath been disposed of; as also to lay before ye Councill copies of all ye Transactions betwixt him and Doctor Cox relating to the aforesaid ffrench refugees. There have been carryed up to Monocantown about 120 Refugees, of whom 6 are dead and about 20 gone away, some for libertinage and lazinesse and some for want of bread, being not able to suffer hunger and take patience when we meet with disappointments (as we did when Bossard and his 'complices stole away upon ye road with force, violence and threatenings the meale from our men and horses, what occasioned almost all ye people to come down and leave ye place), and cannot get meal; but we believe that severall of them and others living in ye English plantations would goe and settle there constantly if they were sure of a peck of meal a head weekly, of a bushell of pease and a peck of salt once for all, and of some blanketts to cover in cold weather such as have none; and we think y't most part of them would doe well, clear ye ground to provide themselves ye next year w'th bread, and afterwards w'th all necessaries, and to pay to his Maj'tie all observances, duty and obedience. We Judge it soe, because we see y't some of y'm who have not been soe sick, and are already pretty well, are encouragement to others; and severall told they would come upp again and settle themselves at work if we could afford them bread to maintain and strengthen them, because they have been so long sick y't they are weak still, and they cannot hope to recover their health and strength in fasting; and so for ye present, their condition being very poor, deserves his maj'tie's charity; and y't some allowance may be made unto them out of the Briefs, money or other to provide y'm w'th corn, clothes, seeds, tools and some cattle, because for want of lands upon Nantsmund River, where they thought to be settled and set down by the Ship altogether w'th their goods without any charge, they have been obliged to goe up about 150 miles into ye woods 25 miles from ye plantations, and to bear great and extraordinary charges for their transportation and of all their goods and victualls, besides ye loss they sufiered at James town by ye sinking of their sloop, where they had their goods lost and spoiled to ye value of 300£, and ye sicknesse they have laid under at ye falls these 4 months, having been above 150 sick at once, w'th soe little help and assistance in a place where provisions are so scarse and dear, y't they have been forced for some small relief and supply to sell their arms, clothes and other goods after having spent what money they had, and so to remain naked and deprived of all commodities till his Maj'tie be pleased to assist and relieve them to enable y'm to make good plantations and to build ye Town; but Capt. Webb or some other must be appointed, w'th power and authority to rule and command y'm, because being come only to endeavour to settle y'm conveniently and comfortably, haveing overgone all ye hardships and difficulties of ye beginning and liveing as Refugees upon His Maj'tie's allowance in England and Ireland, which we cannot receive here, we desire to goe there to enjoy of his Maj'tie's bounty and to return to every one what they have entrusted unto us, to remove all ye prejudices of tales and false reports of ye ffrench and Popish Emissaries, who have alwayes endeavoured to cross and oppose this undertaking, and as we see have prevailed and sent over some men to cross and contradict us and to make us suspect to ye Nation, Governm't and Clergy and to all other people; but we shall prove to ye whole world y't we have taken all these troubles and charges upon us only out of Charity, and done all this w'th honesty and sincerity; and for ye other Refugees settled by Mr de Joux between Manycan Creek and Powick Creek, we doe not know their condition, and though they have given unto us great many subjects of Complaints in troubling and vexing us, we will Charitably spare y'm; and to avoid all disputes and quarrels, desiring to live quietly and peaceably, say nothing of ye malice and tricks they employ every day to blame and accuse us without justice, cause or reason, and leave to ye said de Joux to give what acc't he pleases, since he hath done all without us and kept ye oth'er 'factures and goods sent to us; what we affirme this 2d day of December, 1700.

CH. DE SAILLY,
OLIVER DE LA MUCE.

If the hon'ble assembly like this undertaking and settl't, and has a mind (as we hope) to assist and encourage it, it's necessary, that ye Minister De Joux be ordered to goe up to settle and stay in ye Town to preach, make prayers, and perform other dutys of his ministry; that he be ordered to give and deliver ye accounts, 'factures and goods intrusted unto him and sent to us to sell, exchange, or mortgage y'm for Corn, &c., for the supplys of ye people; that ye people of ye 3d ship and their chiefs be alsoe ordered to doe ye same for ye same use, and particularly for 23£ sterling intrusted unto y'm in a Trunck of Chirurgy and medicine sent unto us for ye Colony, besides ye same money as others; That a proclamation be sent to every parish to forbid to receive, keep and maintain any of them without ye leave and discharge of their directors, and to order to ye s'd refugees, who run up and down, and have no place or condition to go up and work, to settle themselves; and finally that a stock of Corn be provided in good time to supply y'm, or a summe of money to buy it as soon as possible, which may be returned unto such as shall be willing to advance and lend ye s'd Corne or money out of the gratifications they expect from his Maj'tie and from this country, or by themselves, at least in 2 or 3 years, when they shall be settled according to ye account kept by such as shall be appointed to be their directors.

At the City of Williamsburgh, Dec 9th, 1700—

Present: his Excellency in Councill

It is the opinion of ye Councill that his Maj'tie's and the Lord's letter concerning the Marquess de La Muce and the setll't of the French refugees and all papers relating to that matter, the Lord's Letter concerning the building and erecting a house for the Governor, and ye settleing and regulating of all claimes and publick debts, and to see in what state ye Revenue at present stands, be recommended to the Consideration of the House of Burgesses.

Indenture made 2d day of May, 1698, between Daniel Cox, in the County of Middlesex, Proprietary of Carolana and fflorida, on the one part, and Sir William Waller, Knight, Oliver, Marques de la Muce and Monsieur Charles de Sailly, of the other part: "Whereas a discovery being made of a region or Territory in ye parts of America between ye degrees of 31 and 36 North latitude inclusively, King Charles V, by Letters Pat. under the great seal bearing date Westminster, 30 October, in the 5th year of his reign, granted and confirmed unto Sir Robert Heath, Kn'ght, all this land lying within certain boundaries; and also all those Islands of Veanis, Bahamas, and all other Islands or Isletts there or neare thereto, and lying Southwards of and from ye s'd Continent, all w'ch lye within ye degrees of 31 and 36 northern latitude inclusively," &c., &c. Of this land, Daniel Cox sells to the above nam'd parties 500,000 acres, English measure, on ye west side of ye River Spiritu Sancto, which empties itself into ye Bay of apalache at ye N. E'd of ye Gulph of Mexico, which shall be purchased by ye Proprietary of ye Indian natives; To have and to hold the s'd Tract of land to them, the said Sir William Waller, Knight, Oliver, Marques de la Muce and Monsieur Charles de Sailly, their heires and assigns forever; and if ye s'd parties and their associates shall take up 500,000 acres more, they shall have power from ye Proprietary so to doe, Provided it be taken up within ye space of Seaven yeares ensueing the date hereof, paying quit rents for the same," &c., &c. The late King did erect this Territory into a Province, and named it Carolana, and the said Islands the Carolana Islands. The last 500,000 acres to be purchased by the parties to the second part "of ye Indian natives at their own proper charge and expence;" and they shall be allowed "six months' time to view the country in order to their choice of such Lands whereon they intend to settle, and that from and after the time of their choice of such lands, that the said Sir Wm. Waller, Kn'ght, Oliver, Marques de la Muce, and Monsieur Charles de Sailly, or their associates, shall enjoy the said lands Seven yeares, paying only a ripe Ear of Indian Corne in the season if demanded; and from ye Expiring of the said Seaven yeares 5 shillings Sterling money of England, or the value thereof, in either Coine or Bullion of Gold or silver, as a Quitt-rent for every 500 acres of Land soe taken up and purchased by the Proprietary as aforesaid." Dr. Cox also reserved for himself the selection of 2 or more places for Ports or Harbours, with a competent Tract of land adjoining; also stipulates for certain royalties on all mines, quarrys, or pearl fisheries discovered. Also certain concessions are made for the introduction into the country of "100 families or 200 Persons," Protestants. "It is mutually agreed, that if the said parties and their associates doe not within the space of 2 yeares, next ensuing ye date hereof, transport, or cause to be transported, at least 200 families to plant and settle within ye s'd Colony, then this Grant and commission shall cease, Determine, and be utterly void and ineffectuall to all Intents and purposes whatsoever."

DAN'LL COXE.

AN ABSTRACT OF "THE COPPY OF DR. COXE'S TITLE HE CLAIMES IN NORFFOLK COUNTY."[45]

Indenture made "the 22d January, 1639, in ye 13th year of Charles," between Sir John Harvey, Kn'ght, Governour of Virginia, and the R't Hon'ble Henry Lord Maltravers, "assignes and sells out" a competent tract of Land in ye Southern part of the Colony, to beare a name of a County, and be called ye County of Norfolk." Said tract situate, lying and being on the southern side of James River, in the branch of ye said river, hereafter to be called Maltravers' River, towards the head of ye said Nanzimum *alias* Maltravers' River, being bounded from that part of Maltravers' river, where it divides itself into Branches, one degree in Longitude on either side of ye River, and in Latitude to ye height of 35 degrees, Northerly Latitude, by ye name and appelation of ye county of Norfolk." And when Lord Maltravers have peopled and planted said tract, he is allowed to make choice and to enter into as much more land in Virginia, &c.

TO HIS EXCELLENCY, FFRANCIS NICHOLSON, ESQUIRE, HIS MAJ'TIE'S LIEUTENANT AND GOVERNOR-GENERAL OF VIRGINIA.

This humble supplication, by the under written petitioners, in the name and behalfe of all the ffrench Refugees arrived in Virginia, along w'th Monsieur De Joux, as also in the behalfe of the greater part of ye ffrench Refugees, who Landed here both before and since to settle themselves in a Colony—

Sheweth, ... That whereas, the King's most Excellent Maj'tie, out of his gracious good will and pleasure, hath granted the ffrench Refugees a Liberty to Settle a Colony in Virginia. His Maj'tie for the incouragem't of that designe hath given Three thousand pounds Sterling, to defray the charges of 500 persons in crossing the seas and to relieve their owne necessities.

---

[45] Dr. Daniel Coxe was also a landed proprietor in West Jersey. Two companies were formed in London and in Yorkshire, chiefly among the Society of Friends, for the settlement of the province in 1677. Dr. Coxe was the largest shareholder in the former company.

In compliance with his Maj'tie's Order, the Marquis de la Muce and Monsieur De Sailly and severall other ffrench Refugees, to the number of about 200 persons, embarqued themselves last Aprill for Virginia, publishing and giving out that they sailed thither to put themselves in a capacity to receive such of their brethren as should afterwards imitate their Example, And in consideration hereof the above mentioned Sieurs De la Muce and De Sailly requested the Sieurs Jaquean, Belet and others of their ffriends whom they left behind, that at such opportunities of shipping as offered they should use the same care and diligence as they did to promote that designe.

About two months after the first embarquement, there departed a second, bound to the same place, consisting of about 150 Refugees, among whom was Monsieur De Joux, sent along with them to exercise his pastorall function as Minister of all ye s'd Colony, and who for that end was admitted into holy orders by my Lord Bishop of London.

These last haveing landed at Jamestown, understood to their great joy and satisfaction how graciously your Excellency received the first party in letting them feele ye effects of yo'r bounty and generosity so many wayes, and particularly in allotting them for their settlement one of the best tracts of land in the whole country, but to which there is no passing by water, as being 25 miles at least above the falls of James River.

But so far was the second party of ffrench Refugees from receiving that aide and assistance they proposed to themselves from the first, that on ye contrary it was noe small suprisall there to understand that more than one halfe of the first party lay sick at ye ffalls languishing under misery and want, notwithstanding the considerable supplies that the Sieurs De la Muce and De Sailly received, both from y'r Excellency and from the Country, as also y't a great number of 'em was dead, and y't so many of 'em as repaired to their new settlem't were in a distressed condition and in great disorder, complaining of the hard-heartedness of De Sailly, and speaking of him as of one whose conduct was odious and insupportable.

It was a considerable surprisall that instead of seeing this second party kindly received by Mr. De Sailly, and admitted to have a share in those charitable supplies he had in his hands and in those he had received from the country, his answer, on the contrary, to such as addrest him for reliefe was, That he had no bread nor sustenance for 'em. Nay, further, he opposed those who desired to take up such tracts of land as were adjacent to the Lands he had marked out for those of his first party, unless they would swear an oath of fidelity to such particular persons as he had made Justices of the Peace, which oaths those of the second party refused to take, being fully perswaded they lay under no obligation so to doe.

Being, therefore, destitute of all hopes of obtaining provision and reliefe from Mon'r De Sailly, they hindered Monsieur De Joux in his designe of delivering up into the hands of De Sailly those goods with which Messieurs Jaquean, Belet and their company entrusted him. And having had sufficient tryall of the s'd Mons. De Joux's integrity and affection towards them, they requested him to use his utmost care and diligence in procuring some sustenance for 'em and some lands, w'ch they might labour, sow and improve in hopes that God's blessing upon their endeavours may give 'em some subsistence for ye future w'thout being burdensome to ye country And this what the s'd De Joux has done with so much successe by his mediation with those magistrates that ruled ye country in your Excellency's absence, that we have had such supplies as have almost hitherto relieved our necessities.

At the same time ye said De Joux has, by your Excellencie's permission, and to our common satisfaction, shared out among us the Lands we are now clearing, in order to our future subsistance.

For these, and severall other weighty considerations, we humbly supplicate and Petition y'r Excellency, not only in our own behalfe, but also in ye behalfe of the ffrench refugees y't arrived here first along w'th the Sieurs De la Muce and De Sailly, and in the behalfe of the third Party that arrived last of all, and are now disperst about Jamestown, to grant us these following articles:

1st.

That it may please your Excell'y, in continuing your charitable disposition towards your Petitioners, to be instrumentall in procuring food and sustenance for them, with other things necessary for their subsistance, till they are in a capacity to live by the fruits of their own labours.

2d.

And because that tract of Land your Excell'y allotted to ye ffrench Refugees is soe remote from the English plantation, and that there is no carrying of things by water, Your Petitioners being likewise destitute of all necessaries for transporting things by land, and being otherwise unable to attend such postages without neglecting their other labours more than one-halffe of ye yeare, they do therefore petition y'r Excell'y to order that such supplies as you will procure for their s'd subsistance may be carried and transported gratis to ye hithermost frontiers of their plantations.

3d Article.

And being that your petitioners can have noe prospect of any good livelyhood in planting of tobacco, and that they cannot expect to be able in a short time to drive a trade in wings, flax, Silk and hemp, and other effects of their industry, which they aime at, and which cannot turne to any good account till after some years are past, during which they will want many things necessary for their comfortable living, They therefore petition y'r Excell'y to use y'r interest with the King's Maj'tie in procuring some encouragements for their labours, and in endeavouring to obtaine of his Maj'tie, for some years at least, a comfortable subsistance for the Ministry among them.

4th.

That it may please your Excell'y to order Monsieur De Sailly to disburse to ye above mentioned Colony the sum of Thirty Pounds Sterling out of the 230£ Sterling designed for the building of a church, without ornaments, a house for the Minister and a magazin to lay up fresh goods in, as shall be found to belong to ye said Colony in Common till it is in a condition to build a more decent and convenient church.

That the said 30 Pounds be paid down by Monsieur De Sailly to Monsieur De Joux for the said purpose.

That the said Church be built in such a place as Monsieur de Joux shall think proper and convenient for the exercise of his ministeriall function.

5th.

And because ye s'd Monsieur De Sailly (though he has in his custody all ye money that has been given to ye Colony for its subsistance), has refused to afford it any further reliefe or sustenance, under pretense that he hath no more money, not excepting so much as ye above summe of 230£ Sterling, designed for the building of ye Church. Therefore your petitioners doe beseech your Excell'y to order that the said De Sailly may, as soon as possible, give an account before such auditors as your Excell'y shall nominate, how he has employed and laid out all ye money he has received, as well in London as in this Government, for the use of ye said Colony.

6th.

That the remaining summe which Monsieur De Sailly shall be found indebted in after he has made up his account, whether it be in money or goods, may be deposited in the hands of y'r Excell'y, or of such Commissioners as y'r Excell'y shall make choice of, that so it may be preserved for the supplying of the urgent necessities of the Colony.

7th.

It being impossible to keep the said Colony in any good order without Magistrates, as being at too long a distance from the English to receive necessary justice from them, the s'd Colony doth therefore petition y'r Excell'y to give them liberty to choose such a number of Judges for a time, at least, as shall be thought necessary for determining all Civill causes, and that ye s'd Judges be chosen by ye people out of the number of those whose catalogue shall be presented by Monsieur De Joux.

That the Judgements w'ch shall be past by the s'd Judges in Civill causes may be liable to an appeale to the courts next adjacent to the Manakin Towne, excepting when the summe in controversy doth not exceed three pounds sterling.

8th.

To prevent the dissolution of ye said Colony, your petitioners do beseech your Excell'y to give strict order to ye English to entertaine none of the ffrench without permission, and that such ffrench as shall desert their new settlement be ordered to restore the 5£ Sterl'g paid for their passage, as also ye goods w'ch they received and belong to the said Colony.

9th.

That Monsieur La Soséé, physician to ye said Colony, be ordered to returne again thither and carry back with him all ye medecins and instruments that ye Colony had entrusted him with.

Your Petitioners doe most humbly supplicate your Excell'y to take into your serious consideration the most deplorable condition of the ffrench Refugees now under your protection, and to grant them the above mentioned favours, and such other reliefs as your Excellency out of your singular goodness shall think fitt to bestow upon them. And they will always pray to God for ye preservation of your person and for the prosperity and glory of your government.

D. Bleüet,
Jacque Corbelose,
P. Zossard,
N. Mare,
David Menetres,
Daulegre,
Souan,
P. Baudry, p.
Anthoine de Ramberge,
ffrancois Gannard,
Jean Levillanà,
Jean Aboàsson,
Théodore Duronsau,
Pierre Rivers,
Jean Riviol,
Jean Mearyut,
Pierre Leluells,
L. Robàll,
Ettienne Chabran,
LaBarr Eabuyt,
Abraham Foy,
ffrancois Delhapiel,
P. Labady,
Paul Caftes,
Moise Verrüeil,
Brault,
Jacob Capon,
Michael Michell,
Jean Arnaut,
J. Hagault,
Josue Petit,
Jean Rugon,
Elie Gullature,
Poussite,
S. Augustin.

AT A GENERAL ASSEMBLY BEGUN AT HIS MAJ'TIE'S ROYALL COLLEDGE OF WILLIAM AND MARY, ADJOINING TO THE CITY OF WILLIAMSBURG, THE FIFTH DAY OF DECEMBER, 1700, IN THE 12TH YEAR OF HIS MAJ'TIE'S REIGN:

Act 2d.

An act making the ffrench Refugees, Inhabiting at the Mannikin Towne and the parts adjacent, a distinct parish by themselves, and Exempting them from ye payment of publick and County Levies for 7 yeares.

Whereas a considerable number of ffrench Protestant refugees have been lately imported into this, his Maj'tie's Colony and Dominion, Severall of which Refugees have seated themselves above the ffalls of James River, at or near to a place commonly called and Knowne by the name of the Manikin Towne, ffor the Encouragement of the said Refugees to settle and remaine together, as near as may be, to the said Manakin Towne, Be it Enacted by the Governor, Councill and Burgesses of this present General Assembly; and it is hereby Enacted that the said Refugees, inhabiting at the said Manakin Towne and the parts adjacent, shall be accounted and taken for Inhabitants of a distinct parish by themselves, and the land which they now doe, or shall hereafter possess at, or adjacent to, the said Manakin Towne, shall be, and is hereby, declared to be a Parish by itself, distinct from any other parish to be called and Knowne by the name of King William's parish, in the County of Henrico, and not lyable to the payment of parish Levies in any other Parish whatsoever; and be it further enacted by the authority aforesaid, that such and so many of the said refugees as are already settled, or shall hereafter settle themselves as Inhabitants of the said Parish at the Manakin Towne and the parts adjacent, shall themselves and their ffamilies, and every of them, be free and exempted from the payment of Publick and County Levies for the space of 7 yeares next ensueing from the Publication of this act; any Law, custom or usage to the Contrary in any wise notwithstanding.

Copia, Teste:

DIONISIUS WRIGHT.

VIRGINIA—*ss:*

At his Maj'tie's Royall Colledge of William & Mary, 23d Dec'r, 1700—

Present : His Excell'y in Councill.

A Brief being proposed for the relief and support of the ffrench refugees Inhabiting at the Mannikin Towne above the falls of James river, the same was read in Councill and signed, and the Colony seal ordered to be thereto affixed.

DIONISIUS WRIGHT.

VIRGINIA—*ss.*

To all Christian People to whom these presents shall come, I ffrancis Nicholson, Esq're, his Maj'tie's L't and Governor Generall of Virginia, send Greeting: Whereas, severall ffrench Protestant refugees having lately arrived in this, his Maj'tie's Colony and Dominion of Virginia, Imported hither at the sole charge and Pious Charity of his most Sacred Maj'tie, and concerning whom his most Sacred Maj'tie, by his most gracious Letter to mee directed, bearing date at Kensington ye 18 March, 1699 [1700], hath signified his Royall will and pleasure, That all possible Encouragement should be given them upon their arrivall in order to their settlement; And whereas, the Right Hon'ble the Lords Commissioners of Trade and Plantations, by their Letter of Aprill 12, 1700, have also recommended them to my favourable assistance, Pursuant whereunto they are now seated at a place called or known by the name of the Mannikin Town above the ffalls of James River, by virtue of an order in Councill dated at James City the 8 day of August, 1700; But forasmuch as the said refugees having nothing at their arrivall here wherewith to subsist, they have hitherto been supported by the contributions of severall pious and charitable Gentlemen in these parts. And whereas, It is manifest and apparent that unless the same Charitable and Christianlike acts be Continued for their reliefe untill such time as they may reape and receive the fruits of their own Labour by the next ensueing cropp they must inevitably perish for want of ffood, Therefore,

I, the said ffrancis Nicholson, Esq'r, By and with the advice and consent of his Maj'tie's Hon'ble Councill, doe hereby recommend ye sad and deplorable Condition of the aforesaid ffrench refugees to the consideration of all pious, charitable and well disposed Persons within this, his Maj'tie's Colony and Dominion of Virginia, desiring that they will express, by subscriptions to this Briefe, what benevolences or gifts they in their Charity shall think fitt to bestow either in money, Corne, or any other thing for the support and reliefe of these our poor distress'd Christian brethren, And I doe hereby Impower and authorize the Hon'ble Wm. Byrd, Esq'r, and Benj'n Harrison, Esq'r, 2 of his Maj'tie's Councill of State, to receive and distribute amongst the said refugees such and soe many benevolences and gifts as the respective benefactors shall be willing to bestow for the promoting and forwarding of this charitable worke. Given under my hand and seale of the Colony of his Maj'tie's Royall Colledge of Wm. and Mary, this 12 yeare of his Maj'tie's reign, 1700.

Copia, Teste:

DIONISIUS WRIGHT.

SUBSCRIPTIONS TO THIS BRIEF.

	£.	s.	d.	
To buy Pork, - - -	5	0	0	ffra Nicholson.
To buy Wheat, - -	5	0	0	
Tobacco, 1,000.				
Indian Corne, 20 Barrells.				

	£.	s.	d.
William Byrd, - - - - -	10	0	0
Edmund Jennings,[46] - - - -	5	0	0
J. Lightfoot,[47] - - - - -	1	0	0

---

[46] Edmund Jenings, for some time Attorney-General of Virginia, member of the Council, and as its President acting Governor of the Colony from the death of Edward Nott, in August, 1706, until the arrival of Lieutenant-Governor Alexander Spotswood, June 23, 1710.

[47] A John Lightfoot patented lands in "James Cittie" in 1624. The name has since been prominent in Virginia.

	£.	s.	d.
Matthew Page,[48] - - - - -	5	0	0
Benj'n Harrison,[49] - - - -	5	0	0
Rob't Carter,[50] - - - - -	5	0	0
Peter Beverley,[51] - - - - -	4	0	0
Miles Cary, - - - - -	3	0	0
William Leigh,[52] - - - - -	2	0	0
G. Corbin,[53] - - - - -	2	0	0
Edwin Thacker, - - - - -	2	0	0
Nath. Harrison,[54] - - - - -	2	0	0

[48] Matthew Page, son of Colonel John and Alice (Luckin) Page, (emigrants from Middlesex, England,) was born at Williamsburg, Va., in 1659; died January 9, 1703, in Gloucester county; a member of the Council of Virginia, and of the original Board of Trustees of William and Mary College.

[49] This was doubtless Benjamin Harrison, of Surry; born 1645; died 1712; married Hannah ———; member of the Council. Benjamin Harrison patented 200 acres of land in "Warrosquinock" county July 20, 1635.

[50] Robert Carter, (son of John Carter, the emigrant,) from his extensive landed possessions, known as "King" Carter. Upon the death of Governor Hugh Drysdale, July 22, 1726, Colonel Carter, as President of the Council, became acting Governor of the Colony, and so continued until superseded by the arrival of Sir William Gooch, in 1727.

[51] Col. Peter Beverley, eldest son of Major Robert Beverley, from Yorkshire, England; County-Lieutenant of Gloucester; clerk of the House of Burgesses, 1691–'96; Speaker, 1700–'14; Member of the Council and Treasurer of the Colony, 1718-'23.

[52] Colonel William Leigh, County-Lieutenant of King & Queen county. United States Senator Benjamin Watkins Leigh, and Judge William Leigh, of Charlotte county, and William C. C. Claiborne, of Louisiana, were his descendants. There was a Francis Leigh, a member of the Council in 1682.

[53] Gawin Corbin, (third son of Henry and Alice (Eltonhead) Corbin, of Lancaster, England, who died in Virginia, January 8, 1675). Married twice—first, Catherine, daughter of Ralph Wormley, of Middlesex; second, daughter of, and co-heir of John Lane, and relict of William Wilson. He was the ancestor of the Corbin family of Virginia.

[54] Nathaniel Harrison, (brother of Benjamin Harrison, of Surry, above;) member of the Council and Auditor of the Colony; died prior to 1737. His daughter, Anne, married August 9, 1739, Colonel Edward, the eldest son of Honorable Cole Digges, member of the Council.

	£.	s.	d.
William Tayloe,[55] - - - - -	1	0	0
Alexander Spence, - - - -	1	0	0
Wm. Waters,[56] - - - - -	1	0	0
George Marable,[57] - - - -	1	1	0
Robert Beverley,[58] - - - -	2	0	0
Thomas Milner,[59] - - - - -	1	0	0
William Wilson,[60] - - - - -	3	0	0
William ffox, - - - - -	1	0	0
Thomas Ballard,[61] - - - -	1	0	0

[55] William Tayloe, of London, settled in Virginia about 1650, and married Anne, daughter of Henry Corbin. They were doubtless the parents of him of the text.

[56] William Waters, Burgess from Northampton county, 1654-'60; will dated 1685; died soon after, leaving issue—i. William of the text, Naval officer for Accomac, 1713; Burgess for Northampton county, 1718; had son, William, whose only child, Mary, married David Meade, of Nansemond county; ii. Obedience; iii. Thomas. This family probably deduces from Edwin Waters, who patented land in Elizabeth city in 1624.

[57] George Marable, "Gent.," patented land in James City February 25, 1663; and in James City county October 26, 1699.

[58] Robert Beverley, (brother of Peter Beverley above,) of "Beverley Park," King & Queen county; Burgess 1699 1700; author of a "History of Virginia," and compiler of an abridgement of the Laws of Virginia; accompanied Governor Spotswood in his Tra-montane expedition; married Ursula, daughter of the first Colonel William Byrd, of "Westover," Va.

[59] Thomas Milner, of Nansemond county; Clerk of the House of Burgesses, 1681-'84; Speaker, 1691-'93. He was of the family of Appleton Hall, county York, Bart., England, as indicated by his armorial bookplate: Per pale or and sa. a chev. bet. three horse's bits, countercharged. Crest. A horse's head couped or, bridled and maned or.

[60] Colonel William Wilson, Naval officer of the Lower District of James river; High Sheriff of Elizabeth city county; died June 17, 1713, aged 67. His tomb, formerly in St. John's Church-yard, Hampton, Va., was destroyed by the Federal soldiers during our late war. It bore the following arms: Sa. on a cross engrailed between four cherubims or, a human heart of the first, wounded on the left side proper, and crowned with a crown of thistles, vert.

[61] Colonel Thomas Ballard, Burgess from James City county in 1666; Member of the Council, 1673; Speaker of the House of Burgesses, 1680; vestryman of Bruton parish.

	£.	s.	d.
Wm. Cary,[62]	I	O	O
Tully Robinson,[63]	I	O	O
Matthew Godfrey,	I	O	O
Thomas Barber,[64]	I	O	O
John Catlett,[65]	I	O	O
Thomas Hobson,	I	O	O
Wm. Gough,	I	O	O
James Westcomb,	I	O	O
Gideon Macon,[66]	I	O	O
Ja. ffoster,	I	O	O
James Bray,[67]	I	O	O
Sam'll Thompson,	I	O	O
John Pewett,	I	O	O
Mord. Cooke,[68]	I	O	O

[62] William Cary, of Warwick county, a younger son of Colonel Miles Cary, the emigrant; Burgess in 1710; married Martha Seabrook; will dated 1711. Had issue: i. Harwood; died 1720; ii. Miles; died 1766; (among his sons was Richard, Judge of the Court of Appeals of Virginia; died 1785); iii. Elizabeth married Edward Jacquelin.

[63] Tully Robinson, of Accomac county; wealthy and influential. One of his daughters, Scarborough, married John Wise, ancestor of the late Governor Henry A. Wise; the late Judge William T. Joynes, and Professor Levin S. Joynes were also descendants.

[64] Thomas Barber patented lands in New Kent county in 1714.

[65] Colonel John Catlett patented large tracts of land on the Rappahannock river, in what is now Essex county, from 1650; Commissioner to settle boundary line between Virginia and Maryland in 1663; killed by the Indians near Port Royal. His grand-daughter, Rebecca Catlett, married Francis Conway, of Port Conway, King George county, and he was thus the ancestor of President James Madison.

[66] Gideon Macon patented lands in New Kent county in 1694. He was the ancestor of the well-known Virginia family of the name.

[67] John Bray patented land in Warrosquinoack county, June 4, 1636. James Bray, of Bruton parish, James City county, was a member of the Council in 1676. He married Angelica ——, and had issue: i. Colonel David, born 1655; died October 21, 1717; father of David; member of the Council, 1699; died October, 1731; ii. James—who had son Thomas—whose daughter, Elizabeth, married Colonel Philip Johnson, of King & Queen county; iii. Thomas; iv. Anne married Mungo Ingles. Of this family was Elizabeth Bray, wife of Governor Edward Digges.

[68] Mordecai Cooke patented 1174 acres of land on Mobjack Bay in 1650. His family has been prominent in Gloucester county to the present time, and have frequently represented it in the State Assembly.

	£.	s.	d.
Jno. Thorowgood,[69] - - - - -	1	0	0
Thos. Edmundson, - - - - -	1	0	0
Rich'd Blande,[70] - - - - -	1	0	0
Thos. Giles, - - - - -		10	0
Henry Applewhite, - - -		10	0

Copia, Test:

DIONISIUS WRIGHT.

The London Society for promoting Christian knowledge, about the year 1715, took under their protection about 200 French refugees, and out of that number the following were sent to America at the Society's expense:

Elizabeth de la Brouse, - -	Sent to Carolina.
Philip Gouiran, - - -	Gone to Virginia.
Claude la Boire, - - -	Gone to Virginia.
Vincent Pinna, - - -	Gone to Carolina.

COURT HELD AT VARINA FEBRUARY, 1700.

Col. Wm. Randolph presented a letter from the Maquis De La Muce and Monsieur Charles De Sailly.

Superscription:

---

[69] Colonel John Thorowgood, grandson of Adam Thorowgood, who came to Virginia, in 1621 and died in 1640,; married, March 19, 1695, Margaret Lawson; sheriff of Norfolk county; died December, 1701. For a deduction of the Thorowgood Family, see the *Richmond Standard*, December 3, 10, 17, 24, 1881.

[70] Richard Bland, of "Jordan's Point," James river, second son of Theodrick and Anne (Bennet) Bland, of "Berkeley," Virginia, married twice: 1st, Mary, daughter of Colonel Thomas Swann, of "Swann's Point;" 2d, Elizabeth, daughter of Colonel William Randolph, of "Turkey Island." She died at "Jordan's," January 22, 1719. He died there April 6, 1720. Surviving issue only by last marriage: i. Mary, married Henry Lee; ii. Elizabeth, married William Beverley; iii. Richard, "the Antiquary," member of House of Burgesses; of Congress of 1774, and of Virginia Convention of 1775, married Anne, daughter of Peter Poythress; iv. Anne married Drury Bolling. For extended deduction of the Bland Family, see *Slaughter's History of Bristol Parish*.

"*To ye Hondurable Colonell Rumdolph, Att. ye Court of Henrico County—These:*

"Sir,—We think ourselves bound to desire you to acquaint the worshipfull Court of Henrico County that Mr. Sehull,[71] the Goldsmith that came along with us in July last, being Dead a little while . . . . . . plantation, in the sd. County, two Miles from Capt. Webb [leaving?] one Child with two French men servants . . . all ye mony, Jewells and other goods belonging to the . . . very Ill; also one other boy, son to Mr. Rogers, printer to . . Elector of Brandenburg, who, designing to Come over, . . . did Intrust this boy unto the s'd Gold Smith, with a par- . . . of above 80l., which the said men will alsoe Spoil and waste . . -ented by ye s'd Court. In appointing somebody to gathere . . . an Inventory and Secure all, for the supply and Relief of these . . . who came to us to complain of their want and the hardship . . . put upon them, abuseing them and treating them worse than . . . and desireing us to take them with their goods, and to deliver . . . from that misery, to put them into Some other houses . . . find just, Reasonable and necessary; but haveing here . . office or authority to Doe it, Wee apply ourselves to ye Court . . these cases might be taken In Consideracon as Some orders . . Speedily to avoid the Disapacon of the remaining part of Goods, and so provide ye Children, or put them at Liberty To provide themselves with our advices till wee may get an answer from their parents, and so doing you will make a great Charity and oblige much. Your Most humble and most obedient servants,

"Oliver De La Muce,
"Chrse Sailly.

"At Capt. Webb's house, this 29th J'n'y, 1700 [1701]."[72]

---

[71] In an inventory of the effects of Sehult, of record in Henrico county court, March 1, 1700 [1701], the following articles appear: a silver girth with silver buckles; amber necklace; five maps; the Duke of Brandenburg's coat of arms; three maps; two pictures; a large Bible; a great parcel of books; two bales of books; a trunk of unbound books; a pearl necklace; a hand and heart ring, etc.

[72] This and the two succeeding extracts are from the records of Henrico County Court.

COURT HELD AT VARINA AUGUST, 1704.

Col. Byrd notifys the court that Henry Ayscough,[73] who had been guardian of Peter Sehull, orphan of Mr. Tertullian Sehull, one of the French refugees, was dead.

COURT, AUGUST 20TH, 1706.

A Statement that on Feb. 1st, 1702 [1703], Mr. Abraham Salle gave bond as executor of Mr. Soloman Delalua,[74] with Mr. Chas. De Sally and Mr. David Minitrees as security; and that De Sally had since gone to Eng., and Minetrees removed himself to a remote part of the colony.

By his Ex'cy and the hon'ble Council, Mr. Sp'r and Gent'n of the H. of Burgesses:

April 24th, 1704.

His Ex'cy and the hon'ble Council having received diverse petitions heretofore presented by the ffrench Refugees, settled at Manicantown, praying for naturalizacon, with several other papers relating to that settlement, Have thought fitt to recom mend to y'r house the mature consideracon of the s'd peticons and papers as being a case of very great importance.

By ord'r of his Ex'cy and ye hon'ble Council.

W. R., Cl'k Ge. C't.[75]

WILLIAMSBURG, August 14, 1716.

Daniel Bloüett, a French settler, prays for redress against one Dupins who had unlawfully surveyed and seized upon a tract

[73] William Ayscough, of the city of York, England, his brother and heir. William Randolph purchased his land.

[74] His will, of record in Henrico county court, February 1, 1702 [1703], "late of Rochelle, in France," devises to his god-son, Solomon Savery, his servant; to his kinswoman, Mrs. Frances Forrest, of Soho Fields, London, £80; remainder of his estate to his cousin, René Paré, dwelling in Portsmouth. In the inventory of his effects, recorded April 1, 1703 [1704], are enumerated a number of paintings, portraits, landscapes, marine scenes; 20 bottles of Hungary waters; medicines; surgical instruments. &c. Total value, £188 15. 0½.

[75] *Calendar of State Papers of Virginia*, I, p. 84.

of 133 acres of land at Manicantown belonging to the said Bloüett; being the amount of land that had been allowed to each family of French Refugees by the Government.[76]

To the Honourable Presid't and Council:

Sept. 2d, 1707.

The answer of Abraham Salle to the Petition of Mr. Philipe, humbly Sheweth,[77]

That whereas, the s'd Philipe Complained that I affronted him on the 30th day of March last, while he was in the Pulpit, by calling him seditious, and the cheif of ye seditious, I beg leave to represent to your honnors the whole fact as it happen'd, which I flatter myself will be a compleat justification. When Mr. Philipe had finish'd the service of the day, he continued in the Pulpit as his custome is where there is any Parish business to be done, the first thing he did, was to demand the Register of Christenings to be delivered up to him out of ye Clerk of the Vestry' hands, and in case he refused to do it, he would excommunicate him; he was pleas'd to say this with a rage very unbecoming the place, which made me intreat him to have a little patience till the dispute should be ended, whether the Register should be in the Vestry's Custody or his; I assur'd him that the Vestry had no intention either to encroach upon his Rights or to give up their own, and therefor desir'd to inform themselves more fully of that matter; upon this, he flew out into a gretter pasion than before, and frankly told us that he acknowledg'd no Vestry there was, neither would he have the people acknowledge any. Immediately after his nameing the People, sevarol of his party, and particularly Lacaze and Michel, stood up, and in the Church took the liberty to utter many injurious things against me; and the last prest thro' the whole congregation to get up to the place where I was, and then catching me by the coat, he threatened me very hardly, and by his Example, several of the crowd were heard to say, we must assassinate that damn'd fellow with

---

[76] *Ibid*, 189.

[77] *Calendar of State Papers of Virginia*, I, pp. 114–116.

the black beard, and that Bougre de Chien ought to be hanged up out of the way, and several other violent Expressions, not very proper for the Church. The s'd Philipe in the mean time, was so far from endeavouring to appease their tumult, that 'twas observed he did his best to inflame it, and was ——— lowder and more outragious than anybody. I thought it now my duty, as a Justice, to command the peace, putting the people in mind of the day and occasion, and the place where they were, but all to little purpose ; the Queen's name had no effect upon them. When I found matters in that dangerous condition, I thought it prudent to withdraw, and when I came to the Church door, I told Mr. Philipe 'twas visible that he had fomented that sedition, and therefore he was a seditious person, and even the Chief of the Seditious. This is the naked fact as it happened, which I am ready to prove to your honours by sufficient testimony, which, if I do, I have the confidence to hope I need no further Justification.

And then, as far as his petitioning for an Order for Chooseing a new Vestry at Monocantown, I humbly beg leave to represent to your honours the unreasonableness of that Petition.

Not long after the erecting Monocantown into a Parish, the Parishioners were assembled to elect a Vestry, and the Plurality of voices fell upon the following persons:

Jacob Amonner,	Jean Guerin,	Pierre Chastain,
Abra. Soblet,	Jacque Lacaze,	Jean Farcy,
Jacques Brousse,	Abra. Remy,	Jean Foniuelle,
Louis Outartre,	Andre Aubry,	Abra. Salle.

Vestry of Monacantown Parish

In that election the Law of this Country was punctually observ'd; the persons were 12 in number, and were chosen by the Major part of the Parish, called together by Mr. Philipe for that purpose; they were not chosen for one year, according to the electing Elders in france, w'ch Mr. Philipe would insinuate, but were chosen as a lawful Vestry, and for several years have been own'd as such, even by Mr. Philipe himself, and he has always apply'd himself to them for his Salary; they have been called Antiens, because the French have no other word in their language for a Vestryman, and it has never been questioned by any one whether this were a legal Vestry or not, till lately that the Sr. Philipe, upon a quarrel he's had with some particular member of it, would get this Vestry quashed, to introduce his onne Creature that will be ready to Sacrifice . . . of the parish to his extravagance and arbitrary humour, if . . .

AT A COUNCIL HELD AT THE CAPITOL THE 18TH DAY OF NOVEM'R, 1710:

Present the Hon'ble Lieut.-Governour in Councill. On Reading at this Board a Petition of Abraham Sallee and Claude Phillipe de Richbourgh, in behalf of themselves and other French Refugees, Inhabitants of the Mannakin Town, setting forth: "That at their first arrival there was granted for the Settlement of the said Refugees a Tract of Ten Thousand acres of Land, to be laid out according to the rate of a hundred and thirty-three acres to each Family. That the said Refugees did settle upon some part of the said Land, and had about five Thousand Acres then laid out and divided among them; but the said division having Regard to the particular Settlement, . . . so as to give to every man the proportion . . . . adjoining to his House, and therefore proposing that a more equal distribution of the said land may be made, and that those who have not their full proportion in the first Five Thousand Acres may have the same made up out of the last Five Thousand Acres, laid out and appropriated for the aforesaid Settlement.

This Board, taking the said Petition—with the proposals therein contain'd—into consideration, have thought fitt to Order that the Land above mention'd be laid out and distributed in manner following (vizt): That all such heads of Families, and their Representatives as have been constantly resident at the said Manakin Town from the first Settlement, shall, in the first place, draw Lotts, and, according to the priority of their Lotts, shall have liberty to choose; And shall Accordingly have as much Land laid out for them respectively in the last five Thousand Acres as will, with the land they have already, make up their full complement of 133 Acres to each Family. That all persons that have come in since the first Settlement, and have been constantly Resident at the Mannakin Town since their first Coming, shall, in the next place, draw Lotts, and, according to the Priority of their said Lotts, shall have their proportion of Land in the last 5,000 Acres to compleat with what they have already, the quantity of 133 Acres to each Family. And, in the last place, such as have deserted the said Settlement, and afterwards returned to Inhabit there, shall, in like manner, draw Lotts, and be preferr'd to the choice of Land in the last 5,000 Acres, to make up their Complement of 133 Acres for each respective Family, according to the priority of their Lotts. And it is Ordered, that the Surveyor of the county of Henrico do lay out the said respective proportions of Land at the charges of the Person desiring the same. In which he is hereby directed and required to take care that the breadth of the several Shares of Land bear a due proportion to the length, and that no small slips of Land be left between the Lotts that may not be usefull or fitt to be taken up by any Other Person.

And in case it shall be found that any Person hath, in the first five Thousand Acres of Land, more than the said proportion of 133 Acres, and his next Neighbour hath not enough, that such Neighbour shall have the Overplus Added to his Lott to make his said lott the Number of 133 Acres, and if any Improvements be made upon the same, the Owner of that Lott, to which it is added, shall pay to the other the value the said Improvements shall be appraised at.

And it is further Ordered, that such of the French Refugees as have bought the Plantations, or dividents of any other of the said Nation in the first 5,000 Acres, shall have and enjoy the same without prejudice to such Purchaser, to hold the Land due to him for his own share, and to take up as much more as will make his said Share the Compleat quantity of 133 Acres.

Provided, That no Person who hath sold his proportion of the first 5,000 Acres shall be Intitled to take up any more of the second 5,000 Acres than he should have had in case such Sale had never been made. And if any Person hath already Settled upon the last 5,000 Acres of Land, and hath made Improvements thereon, such Person shall have his whole quantity of 133 Acres laid out in the last 5,000, provided there be sufficient over and above the Proportion due to the other Inhabitants, and there be not, then the Houses and clear'd grounds of such Persons shall be reserved to him as part of his Proportion to the said Tract of Land.

And whereas, divers of the first heads of Families settled at the Mannakin Town are since dead, it is Ordered that the Heir or Children of the Deceas'd (if any be), and if not the Widdow, shall have and Enjoy the divident Allotted or which ought to be Allotted . . . . head of Family be dead without Heir or other Representatives, his Share or Proportion of the said Lands shall be confirmed to such person or persons (being of the same Nation) as are now in possession thereof. And to the end the Surveyor of Henrico county may be the better Enabled to Sett out and Assign to each particular person his share of the said land, it is Order'd that Mr. Robert Bolling, who Surveyed the first 5,000 Acres, do grant Certificates of the Bounds and quantities of the several lotts unto the Persons for whom he setts out the same, and to such as claim under them, without demanding any fee or reward, he having been already paid for the same out of his Majestie's Revenues. And if it shall happen that any person shall be contented with less than 133 Acres, so that there shall remain any quantity of land not taken up after the several Allottments above mention'd, it is hereby declar'd that such Overplus land shall be granted to any other French Refugees as shall hereafter come to settle at the Mannakin Town, for the Encouragement of the said settlement. And the Surveyor of the said County of Henrico is hereby ordered and required to lay out the lands aforesaid, having due regard to Rules and directions herein before sett down, and in any case any dispute or controversie shall arise among the said Refugees in the distribution of their several shares of Land, The Hon'ble the Lieut. Governour, with the advice of the Councill, doth hereby Authorize and Impower Colo. Wm. Randolph and Mr. Richard Cocke, of Henrico county, to hear and determine the said disputes, And in case they find any difficulties, that they Report the same specially to the Lieut. Governour for his final determination therein.

[Copia.] WM. ROBERTSON, *Cl'k Co'n.*

LISTE GENERALLE DE TOUS LES FRANCOIS PROTESTANTS REFUGIES, ESTABLYS DANS LA PAROISSE DU ROY GUILLAUME, COMTÉ D'HENRICO EN VIRGINIA, Y COMPRIS LES FEMMES, ENFANS, VEUSES, ET ORPHELINS.[78]

NOMS DES HOMMES.	Femmes.	ENFANS.		Total.
		Garcons.	Filles.	
Jean Cairon, Ministre[79]............	....	3	....	4
Abraham Sallé[80]............	....	5	1	7
Pierre Chastain............	1	2	4	8
Charles Perault............	1	1	3	6
Jean Forquerand............	1	2	....	4
Anthoine Matton............	1	5	....	7
Isaac Lesebure............	1	1	3	6
Jacques Bilbaud............	1	1	....	3
Jacob Amonnet............	....	3	2	6
Michel Cantepie............	1	....	....	2
Jean Voyé............	1	2	2	6
Francois Dupuy............	1	....	1	3
Daniel Guerrand............	1	2	2	6
Barthelemy Dupuy............	1	3	2	7
Jacques Sobler............	1	1	1	4
Pierre Trauve............	1	1	1	4
Mathieu Agé............	1	....	....	2
Thomas Briaus............	1	2	3	7
Jean Chastain............	1	....	....	2
Francois De Clapie............	1	....	2	4
Louis Sobler............	1	1	....	3
Tho. D'allizon............	1	....	....	2
Pre. Dutoit............	1	....	2	4
Jean Calver............	1	3	2	7
Jean Farcy............	1	3	....	5
Estienne Chastain............	1	....	....	2
Estienne Bonard............	1	2	1	5
Abra. Sobler, lesué............	....	....	....	1
Abra. Sobler, le jeune............	1	....	....	2
Gedeon Chambon............	1	1	....	3
Pre. Morisser............	1	1	3	6
31............	27	45	35	138

[78] Extracted from *Papers Relating to the History of the Church in Virginia, A. D. 1650–1776 Edited by William Stevens Perry, D. D. Privately Printed 1870*, pp. 193–195—where it is printed from the "Original MS." It is undated, but may be assigned to the period 1714.

[79] "Jean Cairon, né à Figeac, ci-devant ministre de Cajarc dans la Haute Guyenne, was one of the French pastors who in 1688 had taken refuge in Zurich." *Baird*, II, 145. His will is recorded in Henrico county court, February, 1715 [1716]. Sons: Peter, Daniel and Isaac.

[80] His will probated in Henrico county court, March, 1719 [1720].

FRANCOIS PROTESTANTS REFUGIES—CONTINUED.

NOMS DES HOMMES.	Femmes.	Enfans.		Total.
		Garcons.	Filles.	
Isaac Lafuitte	1	2	....	4
Jean Panetie	1	1	....	3
Jean Joanis	1	....	2	4
Jacq. Bioret	1	1	....	3
Jean Solaigre	1	1	....	3
Daniel Maubain	1	....	....	2
Isaac Parenteau	....	1	2	4
Andre Aubry	....	....	....	1
Gillaume Genin	1	....	....	2
Jean Fonuiele	1	1	....	3
Joseph Cailland	1	....	1	3
Joseph Bernard	....	....	....	1
David Bernard	1	4	1	7
Estienne Regnault	1	....	2	4
Pierre Oliver	....	....	....	1
Pierre Viet	....	....	....	1
Anthoine Giraudan	1	1	1	4
Jean Levillain	1	2	2	6
Jean Filhon	1	....	....	2
Abra. Michaux	1	4	6	12
Adam Vique	1	....	1	3
Abra. Remy	1	1	2	5
Anthoine Trabue	1	3	....	5
Jean Martin	1	3	1	6
Moize Leneveau	1	2	....	4
Jacob Cappon	1	....	....	2
Pierre Delaunay	....	....	....	1
Francois Lassin	1	1	2	5
Jean Powell	1	2	....	4
Jean Dupre	1	....	1	3
Jean Gorner	....	....	....	1
Gaspard Gorner	1	1	....	3
Mathieu Bonsergent	....	....	....	1
Jacques LeGrand[81]	1	....	....	2
Pierre David	1	....	....	2
Claude Garry	1	....	....	2
Nicollas Souille	....	....	....	1
Anthoine Rapinne	1	....	1	3
Gillaume Martin	1	3	....	5
Pierre Deppe	....	....	....	1
40	30	34	25	129

[81] Will of James Le Grand, "late of La Haye, Holland," recorded in Henrico county court September, 1716. Legal portion of his estate to his wife, Elizabeth; residue to his brother, John.

FRANCOIS PROTESTANTS REFUGIES—Continued.

FEMMES VEUVES ET LEURS ENFANS.	Femmes.	Enfans.		Total.
		Garcons.	Filles.	
Lavenne Souillé	....	....	2	3
Lave. Lorange	....	....	....	1
Lave. Gorry	....	....	....	1
Lave. Mallet	....	1	1	3
Lave. Launay	....	....	1	2
5 Femmes Veuves	....	1	4	10
ENFANS ORPHELINS.				
Jean Fauve	....	....	....	1
Estienne Mallet, Suzane Mallet, Marie Mallet,	....	....	....	3
Isaac Gorry, Jean Gorry,	....	....	....	2
Anthoine Berin	....	....	....	1
Pre. Sobriche, Jeanne and Suzanne,	....	....	....	3
Jean Loncadou, Pierre Loncadou,	....	....	....	2
Suzanne Imbert, Jeanne Imbert,	....	....	....	2
	....	....	....	14
RECAPITULATION DU TOUT.				
Pre. Page, 31	27	45	35	138
2d do., 40	30	34	25	129
71	57	79	60	267
Veuves et leurs Enfans	5	1	4	10
Enfans Orphelins	....	....	....	14
71	62	80	64	291

REGISTER CONTAINING THE BAPTISMS MADE IN THE CHURCH OF THE FRENCH REFUGEES AT MANNIKIN-TOWN IN VIRGINIA, IN THE PARISH OF KING WILLIAM, IN THE YEAR OF OUR LORD, 1721, THE 25TH MARCH.[82]—DONE BY JAMES SOBLET,[83] CLERK.

Was baptized by Mr. Fontaine,[84] a girl named Elizabeth, daughter of Pierre Morriset and Elizabeth Morriset; the godfather was Jean Faure and the godmother, Elizabeth, her mother, wife of Pierre Morriset, who have declared that this child was born the first of March, 1721 [1722.]

J. Soblet, Clerk.

. . . . Jeanne Madelene, born the . . . . was baptized the 4th October, by . . . . Madelaine and Evange . . . daughters of Je . . .

Jean Chastain, son of Jean Chastain and of Marianne Chastain, his father and mother, born the 26 of September, 1721, was baptized the 5 October by Mr. Fontainne, he had for godfather and godmother, Pierre David and Anne David, his wife, who have declared that this child was born the day and year above, in faith (of which),

Signed, *Jaque Soblet, Clerk.*

The 18th August, 1721, was born Daniel, the son of Daniel Guerrant and of Francoise Guerrant, his father and mother; he was baptized the . . of October, by Mr. Fontaine; he was presented for baptism by Daniel Guerrant, his grand [father ?] and Madame Lorange, his grand mother, which they have declared that this child was born the day and year above.

J. Soblet, Clerk.

---

[82] This is a translation of the original register in the French language, which is in the possession of the editor. It covers about twenty-five pages of foolscap paper. The barbarous orthography used involves, in many instances, it will be observed, almost a denationalization and mystification of surnames. Many of them are, however, palpably English, the result of intermarriage with the neighboring colonists.

[83] Now rendered Sublett in Virginia.

[84] Reverends Peter and Francis Fontaine appear to have successively served the parish. See Appendix—*A partial list of the descendants of John de la Fontaine.*

. . February, 1720, was born Elizabeth, ... and of Madelaine, ...

Madellene . . . was baptized . . . . . Mr. feene,[85] Minister. She was presented . . . . by Clod Goury and by his wife. . . . . The parties have declared that [this child] was born the day and year above.

Je. Soblet, Clerk.

The 21st February, 1721, was born Jean Gil[mer], . . . of Jean Gaspar [Gil]mer and of Susanne, his wife; was baptized by Mr. Fontaine. He was presented for baptism by Daniel Maubain and Nicolas Soullee, . . . Mary Dupree, wife of Jean Dupree. the parties have declared that this child was born the day and year above. *J. Soblet, Clerk.*

. . . The 17 October, 1722, was b[orn] . . . of Jean Gasp. . . . Ka. . . . *Chastain.*

by Danniele, . . . presented by Danniele guerand, godfather. . . .

I, Marie guerand, godmother, which parties have declared that this child was born the day and year above.

J. Soblet, Clerk.

Le 23 December, 1722, was born anne, daughter of Pierre David and of Anne David, her father and mother; was baptized by Mr. Finee, minister; was presented for baptism by Mr. David and Anne David, her father and mother, and they have declared that this child was born the day and year above.

J. Soblet, Clerk.

The . . . January, 1723, was born Jean [Dupuy ?) . . . Pierre Dupuy, and of J. . . . was baptized. . . .

The 12 january, . . . daughter of Mr. . . . father and . . .

The thirteenth, . . . heur to . . .

The 29th October, 1726, was born [John, the son ?] of Etienne Monford and Elizabeth Monford, his father and mother; was baptized the 14th April, in the year 1727, by Mr. Mordock,[86]

---

[85] Rev. Wm. Finney, M. A. of the University of Glasgow, subsequently recorded "Finee." His will of record in Henrico county court, June 5, 1727. Wife, Mary; son, William, and daughter, Mary.

[86] Rev. William Murdaugh.

minister of St. James. He was presented for baptism by Elie Susain and by Olive Sallie, his godfather and godmother. The parties have declared that this Child was born the day and year above at Mannikintown.

Je. Soblet, Cleark.

The 10th May, 1727, was born Judith, daughter of Jean Chastain and of Charlot Chastain, her father and mother; was baptized the 18 may (?) by Mr. Brook,[87] minister of Hanover. She had for godfather Mr. Pierre Chastain and Magdelaine Chastain, and Anne David, wife of Pierre David, for Godmother. The parties have declared that the child was born the day and year above.

J. Soblet, Cleark.

The 21 April, 1727, was born Jack, a black, to Mr. Barthelemy Dupuy.

The 3d June, 1727, was born Jean, son of Jean Dykar and of Elizabeth Dykar; was baptized the 4th September by Mr. Neirn,[88] minister of Vairren [Varina]. He was presented to Baptism by Jean Jaque dupuy at 10 by (Stephen) Etiene Monford, godmother philip dupuy. The parties have declared that this child was born the day and year above.

J. Soblet, Clerk.

The 23 day of August, 1727, was born Marie Magdelaine, a girl, to Mr. Estiene Chastain and Marthe Chastain, her father and mother; was presented for baptism by Mr. Barthelmie dupuy and Mar[the?] dupuy, his wife. The parties have declared that this child was born the day and year above.

J. Soblet, Cleärk.

The 24th day of the month of July was born to Estienne Chastain a black named Tobye, 1727. The 21st may was born Jean Gori, son of Eglan gori and of Jeanne, his wife; was baptized by Mr. Neirn, minister of the Holy Evangelist; was presented by Jean Pierre Bilbau and Elizabeth Dutoi. The father has declared that this child was born the day and year above.

Jean Chastain, Clerk.

---

[87] Rev. Zachariah Brooke, of Hanover county.

[88] Nearne.

1726.[89] The 9th of November was born judith, daughter of Abraham Salé and of Magdelaine, his wife; was baptized the 14th by Mr. Mordoc, minister of the Holy Evangelist; was presented by Jean Chastain and Charlote, his wife. The father has declared that the child was born the day and year above.

Jean Chastain, Clerk.

The 13th November, 1727, was baptized Jaque Martain by Mr. Neirn, minister of the Holy Evangelist; was presented by Jaque Soblet and Madame Martain. The parties have declared that he was born the 8th September of the said year.

Jean Chastain, Clerk.

The 25th September, 1727, was born to Mr. Gille Allaigre[90] a little negro named Thonberlan.

The 23d December, 1727, was born to Mr. Jean Villain[91] a negro named guillaume.

The 9th April, 1728, was born Louis Soblet, son of Pierre Louis Soblet and of Marte, his wife; was baptized by Mr. Na[irn?] minister of Varaine [Varina?] He had for godfather Jean Martain and Jacob Trabue; for godmother, Marie Martain. The father has declared that the child was born the day and year above.

The 16th April, 1728, anne Tammas was born; was baptized by Mr. Na[irn?] minister of Varaine; had for godfather Guillaume Samson (?) for godmother, Olive Salle and Brigét. The parties have declared that she was born the day and year above.

Jean Chastain, Clerk.

The 8th October, 1727, was born to gedeon Chanbon a black named Jean.

The 28th May, 1728, was born to Jaque billebo a black named Jaque.

The 8th June, 1728, was born a black girl to Estienne Chastain named Janne.

---

[89] Thus in the original, but evidently an inadvertent entry.

[90] The great-grand-daughter of Giles Allaigre (now rendered Allegre). Sophia, daughter of William (a music master) and Jane (daughter of William Battersby) Allegre, married April 23, 1789, at Richmond, Albert Gallatin, the Statesman. She was his first wife.

[91] Le Villain, or Villain.

The 16th June, 1728, was born to gille Allaigre a black, named Anibal.

The 31st May, 1728, was born to Isac Salle a black, named Guillaume.

The 4th July, 1728, was born Elizabeth Salle, daughter of Guillaume Salle and of Elizabeth, his wife; was baptized by Mr. Mason,[92] minister of Nioukaint [New Kent]; had for godfather, Thommas Girodan, and for godmother, Olive malet and anne cal . . t.

1728. 15th Jeane Antoine Dubreuil was born, son of Cristoffe dubreuil and of Mariane, his wife; was baptized the 1st August following by Mr. Mason; was presented by Antoine Benin, and Elizabeth Dutoi was grandmother.

Jean Chastain, Clerk.

The 21st April, 1728, was born a black to Mr. Joannis, named Jean.

The 21st August 1728, was born to Isac Sallé a black, named Pierre.

The 12th October, 1728, was born a boy to Nicolas Soullie.

The 12th October, 1728, was born a daughter to Daniel Guerand, named Francoise; was baptized by Mr. Mason; had for godfather, Claude Rouvierre; for godmother, Francoise Lorange. The parties have declared that the child was born the day and year above.

The 19th October, 1728, was born a girl to Roger Prot.

The 3d November, 1728, was born a boy to Etienne Chastain; he had for godfather, Gillaume Sallé; for godmother, Elizabeth Sallé; was baptized by Mr. Swift; was baptized the 27th December of the said year.

The 9th November, 1728, was born a girl to David le Seur, named Elizabet

The 12th February, 1728 [1729], was born Pierre Dupui, son of Pierre Dupui and Judith Dupuy; was baptized the 20th of said month by Mr. Swift; had for godfather, Etienne Chastain, and for godmother, Philipe Dupui.

Jean Chastain, Clerk.

---

[92] Rev. David Mossom, rector of St. Peter's parish, New Kent county, for forty years, from 1727. He officiated at the nuptials of General Washington.

The 5th September, 1728 [1729], was born Charle Pero,[93] son of Daniel Pero and of Marie Pero; was baptized by Mr. Mason, minister; had for godfather and godmother Antoine Rapine and his wife.

The 12th December, 1728, was born a boy to Jean Faure.

. . . 10? February, 1728 [1729], was born Marie, daughter of Francois Farsi and of Susane Farsi; was baptized by Mr Swift,[94] the 21st of March; she had for godfather, Etienne Chastain, for godmother, Mad. Rapine and Marie Pero. The parties have declared that she was born the day and year above mentioned.

The 24th February, 1728 [1729], was born Pierre Chastain, son of Jean Chastain and of Charlote Chastain; was baptized by Mr. Swift the 24th March; he had for godfather Abraham Sallé, and —— re Amonet; for godmother, Marie Teler.

The 13th March, 1728, was born Elizabeth Sallé, daughter of Abraham Salle and of Magdelaine Salle; was baptized the 21st March by Mr. Swift; had for godfather, Pierre Salle and for godmother, Elizabet Salle.

The 19th March (?) was born a black girl to Estienne Chastain.[95]

The 11th July, 1729, was born a black girl to Jean Levillain, named Ollive.

The 31st May, 1729, was born Joseph Faure son of Pierre Faure and of Judith Faure, his wife; was baptized by Mr. Mason, the 16th July; he had for godfather, Joseph Bingli; for godmother, Judith Bingli; the parties have declared that the child was born the day and year above. *John Chastain, Clerk.*

The 25 July, 1729, was born Elizabet Legrand, daughter of Jean Legrand and of Catherine Legrand; was baptized the 19th October of the said year, by Mr. Teler,[96] in the church of St. James; she had for godfather, Guillame Salle; for godmother,

---

[93] Perault.

[94] He was dead, March 24th, 1734 [1735]. *Perry*, p. 357.

[95] In Henrico county records, February 1, 1706, is noted a payment to "Dr. Chasteen."

[96] Presumably, Rev. Daniel Taylor, rector of Blissland Parish, New Kent county, 1721–1729.

Elizabeth Salle and Ollive Mallet. The parties have declared that she was born the day and year above.

The 9th August, 1729, was born Isac, son of Antoine Benin and of Elizabeth, his wife; was baptized by Mr. Taler; had for godfather, William Landsdon and Estiene Farsi; for godmother, Marriane Dutoi. The parties have declared that the child was born the day and year above. *Jean Chastain.*

The 13th December, 1729, was born to Jean Dupre, a black boy, named Pierre.

The 12th November, 1729, was born Olimpe Dupui, daughter of Jean Jaque Dupui and of Susane Dupui; was baptized by Mr. Swift; had for godfather, Jean Levilain, and for godmother, Philippe Dupui and Judith Dupui. The parties have declared that the child was born the day and year above.

Jean Chastain, Clerk.

The 4th May, 1729, was born a boy to Etiene Monfor, named Jacob; was baptized by Mr. Massom; had for godfather, Jacob Capon; for godmother, Brigit. The parties have declared that he was born the day and year above.

The 21st Xber, 1729, was born Pierre Sassain, son of Elie Sassain; was [baptized] by Mr. Massom; had for godfather, Pierre Sabattie; for godmother, Anne Bernard. The parties have declared that he was born the day and year above.

Jean Chastain, Clerk.

The 21st February, 1729, was born Elizabeth Salle, daughter of guillaume Salle and of Elizabeth Salle; was baptized by Monsieur massom; had for godfather, Isac Salle; for godmother, Magdelaine Salle and Elizabeth Lesueur. The parties have declared that the child was born the day and year above.

The 27th January, 1729, was born to Isac Salle a black named Robert.

The 1st March, 1729, was born Estiene Chastain, son of Estiene Chastain and of Martre, his wife; was baptized the 12 April following by Mr. Massom; had for godfather, Jean Jaque Dupui and Estiene Farsi; for godmother, Philipe Dupui. The parties have declared that he was born the day and year above named. *John Chastain.*

The 1st March, 1729, was born Jean Girodan, son of Thommas Girodan and of Judith, his wife; was baptized the 12th of April following by Mr. Massom; had for godfather, Guillaume Salle and Jaque Martain; for godmother, Md. Martain. The parties have declared that he was born the day and year above.

Jean Chastain, Clerk.

The 8 March, 1730. was born Marie Mallet, daughter of Etiene Mallet and of Olive Mallet, her father and mother; was baptized the 20th of May, 1730, by Mr. Marie;[97] had for godfather, Guillaume Salle; for godmother, Elizabeth Salle and Susane Billiebo. The parties have declared that she was born the day and year above mentioned.

The 2d July, 1730, was born Jean Pierre Martain, son of Jaque Martain and of Janne Martain; was baptized the 20th of the same month by Mr. Marie, minister of St. Jams;[98] had for godfather, Jean Martain and Pierre Sabatie; for godmother, Md. Martain. The parties have declared that he was born the day and year above. *Jean Chastain.*

July 17th, 1730, was born to Barthelemi dupui a black named Jak.

June 30th, 1730, was born Jaque Billiebo,[99] son of Jean Billiebo and of Susane, his wife; was baptized the 16th of August by Mr. Marye; had for godfather, Antoine Rapine and Estiene Mallet; for godmother, Olive Mallet. The parties have declared that he was born the day and year above named.

Jean Chastain, Clerk.

The 20th 7ber, 1730, was born Judith Amonet, daughter of Andre Amonet and of Janne Amonet; was baptized the 27th of the same month by Mr. Marye; had for godfather, Abraham Sallee; for godmother, Magdelaine Salle and Charlote Chastain. The parties have declared that the child was born the day and year above. *Jean Chastain, Clerk.*

The 14th March, 1730 [1731], Jaque Soblet, son of Pierre Louis Soblet and of Marie, his wife, was baptized by Mr. Marye;

---

[97] Rev. James Marye.

[98] Parish of St. James, Northam, Goochland county.

[99] Bilbo, Bilbaux, Bilbaud.

he had for godfather, Jaque Soblet and Jaque Martain; for godmother, Janne Martain. the parties have declared that he was born the 3d of the month of January, 1730 [1731].

Jean Chastain.

20th February, 1730 [1731], Marie Dupui, daughter of Pierre and of Judith Dupui, was born; was baptized by Mr. Marye the 28th of March following; had for godfather, Jean Levilain; for godmother, Philipe Vilain. The parties have declared that she was born the day and year above named.

The 8th March, 1730 [1731], was born Marie Bernard, daughter of David Bernard and of Anne Bernard, his wife; was baptized the 28th of the same month; had for godfather, Antoine Villain; for godmother, Susane Sasin and Janne Amonet. The parties have declared that she was born the day and year above named. *Jean Chastain.*

15 April, 1731, was born a black girl, who belongs to Gille Allaigre, named Nelly.

15 March, 1730 [1731], was born a black boy named Jame to Jan Dupre.

12 April, 1731, was born Joseph Peen, son of Jean Peen and of Elizabeth Peen; was baptized by Mr. Marye the 9th of May; had for godfather, Estiene Malet and Guiliaume Baton; for godmother, Olive Mallet. The parties have declared that he was born the day and year above.

The 11th April, 1730, was born Lousi, daughter of Daniel Faure; was baptized the 9th July of the year 1731.

The 9th May, 1731, was born Jean Bryer, son of Edward Brier and of Sara, his wife; was baptized the 9th July.

The 13th April, 1731, was born a girl to Mr. Giles Allaigre, a girl named Anne.

The 20th June, 1731, was born to Mr. Giles Allaigre a black girl named Janne.

The 28th July, 1731, was born to Jean Levilain a black girl named Julienne.

The 20th August was born to Maglaine Salle a girl named Marriane; was baptized the 12th 7ber by Mr. Marie; had for godfather, Charle Amonet; for godmother, Md. Barriere and Mariane Chastain.

7ber 1s, 1731, Sara Teler, daughter of Jaque Teller and of

Marye, his wife, was born to them; was baptized the 24th 8ber following; had for godfather, Jaque Martain; for godmother, Mde. Martain and Elizabeth Chastain. The parties have declared that she was born the day and year above.

Jean Chastain.

Marye Villain, daughter of Jean Villain and of Philipe Villain, was born the 2d 8bre, 1731; was baptized by Mr. Marye the 27th 8ber following; had for godfather, Barthelemi Dupuy; for godmother, mad. Dupui and md. Chastain. The parties have declared that she was born the day and year above named.

Jean Chastain.

The 27th 8ber, 1731, was born Judith Bernard, daughter of Jean Bernard and of Anne, his wife; was baptized by Mr. Marye; had for godfather David Bernard; for godmother, Judith Girodan and Anne Bernard; was baptized the 5th 9ber of the said year.

Jean Chastain.

28th 9ber, 1731, was born a little black girl, named Janne, to Antoine Rapine.

26th november, 1730, was born a black to Jean Martain, named Francoi.

25th october, 1731, was born to Judith Girodan a black named Guillieaume.

15th february, 1731 [1732], was born to Anne David a black girl named Jane.

The 24th february, 1730, was born a black to Antoine Benain.

The 25th november, 1731, was born Estiene Malet, son of Estiene Malet and of Olive Malet; was baptized by Mr. Marye, the minister; had for godfather, Pierre Salle and Jean Pierre Billiebo, and Magdelaine Salle for godmother.

Jean Chastain.

The 7th 7ber, 1731, was born Judith Benain, daughter of Antoine (?) Benain and of Elizabeth Benain; had for godfather, Thomas Porter; for godmother, Ester Joannis and Barbarie Dutoy; was baptized by Mr. Marye, minister.

The 5th January, 1731 [1732], was born Magdelaine Chastain, daughter of Jean Chastain and of Charlote Chastain; was baptized by Mr. Marye, minister; had for godfather, Charle Amonet; for godmother, Magdelaine Salle and Elizabeth Chastain.

John Chastain.

The 4th March, 1730, was born william porter, son of Thomas Porter and of Elizabet Porter; had for godfather, Antoine Benin and Francoi Farsi; for godmother, Mariane Dutoi.

John Chastain.

The 16 March, 1732, was born Elizabet Porter, daughter of Thommas Porter, and of Elizabet Porter; had for godfather, Joseph Benin, for godmother, Elizabet Dutoi and Elizabet Benin. *Jean Chastain.*

The 17th February, 1731 [1732], was born to Estienne Chastain a black girl named Suson.

The 17th April, 1732, was born Guillieaume Salle, son of Guillieaume Salle and Elizabet Salle; was baptized by Mr. Marye; had for godfather, David Leseur and Estienne Mallet; for godmother, Olive Malet.

The 20th May was born a black girl named Jene to Antoine Rapine.

The 15th June was born Jacob Amonet, son of Andre Amonet and of Janne, his wife; had for godfather, Pierre Faure and Charle Amonet; for godmother, Anne David and Marie Stonebane. The parties have declared that the child was born the day and year above named.

The 18th July, 1732, was born Judie, a black girl, to Estiene Chastain. *Jean Chastain.*

The 7th February, 1732 [1733], was born Isaac Dupuy, son of Pierre Dupuy and of Judith Dupuy; was baptized by Mr. Marye; had for godfather, Jaque Brian and Antoine Villain; for godmother, Elizabeth Brian. The parties have declared that he was born the year and day above named.

Jean Chastain.

The 28th December, 1732, was born to Jean Dupre an black named Aubaie.

1732. The 4th October was born Jean Sassain, son of Elie Sassain and of Susane Sassain, his wife.

Le 4 Janvier, 1732 [1733], was born Joseph Trabu, son of Jacob Trabu and of Marie Trabu, his wife.

The 19 March, 1732 [1733], was born Mariane Witt, daughter of Benjamin Witt and of Mariane Witt, his wife; had for godfather, Jean Chastain; for godmother, Anne David and Charlote Chastain. *Jean Chastain.*

The 15 Xber, 1732, was born a black to Pierre Louis Soblet, his name is Prymus.

The 22 April, 1733, was born a black girl to Gédéon Chambon, her name is Marye.

The 21st August, 1732, was born a boy to Francoi Dupuy,[100] his name is Jean.

The 23d April, 1733, was born Bainjamain Soblet, son of Pierre Louys Soblet and of Marte, his wife; had for godfather, gedeon Chanbon and Wollter Stot; for godmother, Anne David. The parties have declared that he was born the day and year above named. *Jean Chastain.*

The 20th May, 1733, was born fransoise Scot, daughter of Edward Scot and of Anne, his wife; was baptized the 1st of June of the said year; had for godfather, Antoine Rapine; and Mart Soblet and Mariane Bariere for godmother.

The 28th May, 1733, was borne Susane Villain, daughter of Jean Villain and of Philipe, his wife; was baptized the 7th of July; had for godfather, Pierre Dupuy; for godmother, Judith Dupuy and Susane Dupuy.

The 28 June, 1732, was born Alexandre Robinson.

Jean Chastain.

The 18th December, 1732, was born Judith, daughter of Giles Allegre.

The 24th May, 1733, was born a black, belonging to Giles Allegre, named Chamberlain.

The 17th July, 1733, was born Jean Gueran, son of Pierre gueran and of Magdelaine Gueran; had for godfather, gedeon Chambon and Antoine Trabut; for godmother, Mariane Loucadou and Marte Chastain; was baptized by Mr. Marye.

Jean Chastain.

---

[100] Francis Dupuy was presumably a near relative of Bartholomew Dupuy, the *propositus* of the Dupuy family in the United States; but the connection does not appear to have been preserved by tradition or "family tree."

The 8th January, 1731, was born a black girl to Guilieaume Salle, named anna.

The 4th February, 1732 [1733], was born to Guilieaume Salle a black girl named Mall.

The 7th August, 1733, was born a black girl to Jean Levilain, named Agar.

The 25 9ber, 1733, was born David Lesueur, son of David Lesueur and of Elizabet Lesueur ; had for godfather, Jean Chastain ; for godmother, Anne David ; was baptized by Mr. Marye, minister. *Jean Chastain.*

13 March, 1732 [1733], was born Elizabet Edmon, daughter of Jean Edmon ; had for godfather, Jean Pierre Bilbo ; for godmother, Marte Chastain and Elizabet Karner.

Jean Chastain.

24th December was born a black girl to Antoine Rapine.

Jean Chastain.

The 15th December, 1733, was born Zacarie, son of Jaque Robinson and of Susane Robinson ; was presented to baptism by Jean Chastain and Rene Chastain ; for godmother, Marye Prouit. *Jean Chastain.*

The 15th March, 1733 [1734], was born Isaac Chastain, son of Rene Chastaine and of Judith, his wife ; was presented for baptism by Jean Chastain and Jean Martain, the younger ; for godmother, Jeanne Martain.

The 9th April, 1734, was born David Bernard, son of David Bernard and of Anne, his wife ; was presented for baptism by Etiene Calvet ; for godmother, Elizabet Calvet.

Jean Chastain.

The 10th February, 1733 [1734], was born Joseph Benin, son of Antoine Benin and of Elizabeth Benin.

Jean Chastain.

The 25th May, 1734, was born a black girl to Antoine Benin named Nelley.

The 28th January, 1733 [1734], was born Guilieaume Malet, son of Etiene Malet and of Olive Malet.

Jean Chastain.

The 25th April, 1734, was born Susane Dupuy, daughter of

Jean Jaque Dupuy and of Susane Dupuy; had for godfather, Pierre Dupuy; for godmother, Philipe Vilain and Brogit Melone.

Jean Chastain.

The 8th May, 1734, was born Guilieaume Salle, son of Guilieaume Salle and of Elizabet, his wife; was baptized by Mr. Marye; for godfather, David Lesueur and the father; for godmother, Sara Porter. The parties have declared that he was born the day and year above.

The 24th April, 1734, was born a little black girl to Guilieaume Salle, named Sarrá.

The 29th July, 1734, was born a black to Jean Levilain, named Gedeon. *Jean Chastain.*

The 6th August, 1734, was born Jean Andre Amonnet, son of Andre Amonnet and of Janne Amonet, has been baptized by Mr. Marie; had for godfather, Jean Chastain; for godmother, Magdelaine Salle.

The 3d 8ber, 1734, was born Janne Chastain, daughter of Jean Chastain and of Judith, his wife; had for godfather, David Lesueur; for godmother, Janne Martain and Janne Amonnet.

Jean Chastain.

The 11th 8ber, 1734, was born Judith Dupuy, daughter of Pierre Dupuy and of Judith Dupuy; had for godfather, Jean Levilain, Jr.; for godmother, Magdelaine Salle and Anne Bernard, wife of Jean Bernard.

The 9th 7ber, 1734, was born Mariane Farsi, daughter of Estiene Farsi and of Mariane, his wife.

Jean Chastain.

The 8th 8ber, 1734, was born Judith Dupuy, daughter of Francoi Dupuy and of Marie Dupuy, his wife; had for godfather, Pierre Dupuy; for godmother, Judith Dupuy and Philipe Villain. *Jean Chastain.*

The 22d 8ber, 1734, was born John Porter, son of Thomas Porter and of Elizabet Porter.

The 5th 8ber, 1734, was born Isaac Salle, son of Pierre Salle and of Francoise Salle.

23d June, 1733, was born Marie Bilbo, daughter of Jean Pierre Bilbo and of Susane, his wife; had for godfather, Antoine Benin; for godmother, Barbarie and Mariane Dutoy.

The 24th Xber, 1734, was born Anne Elizabet Chanbon, daughter of Gedeon Chanbon and of Janne, his wife.

The 13th July, 1734, was born Francoise Dikins,[101] daughter of Thomas Dikins and of Anne Dikins, his wife.

Jean Chastain.

The 11th April, 1735, was born Louy Sasain, son of Elie Sasain and of Susane, his wife.

The 16th May, 1735, was born a black to Jaque Martain, named Dic. *Jean Chastain.*

The 24th May, 1735, was born Guillieaume Martain, son of Jaque Martain and of Janne Martain, his wife; was presented for baptism by Jean Chastain and Rene Chastain; for godmother, Charlote Chastain. *Jean Chastain.*

The 8th June, 1735, was born Magdelaine Bernard, daughter of David Bernard and of Anne Bernard, his wife; had for godfather, Antoine Bernard; for godmother, Magdelaine Salle, the mother and the daughter.

19th June, 1735, was born Nanni Soulie, daughter of Nicolas Soulie and of Francoise Soulie, his wife; had for godfather, the father of the child; for godmother, the mother and Anne gining. *Jean Chastain.*

17th July, 1735, was born a black to Antoine Rapine named Bili. *Jean Chastain.*

22d 7ber, 1735, was born to Jean Levilain, Sr., a black named Estiene. *Jean Chastain.*

The 29th August, 1732, was born David Stanford, son of William Stanford and of Caterine, his wife.

The 6th January, 1734 [1735], was born Mariane Stanford, daughter of William Stanford and of Caterine, his wife.

Jean Chastain.

The 12th 8ber, 1735, was born Jean Villain, son of Jean Vilain, the younger, and of Philipe, his wife; had for godfather, Jean Vilain, his grandfather; for godmother, Charlote Chastain.

Jean Chastain.

---

[101] Doubtless Dickens.

The 28th August, 1735, was born Jean Trabu, son of Jacob Trabu and of Marie Trabu.

The 12th 9ber, 1735, was born Caterine Lesueur, daughter of David Lesueur and of Elizabeth, his wife; had for godfather her father; for godmother, Charlote Chastain and Elizabet Brian.

The 26th 9ber, 1735, was born Jean Bilbo, son of Jean Pierre Bilbo and of Susane, his wife; he had for godfather, Jean Panetie and Isaac Dutoi; for godmother, Janne Janbon and Ester Lafuite; baptized the 18th March.

The 2d Xber, 1735, was born Ester Guerant, daughter of Pierre Guerrant and of Magdelaine Guerant; for godfather, Guilieaume Salle; for godmother, Elizabet Salle and Judith Trabu; baptized the 18th March, 1735 [1736].

Jean Chastain.

The 15th March, 1735 [1736], was born to Anne David a black named Jeck.

The 22d 9ber, 1735, was born Samuel Edmon, son of Jean Edmon; had for godfather, Antoine Trabu and Pierre Loucadou; for godmother, Elizabet Loucadou. *Jean Chastain.*

The 21st January, 1735 [1736], was born george Smith, son of George Smith and of Anne, his wife; had for godfather, Estiene Farsi and Jaque Brian; for godmother, Elizabet Brian.

Jean Chastain.

The 26th February, 1735 [1736], was born Marie Dupuy, daughter of Jean Jaque Dupuy and of Susane, his wife.

Jean Chastain.

The 20th November, 1735, was born Estiene Perault, son of Daniel Perault and of Marie, his wife.

The 1st June, 1736, was born a black boy to Marie Farsi; his name is Jaque. *Jean Chastain.*

The 4th April, 1736, was born Jean Bernard, son of Jean Bernar and of Anne Bernar, his wife; he had for godfather, Charle Amonnet; for godmother, Judith Trabu. The Parties have declared that the child was born the day and year above.

Jean Chastain.

The 22d 8ber, 1735, was born to Antoine Benin a little black girl named Sara.

The 20th of May, 1736, was born Elizabet Porter.

Jean Chastain.

The 15th March, 1735 [1736], was born Jean Forqueran, son of Moyse Forqueran and of Susane, his wife; had for godfather, Pierre Forqueran; for godmother, Janne Dupre.

Jean Chastain.

The 28th July, 1736, was born to Jean Vilain a black girl named Pegg.

The 28th July, 1736, was born to Daniel Perault a black boy named Guilieaume.

17th 7ber, 1736, was born Elizabet Benin, daughter of Antoine Benin and of Elizabet Benin.

The 28th 7ber, 1736, was born Marie Magdelaine Dupuy, daughter of Pierre Dupuy and of Judith Dupuy; had for godfather, Jean Jaque Dupuy; for godmother, Marie Chastain and Philipe Vilain. *Jean Chastain.*

The 2d 7ber, 1736, was born Judith Malet, daughter of Etiene Malet and of Olive, his wife; had for godfather, James Goss; for godmother, Elizabet Sale and Magdelaine Salle.

Jean Chastain.

The 8th 8ber, 1736, was born Thomas Robinson, son of Isaac Robinson and of Anne, his wife; had for godfather, Jacob Trabu; for godmother, Marie Trabu.

The 5th 9ber, 1736, was born Elizabet Loucadou, daughter of Pierre Loucadou and of Elizabet, his wife.

Jean Chastain.

The 6th 9ber, 1736, was born Pierre Chastain, son of Rene Chastain and of Judith Chastain.

The 2d 7ber, 1730, was born Marie Faure, daughter of Jaque Faure and of Anne, his wife.

The 6th 7ber, 1733, was born Judith Faure, daughter of Jaque Faure and of Anne, his wife.

The 11th January, 1733 [1734] was born Pierre Faure, son of Jaque Faure and of Anne, his wife.

The 20th August, 1736, was born Magdelaine Faure, daughter of Jaque Faure and of Anne, his wife.

The 9th January, 1736 [1737], was born a black to Jean Porter named Ben.

The 27th August, 1735, was born Filis, a black girl, to Estiene Chastain.

The 12th January, 1728, was born Antoine Chaveron, son of Antoine Chaveron and of Anriette, his wife.

The 6th 9ber, was born Antoine Apperson, son of William Apperson and of Anne, his wife.

The 8th May, 1737, was born to Estiene Chastain a black named Ben. *Jean Chastain.*

The 29th Xber, 1736, was born Alexander Bryers, son of Edward Bryers and of Sara, his wife; for godfather, Jean Levilain. *Jean Chastain.*

The 29th Xber, 1736, was born Sara Bryers, daughter of Edward Bryers and of Sara, his wife; for godfather, Jean Pierre Bilbo; for godmother, Judith Chastain. *Jean Chastain.*

The 25th July, 1734, was born Edward Bryars, son of Edward Bryers and of Sara, his wife; for godfather, Moyse Forqueran; for godmother, Mariane Loucadou.

The 14th June, 1735, was born to Estiene Malet a little black girl named Nanni.

The 28th July, 1732, was born Sabary Willeamson, daughter of Jean Willeamson and of Sara, his wife.

The 15th July, 1734, was born Mathiew Williamson, son of Jean Williamson and of Sara, his wife.

The 20th 8ber, 1734, was born Jean Williamson, son of John Williamson and Sara, his wife. *Jean Chastain.*

The 18th 9ber, 1736, was born Abraham Salle, son of Pierre Salle and Francoise, his wife; had for godfather Pierre Bonduran and Joseph Bonduran; and for godmother Ann Faure. *Jean Chastain.*

The 9th March, 1736 [1737], was born Charle Amonet, son of Andre Amonet and of Janne, his wife; had for godfather, Jean Moriset; for godmother, Cattrine Taboi.

The 7th March, 1736, was born Anne Farsi, daughter of Estiene Farsi and of Marie, his wife; had for godfather, Daniel Pero; for godmother, Anne Apperson.

The 6th August, 1731, was born a black to the widow Gueran named Francoi. *Jean Chastain.*

The 30th April, 1735, was born a black girl to Nicolas Soulie; she is named Hanna.

The 4th July, 1735, was born a black to the widow Soulie; he is named James. *Jean Chastain.*

The 24th 7ber, 1737, was born Janne Forquerant, daughter of Moyse Forquerant and of Susane, his wife; had for godfather, Jean Robert; for godmother, Elizabet Haneri and Janne Levrant; was baptized by Mr. Brook.

The 7th 8ber, 1737, was born Marey Taler, daughter of Charle Taller; had for godfather, Joseph Bingley; for godmother, Judith Bingley; was baptized by Mr. Brook.

The 9th of 9ber, 1737, was born Estiene Chastain, son of Jean Chastain and of Charlote Chastain; had for godfather, Pierre David and Jean Chastain, his brother; for godmother, Magdelaine Salle, the younger; was baptized by Mr. Brook.

Jean Chastain.

The 28th 9ber, 1737, was born to Jean Levilain, a daughter named Elizabet; had for godfather, Estiene Chastain; for godmother, Elizabet Brian and Martre Chastain.

Jean Chastain.

The 27th 7ber, 1737, was born Antoine Martain, son of Pierre Martain and of Mariane, his wife; had for godfather, Rene Chastain; for godmother, Janne Martain the younger.

Jean Chastain.

The 16th Xber, 1737, was born to Estiene Chastain a little black girl named Lucy.

The 10th Xber, 1737, was born Jean Benin, son of Antoine Benin and of Elizabet Benin; had for godfather, Jams Gose and Pierre Bilbo; for godmother, Ester Lafite.

Jean Chastain.

The 17th Xber, 1737, was born Pierre Gueran, son of Pierre Gueran and of Magdelaine, his wife; had for godfather, Pierre David; for godmother, Anne David, the younger; Pierre Guerant, the younger.

The 10th Xber, 1737, was born David Trabu, son of Jacob

Trabu and of Marie, his wife; had for godfather, Antoine Trabu and Edward Wooldrig;[102] for godmother, Judith Trabu.

Jean Chastain.

The 26th 9ber, 1737, was born to Estiene Malet a black named George.

The 17th February, 1737 [1738], was born Dutoy Porter, son of Thomas Porter and of Elizabet, his wife; had for godfather, Antoine Benin and Isaac Dutoy; for godmother, Ester Lafite.

Jean Chastain.

The 10th Xber, 1737, was born David Trabu, son of Jacob Trabu and of Marie Trabue; had for godfather, Antoine Trabu and Edward Wooldrig; for godmother, Judith Trabu; was baptized by Mr. Brook.

The 27th March, 1738, was born to Jean Levilian a black named Pedro.

The 17th March, 1737 [1738], was born Jean Dupuy, son of Jean Jacque Dupuy and of Susane, his wife; had for godfather, Jean Levilian, the younger; for godmother, Marte Chastain; was baptized by Mr. Brook.

The 14th April, 1738, was born to Jean Levilian a black named Jo.

The 28th March, 1738, was born a black girl to Antoine Bennin; her name is Moll.

The 30th March, 1738, was born Marie Porter, daughter of Jean Porter and of Marie, his wife.

The 17th May, 1738, was born Mariane Chastain, daughter of Rene Chastain and of Judith, his wife; had for godfather, Jean Chastain; for godmother, Magdelaine Chastain and Janne Martain.

Jean Chastain.

Judith Dupuy, daughter of Pierre Dupuy and of Judith Dupuy, his wife, was born the 24th June, 1734; had for godfather, Jaque Brian; for godmother, Elizabet Brian and Judith Salle; was baptized the 8th August by Mr. Brook.

The 31st July, 1738, was born Susane Elizabet Elson, daughter of Thomas Elson and Elizabet Elson; had for godfather, Jean Pierre Bilbo; for godmother, Susan Bilbo and Barbari Dutoy.

Jean Chastain.

---

[102] Wooldridge; a name estimably represented in Virginia.

The 4th of 8ber, 1738, was born David Lesueur, son of David Lesueur and of Elizabet Lesueur; had for godfather, Jaque Brian and Jean Chastain; for godmother, Anne David.

Jean Chastain.

The 6th 8ber, 1738, was born Anne Bernard, daughter of Jean Bernard and of Anne, his wife; had for godfather, Jean Chastain; for godmother, Charlote Chastain and Magdelaine Guerran.

The 27th 7ber, 1738, was born Jean Loucadou, son of Pierre Loucadou and of Elizabet, his wife; had for godfather, David Tomas and Jaque Solaigre; for godmother, Anne Bore.

The 5th 8ber, 1738, was born Willeam Bantan, son of Willeam Bantan; had for godfather, Jean Pierre Bilbo and Antoine Trabu; for godmother, Marte Chastain. *Jean Chastain.*

The 15th August, 1736, was born to Marie Dupuy a black named Tobie.

The 10th 8ber, 1737, was born Anne Pene, daughter of Charle Pene and Marie, his wife.

The 11th 9ber, 1738, was born a black to Daniel Pero, named Judith.

The 23rd 8ber, 1738, was born Jean Roberd, son of Jean Roberd and of Janne, his wife; had for godfather, Moyse and Pierre Forqueran; for godmother, Janne Dupre.

Jean Chastain.

The 25th 8ber, 1738, was born Elizabet Gore, daughter of Jamse Gore[103] and of Mariane, his wife; had godfather, Mathieu Bingli; for godmother, Barbari Dutoy and Elizabet Porter; was baptized by Mr. Brook.

The 27th 9ber, 1738, was born Ester Malet, daughter of Etiene Malet and of Olive, his wife; had for godfather, Jaque Faure; for godmother, Ester Lafitte and Anne Oge.

The 15th January, 1737 [1738], was born Anne David, daughter of Pierre David and of Elizabet, his wife; had for godfather, Jean Chastain; for godmother, Anne David and Charlote Chastain. *Jean Chastain.*

The 13th February, 1738 [1739], was born Elizabet Bilbo, daughter of Jean Pierre Bilbo and of Susane, his wife; and died the 20th March, 1738 [1739].

---

[103] Gaure.

The 1st March, 1738 [1739], was born a black to Marie Hamton, named Isaac.

The 25th March, 1739, was born Diane Robinson, daughter of Isaac Robinson and of Anne, his wife. *Jean Chastain.*

The 28th April, 1739, was born a black girl to Guillieaume Salle, and her name is Dorotie.

The 28th May, 1739, was born to Guillieaume Salle a black girl named Fillis.

The 12th May, 1739, was born to Estiene Malet a black girl named Agar. *Jean Chastain.*

The 18th June, 1739, was born a black to Antoine Benin, named Pompe.

The 10th July, 1739, was born a black to Marthe Chastain, named Samiel.

The 27th July, 1739, was born a black to Pierre Martain ; his name is Franky. *Jean Chastain.*

The 27th July, 1739, was born Isaac Salle, son of guillieaume Salle and Elizabet, his wife; had for godfather, Estiene Mallet and the father of the child; for godmother, Anne David [and the] mother.

The 12th August, 1739, was born Isaac Brian, son of Jaque Brian and of Elizabet Brian; had for godfather, David Lesueur; for godmother, Judith Bingli.

The 24th February, 1738, was born Anne Faure, daughter of Jaque Faure and of Anne, his wife. *Jean Chastain.*

The 27th August, 1739, was born Rachel Faure, daughter of Jaque Faure and Anne, his wife.

The 29th August, 1739, was born Jane Farsi, daughter of Estiene Farsi and of Marie Farsi, his wife.

The 4th May, 1739, was born Frederick Don, son of Nathanael Don and of Elizabet Don; had for godfather, David Lesuer and Rene Chastain; for godmother, Judith Chastain, the wife of Rene Chastain. *Jean Chastain.*

The 17th November, 1739, was born to Joseph Bingli a black girl named Hanna.

The 7th 8ber, 1739, was born Elizabeth Forqueran, daughter of Moyse Forqueran and of Susane, his wife; was baptized by

Mr. Gavain; had for godfather, Jean Chastain; for godmother, Magdelaine Gueran and Jyse Forqueran.

The 27th February, 1739, was born a black girl to Marte Chastain, named Pegg. *Jean Chastain.*

The 23d March, 1739, was born a boy to Jacob Trabu, named William; had for godfather, Robert Wooldrig and Edward Parrat; for godmother, Marrie Arrison.

The 12th 9ber, 1739, was born Laraus Bryers, son of Edward Bryers and of Sara, his wife; had for godfather, Mattieu Bingly and Rene Chastain; for godmother, Janne Dupre.

The 9th April, 1740, was born a black girl to Jean Levilian, Jr.; her name is Judith; she died the 19th June, 1740.

Jean Chastain.

The 6th May, 1739, was born Daniel Wever, son of Samuel Wever and of Francoise, his wife; had for godfather, John Chandler and William Wever; for godmother, Elizabeth Wever.

The 30th January, 1738, was born a black girl to Samuel Wever.

The 1st April, 1740, was born Marie Wattkins, daughter of Stephen Watkins[104] and Judith, his wife; had for godfather, William Hampton; for godmother, Magdelaine Chastain and Marie Farci. *Jean Chastain.*

The 29th May, 1740, was born to Jean Levilain, Sr., a black named William.

The 26th May, 1740, was born to Pierre Martain a black named Hanna.

The 11th July, 1740, was born Jean Martain, the son of Pierre Martain and of Mariane, his wife; had for godfather, Jaque Martain and Daniel Perro; for godmother, Janne Martain, wife of Jaque Martain. *Jean Chastain.*

The 4th 7ber, 1740, was born Elizabet Dupuy, daughter of

---

[104] The name Watkins was early seated in Virginia, and has been continuously prominent in its annals. John Wattkins patented 850 acres of land in James City county, July 3, 1648, *Virginia Land Registry* (Book No. 1, page 144); and there are numerous subsequent grants to the name of record. The Watkins blood is represented by the names of Bouldin, Cabell, Carrington, Coleman, Daniel, Edmunds, Ellet, Flournoy, Leigh, Morton, and numerous others as worthy.

Jean Jaque Dupuy and of Susane, his wife; had for godfather, Jean Barthelemi Dupuy; for godmother, Elizabet Porter and Marie Chastain.

The 31st August, 1740, was born Magdelaine Guerant, daughter of Pierre Guerran and of Magdelaine, his wife; had for godfather, Jean Trabu; for godmother, her mother and Clere Trabu

21st 7ber, ——, was born David Bernar, son of Jean Bernar and of Anne, his wife; had for godfather, Andre Amonnet and Pierre Dupuy, and Janne Amonnet for godmother.

Jean Chastain.

The 31st August, 1740, was born David Sassain, son of Elie Sassain and of Susane, his wife; had for godfather, Jean Bernard and the father; for godmother, Anne David.

The 3d August, 1740, was born Sara Gase, daughter of James Gase and of Mariane, his wife.

The 6th Xber, 1740, was born a black girl to Marie Chastain; her name is Nani.

The 25th Xber, 1740, was born Jaque Lesheur, son of David Lesueur and of Elizabet, his wife.

The 31st Xber, 1740, was born a black girl to Marte Chastain, her name is Moll; she died the 11th January, 1740 [1741].

The 18th January, 1740 [1741], was born a black girl to Jaque Brian; her name is Janne. *Jean Chastain.*

The 15th Xber, 1740, was born a black girl to Daniel Perro; her name is Catterine.

The 10th February 1740 [1741], was born to Jean Chastain a black girl; her name is Batte.

The 1st 7ber, 1740, was born a black girl to Thomas Porter; her name is Amee.

The 27th 9ber, 1740, was born William Porter, son of Thomas Porter and Elizabeth, his wife.

The 12th February, 1740 [1741], was born a black girl to Jean Chastain; her name is Bette.

The 19th February, 1740 [1741], was born a black girl to Pierre Gueran; her name is Louci. *Jean Chastain.*

The 1st 8ber, 1737, was born Jean Bonduran, son of Jean Bonduran.

The 22nd August, 1740, was born Richard Bonduran, son of Jean Bonduran.

The 20th January, 1740 [1741], was born Elizabet Mallet, daughter of Estiene Mallet and of Olive, his wife; had for godfather, Jean Chastain; for godmother, Charlote Chastain and Anne David, the younger. *John Chastain.*

The 22nd April, 1741, was born Isaac Salle, son of Guillieaume Salle and of Magdelaine, his wife; had for godfather, his father and Jean Chastain; for godmother, Charlote Chastain.

The 2nd May, 1741, was born to Joseph Bingli a black; his name is Napton.

The 24th April, 1734, was born Rebeca Bernard, daughter of Jean Bernar and of Anne, his wife; had for godfather, Pierre Martain; for godmother, Janne Martain, the younger, and Elizabet Roberd. *Jean Chastain.*

The 28th April, 1741, was born David Lacy, son of William Lacy; had for godfather, Mattieu Bingly; for godmother, Elizabet Robert.

The 14th June, 1741, was born a black girl to Rene Chastain; her name is Janne. *Jean Chastain.*

The 30th June, ——, was born Rene Chastain, son of Rene Chastain and of Judith, his wife; had for godfather, his father, and for godmother, Judith Chastain, wife of Jean Chastain.

The 14th June, 1741, was born Jesse, reputed son of John Harris and of Elizabet Roberd; had for godfather, John Bernar and Jean Chastain; for godmother, Charlote Judith Chastain.

The 5th Xber, 1740, was born Elizabet Bilbo, daughter of Jean Pierre Bilbo and of Elizabet, his wife; had for godfather, Pierre Gueran, Jr.; for godmother, Elizabet Wever and Marie Wever.

8ber 1st, 1741, was born Marie Salle, daughter of Pierre Salle and Francoise Salle, his wife. *Jean Chastain.*

9ber the 25th, 1741, was born Elizabet, daughter of Ethiene Farci and of Marie Farci, his wife.

15th March, 1741 [1742], was born to Jaque Brian a black girl; her name is Anna.

The 12th April, 1731, was born Anne Robinson, daughter of Jamse Robinson and of Susane, his wife. *Jean Chastain.*

The 7th June, 1735, was born Jamse Robinson, son of Jamse Robinson and of Susane, his wife.

The 20th May, 1739, was born Marie Robinson, daughter of Jamse Robinson and of Susane, his wife.

The 19th July 1741, was born a black to Jamse Robinson; his name is Will. *Jean Chastain.*

The 15th March, 1741, was born Lucy and Magdelaine Robinson, daughters of Isaac Robinson, and of Anne, his wife; they had for godfather, Pierre David and Andre Amonet; for godmother, Anne David, the mother, and Anne David the younger, and Janne Amonet and Susane Sassain.

Edmond Bryer, son of Edward Bryer, was born the 27th day of May, 1742; had for godfather, Jaque Martain; for godmother, Judith Dupuy. *Jean Chastain.*

The 6th May, 1742, was born a black girl to Md. Dutoy; her name is Agge,

The 16th May, 1742, was born a black to Thomas Porter; his name is Dick.

The 24th March, 1742, was born Elizabet Trabu, daughter of Jacob Trabu; had for godfather, Jean Trabu; for godmother, Elizabet Salle, daughter of Abraham Salle, and Elizabet Salle, daughter of Guilleame Salle. *Jean Chastain.*

The 19th 7ber, ——, was born a black to Estiene Malet; her name is Janne.

The 21st August, 1742, was born a black to Jean Jaque Dupuy; her name is Marie.

The 14th October, 1741, was born a black to David Le Sueur; his name is Robin. *Jean Chastain.*

Was born to Guilliaume Salle, two negro girls—one on the 20th February, 1741 [1742]; her name is Moll; the other, born 6th April, 1741 [1742], and her name is Nanney.

The 14th 7ber, 1742, was born Ester Bernar, daughter of Antoine Bernar and of Sara, his wife; had for godfather, Hanry Godsy; for godmother, Febe Lacy and Marie Godse.

The 10th 9ber, 1742, was born Marie Magdelaine Malet, daughter of Estiene Malet and of Olive, his wife; had for godfather, Matthieu Bingly; for godmother, Judith and Mariane Salle.

Jean Chastain.

The 16th May, 1742, was born a black girl to Jaque Martain; her name is Sara.

The 21st February, 1742 [1743], was born a black to Jaque Martain, his name is Caesar. *Jean Chastain.*

The 22d 7ber, 1742, was born ——— Watkins, daughter of Estiene Watkins and of Judith, his wife; for godfather, Jacob Trabu; for godmother, Magdelaine Gueran and Marie Vilain.

The 3d February, 1742 [1743], was born a black girl to Joseph Bingly; her name is Janne.

The 2d 8ber, 1742, was born Binjamen Joss, son of Jamse Joss and of Mariane, his wife.

The 27th March, 1743, was born a black girl to Jaque Brian; her name is Nanne. *Jean Chastain.*

The 14th March, 1742 [1743], was born Jaque Faure, son of Jaque Faure and of Anne, his wife.

The 12th April, 1743, was born a black girl to Estiene Malet; her name is Aimi.

The 2d April, 1743, was born Guilieaume Loucadou, son of Pierre Loucadou and of Elizabeth, his wife; had for godfather, Jean Chastain, Jr., and Joseph Bonduran; for godmother, Susane Gaspar. *Jean Chastain.*

The 28th March, 1742, was born Anne Kempe, daughter of Thomas Kempe and of Mary, his wife; had for godfather, Pierre Faure; for godmother, Anne Garret and Mary Davis.

The 28th June, 1743, was born to Estiene Malet a black girl; her name is Nane.

The 28th April, 1743, was born Jean Howard, son of William and of Rebecca Howard; had for godfather, Jean Bernard; for godmother, Judith Salle. *Jean Chastain.*

The 24th January, 1742 [1743], was born Francoi Bernar, son of Jean Bernar and of Anna, his wife; had for godfather, Antoine Trabu; for godmother, Claire Trabue.

The 2d 9ber, 1742, was born a black girl to Jean Vilain, Sr.; her name is Moll.

The 23d January, 1743 [1744], was born Magdelaine Chastain, daughter of Jean Chastain and of Judith, his wife; had for godfather, Guilieaume Salle; for godmother, the wife of Guiliaume Salle and Magdelaine Salle, her aunt. *Jean Chastain.*

The 12th February, 1743 [1744], was born a black girl to Jacob Trabu; her name is Nanni.

The 18th 9ber, 1743, was born Henry Lacy, son of William Lacy and of Elizabet, his wife.

The 13th 9ber, 1743, was born Chastain Cocke, son of Jamse Cocke[105] and Marie, his wife; had for godfather, Jean Jaque Dupuy and Hanry Godse; for godmother, Anne David, the younger. *Jean Chastain.*

The 4th March, 1743 [1744], was born to Jamse Cocke a black; his name is Isham.

Jacob Salle, son of Pierre Salle and of Francoise, his wife, was born the 9th February, 1743 [1744].

The 27th April, 1744, was born to David Lesueur a black girl, named Moll. *Jean Chastain.*

The 25th 8ber, 1744, was born a black girl to Pierre Gueran; her name is Hannor.

The 3d August, 1744, was born to Estiene Malet a black; his name is Hemton.

The 21st Xber, 1744, was born Marie Howard, daughter of William and Rebecca Howard. *Jean Chastain.*

The 29th 9ber, 1744, was born Marie Trabu, daughter of Jacob Trabu and of Marie, his wife; had for godfather, William Woodreg; for godmother, Magdelaine Wooldreg and Magdelaine Gueran.

The 29th January, 1744 [1745], was born Jaque Dupuy, son of Jean Jaque Dupuy and of Susane, his wife. *Jean Chastain.*

The 19th March, 1744 [1745], was born Joseph Watkins, son of Estiene Watkins and of Judith, his wife.

The 7th February, 1743 [1744], was born Sara Porter, daughter of Thomas Porter and of Elizabet, his wife; had for godfather, James Cox; for godmother, Madame Gavain.

Judith Farci, daughter of Estienne Farci and of Marie, his wife, was born the 19th of October, 1744; had for godfather,

---

[105] James Powell Cocke married Mary Magdalene, daughter of Stephen and Martha Chastain. Their descendants embrace, with other estimable names, those of Allen, Anderson, Archer, Barnwell, Boston, Boyd, Browne, Cannon, Carter, Christian, Churchill, Deane, Eggleston, Ellis, Field, Harvie, Hemphill, Hobson, Lewis, Mosby, Murray, Old, Parkhill, Richardson, Ronald, Royall, Sharp, Southall, Taylor, Venable, Webb and Weisiger.

Thomas Smith; for godmother, Marie Farci and Olimpe Dupuy.

The 3d 9ber, 1743, was born Judith Faure, daughter of Pierre Faure and of Marie, his wife.

Joseph Faure was born the 31st of May, 1744; son of Pierre Faure and of Marie, his wife. *Jean Chastain.*

The 25th 9ber, 1745, was born Pierre Faure, son of Pierre Faure and of Marie, his wife.

The 14th January, 1745 [1746], was born Mike. Pembreton, daughter of Richard Pembreton and of Elizabeth, his wife.

The 17th 8ber, 1745, was born Judith Gueran, daughter of Pierre Gueran and of Magdelaine, his wife; had for godfather, Estiene Watkins; for godmother, Marie Trabu and Judith Bernar. *Jean Chastain.*

The 17th March, 1745 [1746], was born a black girl to Jaque Brian, named Filis.

The 9th March, 1745, was born Joseph Salle, son of Pierre Salle and of Francoise, his wife.

The 24th March, 1745 [1746], was born a black girl to Jean Chastain; her name is Fillis.

The 20th of June, 1746, was born a black to Pièrre Gueran; his name is Sesar.

The 10th of 9ber, 1745, was born Anne Bonduran, daughter of Joseph and Agnes Bonduran.

Ruth Faure was born the 14th February, 1745; daughter of Jaque and Anna Faure. *Jean Chastain.*

The 24th December, 1744, was born Chastain Le Sueur, son of David Le Sueur and of Elizabeth, his wife; had for godfather, Jean Chastain, the younger, and Matthieu Bingly; and for godmother, Magdelaine Salle.

The 2d of November, 1745, was born Jean Salle, son of Guilliaume Salle and of Magdelaine, his wife; had for godfather, Abraham Salle and Jean Chastain, the younger; for godmother, Elizabeth Le Sueur.

The 16th July, 1731, was born a black to Jean Harris; his name is George.

The 15th Xber, 1732, was born a black girl to Jean Harris; her name is Debora.

The 23d April, 1739, was born a black girl to Jean Harris; her name is Hanna.

The 3d December, 1741, was born a black girl to Jean Harris; her name is Jene.

The 23d February, 1743, was born a black girl to Jean Harris; her name is Nell.

The 24th February, 1744, was born a black girl to Jean Harris; her name is Judith.

The 15th February, 1744, was born a black girl to Jean Harris; her name is Magdelin.

The 12th February, 1745, was born a black to Jean Harris; his name is Franck.

The 29th January, 1746 [1747], was born a black to Jean Harris; his name is Fill. *Jean Chastain.*

The 6th January, 1746 [1747], was born a black girl to Mariane, whose name is Jene.

The 6th April, 1746, was born Jerusha Godsy, daughter of Thomas Godsy and of Febe Godsy, his wife.

The 12th June, 1747, was born to Jean Chastain a black; his name is Will. *Jean Chastain.*

The 21st May, 1747, was born Marie Dupuy, daughter of Jean Jaque Dupuy and of Susane, his wife; had for godfather, Jean Trabu; for godmother, Olimpe, his wife.

The 16th Xber, 1745, was born a black to Jaque Martain; his name is Tom.

The 19th July, 1747, was born a black to Jaque Martain; his name is Harry.

On the 14th July, 1747, was born Pierre Bernard, son of Jean Bernard and of Anne, his wife.

The 1st July 1747, was [born] Pierre David, son of Pierre David and of Elizabet, his wife; had for godfather, Pierre Gueran and Jean Papham; for godmother, Elizabet Papham.

Jean Chastain.

The 4th 9ber, 1747, was born Josue Trabue, son of Jacob Trabu and of Marie, his wife; he had for godfather, Jean Gueran and Joseph Trabu; for godmother, Marie Wooldrig.

The 7th 9ber, ——, was born a black to Jacob Trabu.

The 22d January, 1747, was born a black to Jean Jaque Dupuy; his name is Dick.

The 23d April, 1748, was born Daniel Gueran, son of Pierre Gueran and of Magdelaine Gueran, his wife; had for godfather,

David Lesueur and Jean Gueran; for godmother, Olimpe Trabu.

The 30th June, 1740, was born a black girl to Abraham Salle; her name is Moll. *Jean Chastain.*

The 14th 9ber, ——, was born a black girl to Abraham Salle; her name is Agar.

The 25th January, 1746, was born a black to Abraham Salle; his name is Jamse.

The 17th January 1747, was born a black to Judith Salle; his name is Matt.

The 10th 8ber, 1748, was born to Pierre Gueran, a black girl; her name is Moll.

The 15th May, 1746, was born Marie Brian, daughter of Jaque Brian and of Clere, his wife; she had for godfather, Louy Soblet, Jr.; for godmother, Caroline Short.

The 21st June 1748, was born a black girl to Jaque Brian; her name is Doll.

The 15th April, 1745, was born a black girl to Samuel Wever; her name is Cloe. *Jean Chastain.*

The 25th March, 1743, was born a black girl to Samuel Wever; her name is Sara.

The 30th January, 1748 [1749], was born William Pambreton, son of Richard Paimbreton and of Elizabeth, his wife.

The 12th July, ——, was born to Jean Levilain a black, named Limbo.

The 7th August, 1748, was born to Jean Levilain a black, named Peter.

The 25th 8ber, 1749, was born Judith Salle, daughter of Pierre Salle and of Francoise, his wife; had for godfather, Estiene Mallet, the younger; for godmother, Judith Salle and Judith Faure.

The 12th July, 1748, was born a black to Jean Levilain; his name is Limbo. *Jean Chastain.*

The 20th August, 1748, was born a black to Jean Levilain; his name is Peter.

The 2d June, 1749, was born Boos Ford, son of Jaque Ford.

The 13th May, 1749, was born a black girl to Jean Ford; her name is Jean.

The 7th January, 1749 [1750], was born to Jean Chastain a black girl; her name is Nell.

Archelaus Faure, son of Pierre Faure, was born the 22d June, 1747.

William Faure, son of Pierre Faure, was born the 2d May, 1749.

The 13th May, 1749, was born to John Faure a black girl; her name is Jeen.

The 13th July, 1743, was born Pierre Salle, son of Guillieaume Salle and of Magdelaine, his wife. *Jean Chastain.*

The 5th November, 1749, was born Olive Salle, son of Guillieaume Salle and of Magdelaine, his wife.

The 28th April, 1750, was born a black girl to Jean Jaque Dupuy; her name is Hannah.

The 17th Xber, 1747, was born Charle Peane; had for godfather, William Shepard and Richard Sumter; for godmother, Marie Delpich.

The 20th Xber, 1750, was born to Jean Levilain a black; his name is Franc.

The 28th February, 1746, was born Martain Goouge, son of Andrew Martin and of Marie Goouge.

The 12th 9ber, 1750, was born to Jaque Brian a black; his name is Buttler. *Jean Chastain.*

The 3d of 7ber, 1746, was born Mariane Esly,[106] daughter of Daniel Esly and of Anne, his wife.

The 15th July, 1749, was born a black girl to Daniel Esly; her name is Judith.

The 20th July, 1750, was born Marte Esly, daughter of Daniel Esly and of Anne, his wife. *Jean Chastain.*

Henry Godsey, son of —— Godsey and of Febe ———, was born the 11th February, 17—.

The 1st April, 1750, was born Elize Lacy, son of Thomas Lacy and of Caterine Lacy.

Susanah Lacy, daughter of Nathanael Lacy and of Marie, his wife, was born the 6th April, 1750. *John Chastain.*

The 29th May, 1751, was born Louicea, daughter of Nathanael Lacy and of Marie, his wife.

The 15th 8ber, 1747, was born Samuel Lesueur, son of David Lesueur and of Elizabeth, his wife.

---

[106] Now rendered Easley.

The 23d 8ber, 1750, was born Peter and John Lesuer, sons of David Lesuer and of Elizabeth, his wife.

The 28th March, 1752, was born to Jean Jaque Dupuy a black girl; her name is Lousi. *John Chastain.*

The 25th Xber, 1751, was born Marie Porter, daughter of Thomas Porter and of Elizabeth Porter, his wife.

The 19th February, 1751 [1752], was born to Jean Levilain a black; his name is Matt.

The 22nd January, 1753, was born to Janne Martain a black; his name is Maroco.

The 9th April, 1753, was born a black to Janne Martain; his name is Ned. *Jean Chastain.*

The 29th February, 1753, was born Jean Amonnet, son of Charle Amonnet and of Diane, his wife; had for godfather, Jean Chastain, Jr., and Andrew Amonnet; for godmother, Magdelaine Salle.

23d July, 1753, was born Isaac Porter, son of Thomas Porter and of Elizabet, his wife.

The 20th November, ——, was born to Jean Jaque Dupuy a black; his name is Jo. *Jean Chastain.*

The 14th 8ber, was born Daniel Trabu, son of Jacob Trabu and Marie, his wife.

The 8th 9ber, 1751, was born a black to Estiene Farci; his name is Sam.

The 2d 9ber, 1750, was born Estiene Farci, son of Estine Farci and of Marie, his wife; had for godfather, Estiene Malet; for godmother, Judith Farci.

The 10th January, 1751, was born to Magdelaine Gueran a black; his name is Bosen. *Jean Chastain.*

The 15th 8ber, 1750, was born to Jacque Brian a black; his name is Buttler.

The 8th March, 1721, was born Thomas Brian, son of Jaque Brian and of Clere Brian.

The 7th 7ber, 1751, was born a black to Jaque Brian; his name is Cyrio. *Jean Chastain.*

The 10th May, 1752, was born to Thomas Trabu, son of Jacob Trabu and of Marie, his wife; had for godfather, William Martain; for godmother, Judith Salle.

The 17th October, 1752, was born Marthe Pimbreton, daughter of Richard Pimbreton and of Elizabeth, his wife; had for godfather, Willeam Streef; for godmother, Cloreck Brian and Caterine Leseur.

The 28th March, ——, was born to Jean Levilain a black girl; her name is Jeen. *Jean Chastain.*

The 5th April, 1753, was born to Jean Levilain a black girl; her name is Ester.

The 15th September, 1753, was born to Magdelaine Gueran a black; his name is Tom.

The 3d March, 1753, was born a black to —— Brian; his name is Samuel.

The 12th September, 1754, was born to Jean Jaque Dupuy a black; his name is Simon. *Jean Chastain.*

The 12th June, 1753, was born a black girl to Jean Chastain; her name is Philis.

The 12th June, 1754, was born a black girl to Jean Chastain; her name is Martila.

The 12th January, 1754, was born Marte Brian, daughter of Jaque Brian and of Cleek, his wife.

The 11th March, 1753, was born a black to Jaque Brian; his name is Sam.

The 21st July, 1754, was born a black girl to Jaque Brian; her name is Sara. *Jean Chastain.*

FRAGMENT OF A REGISTER OF DEATHS.

Janne La Fitt, wife of Tobit Lafitt, 15th December, 1722, aged about ——teen years, daughter of Estienne Malet and of Marie Malet, her father and mother. *J. Soblet, Clerk.*

The 12th January, 1722 [1723], died Janne Chastain, daughter of ——ieur Chastain and of Anne Chastain, her father and mother, aged about 6 years; was buried the thirteenth of the month, on Sunday, at three o'clock in the afternoon.

3 April, 1723, died Anne Soblet, the ——sieur Pierre Chastain, aged about —— years; was buried the fourth of the month.

January, 1723 [1724], died the Sieur Anthony [Trabue ?], aged about fifty-six or seven years; was buried the 30th of the same.

J. Soblet, Clerk.

Died, Francois de Clapie, aged about sixty-one years; was buried ———— of the year 1724.

J. Soblet, Clerk.

——— Magdelaine Le Fevre, daughter of Isaac Le Fevre and of Magdelaine Le Fevre, her father and mother; —— was buried on Sunday, the 26th of the month.

—— August, 1724, died Mariane ———n Chastain; aged 28 years; ——— was buried the 21st of the same month at five o'clock in the afternoon.

The 26th February, 1724 [1725], died Jeanne ———, wife of Francois La Fitt; aged 69.

The 6th F–b., 1724 [1725], died Marie, daughter of a black woman of Barthelemis Dupuy. *J. Soblet, Clerk.*

1725.

The 24th December, 1725, died Marthe ———, wife to Monsieur Estiene Chastain; aged about fifty-two or three years.

The 9th of January, 1725 [1726], died Jean Gaspar ———; aged 29 years, or thereabouts. *J. Soblet.*

The 3 of January, 1725 [1726], died Daniel ———; aged about 44 years; was buried the —— of the month —— Sunday.

The 24th January, 1725 [1726], died ———, wife of ——— Chastain; aged ——; buried the 25th of the month.

The 19th of January, 1720 [1725] [1726], died Jean ———; about ——— was buried.

The 5 8ber died Jacob Amonnet.

William Porter, son of Tomas Porter, died the ——.

Elizabeth Benin, daughter of Antoine Benin, died the 20th 8ber.

One black to Antoine Benin, named Nelley; died the 20th 8ber.

——— ———; he died the 10th ———.

——— ———; she died the ———.

Jean Chastain.

INHABITANTS OF KING WILLIAM PARISH, IN MANACAN TOWN, VIRGINIA, TO MR. NEARNE.[107]

[Extract.]

4TH JULY, 1728.

Rev'd Sir:

Your near departure out of this country obliges us, the Church Wardens and Vestries of King William's Parish, with humble submission, to beg your Assistance when, please God, you are arrived in London. We are very sorry that we can no longer enjoy the pleasure of your good presence and Education.

We thought ourselves happy in our late settlement with your Reverence.

We had above 110 or 120 tithables, but at present our number is 130. You see, therefore, the impossibility for us to raise a sum sufficient to keep our own Minister, and since we are conformed to the Laws and Disciplines of the Church of England, and that our Parish is a Royal Gift to us French Refugees, we think we ought not to consent to be dissolved and incorporated into another Parish.

Many of our Parishioners understand no English; but for the sake of our Children and the English Families settled amongst us, we should be heartily Glad to have the Common Prayers and Sermons in English as well as French.

JUNE, 1744.—A LIST OF KING WILLIAM PARISH.

The estate of John James Flournoy, viz: Jos. Akin, Yarmouth, Charles, Will, Sue, Sara,	6
John James Dupuy, Dick, Betty,	3
John James Levilin, Betty,	2
James Ford, Stephen Ford,	2
Thos. Bradley,	1
Stephen Mallet, Robin, Lucy, May,	5
John Levilin, Jack, Dick, Mary, Nan,	5

[107] *Perry's Church Papers of Virginia*, p. 353.

James Cocke, Henry Godsie, Jack, Dick, Sarah, Hannah, Betsy, Jane,	8
Wm. Salle, George, Betty, Jenny, John Proan,	5
Peter Salle, Jemine,	2
Peter Bondurant,	1
John Bondurant,	1
Joseph Bondurant, Thomas Miles,	2
Richard Annis, Constable,	2
William Meginson, Tom, Abram, George,	4
Peter Ford, Daniel Ford, Jogg,	3
Peter Soblet,	1
John Young,	1
John Harris, Demetius Young, Bob, Chloe, Phillis, Moll,	6
Peter Lewis Soblet,	1
Thomas Porter, Isaac Dutoy, Hamton, Joe, Cæsar, Judy, Sarah,	7
John Peter Bilbo, John Gory, Sara, Will,	4
John Porter, Judy,	2
John Chandler, Jos. Chandler,	2
Stephen Forssee, Sam,	2
Thomas Smith, James Smith, Will	3
Peter Guerrant, John J.,	0
Tom, Betty,	0
John Burner,	1
For Mrs. Elize Bernard: Will'm Howard, James, Charles, Will, Adam, Essex,	6
Edmund Goin,	1
Stephen Reno, Jno. Weaver,	2
Mattie Ayce, Jas. Ayce, Francis Hilguro, Ege Edins,	4
John Butler: George, Jack, Betty,	0
David Lesueur, Dick, Philis,	3
Thomas Kemp,	1
John Ford,	1
Benjamin Harris, Ben, Harry, Matt, Lasey,	5
David Thomas, Betty,	2
James Robinson, Moll,	0
John Carner, William Carner,	2
For Am't Bennj: Matt. Bingley, Am't Debril, Betty, Cassy, Jenny, Jack,	6
Peter Depp, Peter Orringe,	2

James Drowen,	1
Andrew Ouinet, Jno. Ford,	2
Eliza Hampton, Left.,	0
John Sullavant, Phillis, Sarah, Moll,	4
Jno Pankey, Lucy,	2
	126

Daniel Gory,	1
For Rene Chastain: Thos. Godsee, Betty,	2
Sam. Weaver, Sam'l Weaver, Jr., Wm. Young, Sam. Robîn,	0
Henry Trent, Jno. C'k,	0
Dilsey Aggy,	0
Chastain, Jno. Chastain, Jun., Charles, Prince, Belinda,	5
Charles, Ominett,	2
William Platt, Charles, Stannad, Phillis,	4
Mrs. Anne Scott: Dan'l Scott, Thomas Mansfield, Sampson, Jerry, Cooper, Jupiter, Pope, Dick,	8
Talb Dillery,	0
Anthony Ayce,	1
John Edins,	1
Wm. Banton,	1
John Young,	1
Peter Lookado,	1
Peter Ford, Jr.,	1
Clarke Trabue: June,	1
Joseph Bingley, Butler, Judy,	3
James Bryant, Sec'y,	2
Jeremiah Rasceine,	1
James Stelman, Jr., Watt, Jonathan, Cæsar, Lucy, Effe,	6
Widow Martin: Wm. Kemp, Peter, Daniel, Jack, Dick, Jenny, Kate,	7
Peter, David, Dick Manowa, Jupiter, Dina,	5
John Jas. Flornoir,	6
John Young,	1
Giles Ford,	1
Stephen Reno,	1
Samuel Wever,	0
Antony Benin,	6
Peter Loucadou,	1

Daniel Peros, - - - - - -	3
Louis Soblet, - - - - - -	1
Jno. Bartholomew Dupuy, - - - - -	1
Charle Pean, - - - - - -	2
Jean Faure, - - - - - - -	5
Richard Sumpter, - - - - - -	1
Richard Sumter, - - - - - -	1
Jean Moriset, - - - - - -	1
Isaac Robinson, - - - - - -	3
Wm. Guettle, - - - - - -	1
Eli Sassin, - - - - - - -	1
Jacob Trabu, - - - - - -	4
Jaque Martain, - - - - - -	4
Janne Dupres Tevis, - - - - -	2
Antoine Bernard, - - - - - -	1
Samuel Jordins, - - - - - -	3
Pierre Forqueran, - - - - -	1
Richard Deen, - - - - - -	1
Magdelaine Salle, - - - - - -	2
Abraham Salle, - - - - - -	2
	113

APPENDIX OF GENEALOGIES.

A PARTIAL LIST OF THE DESCENDANTS

OF

JOHN DE LA FONTAINE,[a]

PRESENTING DATA OF THE FONTAINE, MAURY, AND OTHER FAMILY NAMES.

John de la Fontaine, of noble origin,[b] was born in the Province of Maine, near its borders, about the year 1500. He received at an early age a commission in the household of Francis I, in what was then called "Les Ordonnances du Roi," a command which he retained with honor through the succeeding reigns of Henry II, Francis II, and until the second year of that of Charles IX, when he voluntarily resigned. He had desired to retire to private life at an earlier period, but had remained in the royal service as a safeguard against religious persecution, having with his father embraced Protestantism about the year 1535. He had married and had had born to him four or more sons. Under the Edict of Pacification of January 17th, 1561 [1562], he was deluded into retiring to his paternal estates in Maine. He, his wife and eldest son were martyred there, in 1563.[c]

---

a Compiled from "*Memoirs of a Huguenot Family*," "*Chart of the Fontaine and Maury Families*," and other sources.

b The arms are emblazoned on the "*Chart of the Fontaine and Maury Families*," as follows: "Ar. a fisse embattled, two elephants' heads erased, with tusks depressed, in chief, and in base a three-masted ship with sails spread and pennant at the prow. Crest—an elephant's head erased, with tusks elevated.

c "*Memoirs of a Huguenot Family*," page 16, *et seq.*

Issue of John[1] de la *Fontaine:*

i. ——, son,[2] martyred 1563.

ii. Jacques,[2] *b.* 1549; *d.* 1633; *m.* twice; left property at Rochelle, amounting to 9,000 livres.

iii. Abraham,[2] *b.* 1551; *m.* ——, and had issue, —— daughter;[3] *m.* —— Brousseaux.

iv. ——, son.[2]

Issue of Jacques[2] *Fontaine:*

i. ——, daughter;[3] *m.* —— Bouquet.

ii. Rev. James,[3] *b.* 1603; *d.* 1666; Pastor of Vaux and Royan; *m.* 1st, in 1628, Miss Thompson (*d.* 1640); 2d, in 1641, Marie Chaillon, who died, aged 63 years.

iii. ——, daughter,[3] *m.* —— Reaud.

Issue, by his two marriages, of Rev. James[3] *Fontaine:*

i. Jane,[4] *b.* 1628; *m.* L. Hommeau.

ii. Judith,[4] *b.* 1630; *m.* —— Guiennot, who died, leaving issue four daughters, who escaped with their mother from France.

iii. Rev. James,[4] *b.* 1633; Pastor of the church at Archiae, in Saintonge, which province is now embraced in the Department of Charente-Inférieure; *d.* prior to 1685, and his widow reached London with her three sons, one of whom became a Protestant minister in Germany.

iv. Elizabeth,[4] *b.* 1636; *m.* Rev. —— Sautreau, minister at Saujon, in Saintonge. He escaped with his wife and children to Dublin, where he entered the Presbyterian church; embarked for America, and with his wife and five children were wrecked opposite the harbor of Boston, Mass.

v. Rev. Peter,[4] *b.* 1638; assistant to his father in the pastorate of Vaux and Royan, and, succeeding him, remained until the demolition of his church, when he was banished. Ended his days as Chaplain of the Pest-House, in London. His youngest daughter, Esther, *m.* John Arnauld, grandson of M. Bouquet.

vi. Francis,[4] *b.* 1640; *d.* young.

————[d]

vii. Susan,[4] *b.* 1643; *m.* Stephen Gachot, grandson of Rev. ——

---

d These division lines indicate the issue by the several wives.

Merlin, of Rochelle; Pastor of St. Saurin, in Saintonge, and then of the church at Salles, in Aunix; remained in France with his wife and two daughters.

viii. Rev. Peter,[4] *b.* 1646; *m.* —— Oissard.

ix. Mary,[4] *b.* 1648; *m.* Rev. Peter Forestier, pastor of the church of St. Mesme, in Augnomois. They escaped to England with their two children.

x. Anne,[4] *b* 1651; *m.* Leon Testard, sieur des Meslars. They escaped to England.

xi. Rev. James,[4] *b.* April 7, at Jenouille, of which estate, and that of Jaffé, he became possessed; received degree of M. A. from College of Guienne; imprisoned, 1658; *m.* Feb. 8, 1686, Anne Elizabeth Boursiquot; escaped, after the Revocation of the Edict of Nantz, to England, with his sister, Elizabeth, and niece, Janette Fontaine; landed December 6, 1685; admitted to Holy Orders by the Protestant Synod, at Taunton, June 10, 1688. His life, as further set forth in his Memoir, which has quite the interest of a romance, was one exhibiting marked mental fertility, courage, and determination of character.[e]

Issue of Rev. Peter[4] and —— (Oissard) *Fontaine:*

i. Benigne,[5] *m.* —— Reau.

ii. Anne,[5] *m.* ——Boussie.

iii. Susan,[5] *m.* —— Grange.

iv. Esther,[5] *m.* John Arnauld.[f]

v. Lewis.

Issue of Rev. Peter and Mary[4] (Fontaine) *Forestier:*

i. Paul.[5]

ii. Janette.[5]

iii. Henriette,[5] became a nun.

iv. Peter,[5] *m.* —— Arnauld.

Issue of Rev. James[4] and Anne Elizabeth (Boursiquot) *Fontaine:*

i. James,[5] *b.* 1686; *m.* ——— in Ireland; arrived in Virginia in October, 1717.

---

e "*Memoirs of a Huguenot Family.*"

f These statements as to the number and the issue of two sons of Rev. James[3] Fontaine, are presented both in the "*Memoir of a Huguenot Family*" and in the "*Fontaine and Maury Chart.*"

ii. Aaron,[5] *b.* 1688; *d.* 1699.

iii. Mary Anne,[5] *b.* April 12, 1690, at Taunton, England; *d.* December 30, 1755, in Virginia; *m.* October 20, 1716, in Dublin, Ireland, Matthew Maury, of Castel Mauron, Gascony (*d.* 1752); emigrated to Virginia, 1718.

iv. Moses,[5] *b.* 1694; received degree of B. A., but became an engraver.

v. Elizabeth,[5] *b.* August 3, 1701; *m.* Daniel Torin.

vi. Rev. Peter,[5] B. A., *b.* 1691; ordained by the Bishop of London; *m.* 1st, March 29, 1714, Elizabeth Fourreau, granddaughter of Captain Boulay, of the French army (who *d.* March, 1715); 2d, E. Wade; emigrated to Virginia in 1716; Rector of King William and Westover Parishes; Chaplain to the Virginia Commission which ran the boundary line between Virginia and North Carolina in 1728–'29, the history of which is so entertainingly and graphically depicted by Col. Wm. Byrd;[g] *d.* July, 1757.

vii. John,[5] *b.* 1693; appointed, October 16, 1710, Ensign in the British army, and served in Spain; visited Virginia in 1714;[h] returned to England; *m.* M. M. Sabatiere; became a watchmaker.

viii. Rev. Francis,[5] M. A., *b.* September 16, 1697; *m.* 1st, Mary Glanisson; 2d, (before 1745), ——, daughter of —— Brush, gunsmith to Governor Spotswood; Professor of Oriental Languages William and Mary College, 1729; Rector of York-Hampton Parish; *d.* 1749; had issue:

i. Francis,[6] *b.* 1721; removed to Newberne, N. C.; *m.* —— and had issue: Francis, Mary, and a son.

ii. Mary,[6] *b.* 1724.

iii. John,[6] *b.* 1726; removed to Newberne, N. C.; *m.* ——; had issue.

iv. Thomas,[6] *b.* 1730; *d.* young.

---

v. James Maury,[6] *b.* 1738.

vi. Judith,[6] *b.* 1740.

Issue of James[5] Fontaine:

i. Elizabeth.[6]

---

g *Westover MSS.*

h This Journal appears in the *Memoirs of a Huguenot Family.*

ii. Lucretia.[6]
iii. James,[6] *m.* Anne Fontaine.
iv. Jane.[6]
v. John.[6]
vi. Anne,[6] *m.* Thomas Owen.

Issue of Matthew and Mary Ann[5] (Fontaine) *Maury:*

i. Rev. James,[6] *b.* 1717; *d.* 1769; Rector of Fredericksville Parish, Virginia; *m.* Mary Walker, niece of Dr. Thomas Walker, the Kentucky explorer.
ii. Mary,[6] *b.* 1728; *m* D. Claiborne.
iii. Abraham,[6] *b.* 1731; *m.* Susanna Poindexter.

Issue of Rev. James[6] and Mary (Walker) *Maury:*

i. Matthew,[7] *b.* 1744; *m.* Mary Walker.
ii. James,[7] *b.* 1746; United States Consul to Liverpool, England; *m.* 1st, C. Armistead; 2d, Mary Rutson.
iii. Leonard Hill.[7]
iv. Anne,[7] *b.* 1748.
v. Mary,[7] *b.* 1750; *m.* T. Strachan.
vi. Catharine,[7] *b.* 1752; *m.* —— Barrett.
vii. Rev. Walker,[7] *b.* 1754; *m.* M. Grymes; *d.* September, 1788, in Norfolk, Va.
viii. Elizabeth,[7] *b.* 1756; *m.* 1st, T. Lewis; 2d, E. Herndon.
ix. Abraham,[7] *b.* 1758; *m.* Mildred Thornton.
x. Fontaine,[7] *b.* 1761; *m.* E. Brooke.
xi. Benjamin,[7] *b.* 1763; *m.* E. Grant.
xii. Richard,[7] *b.* 1766; *m.* Diana Minor.
xiii. Matilda Hill,[7] *b.* 1769; *m.* —— Eggleston.

Issue of Matthew[7] and Mary (Walker) *Maury:*

i. Mary,[8] *m.* W. Michie.
ii. James Bickerton.[8]
iii. Matthew,[8] *m.* M. Fry.
iv. Elizabeth Walker.[8]
v. Mildred,[8] *m.* —— Fry.
vi. Thomas Walker,[8] *m.* E. Clarkson.
vii. Francis Fontaine,[8] *m.* Matilda Fry.
viii. Reuben,[8] *m.* E. Lewis.
ix. Catherine,[8] *m.* E. Lightfoot.
x. John,[8] *m.* Mrs. ——.

Issue of W. and Mary[8] (Maury) *Michie:*

i. Matthew Fontaine.[9]
ii. Betsy,[9] *m.* —— Fry.
iii. Mary,[9] *m.* —— Fry.
iv. William.[9]
v. Eliza.[9]
vi. Walker.[9]
vii. Peachy.[9]
viii. Reuben.[9]
ix. John.[9]

Issue of James[7] *Maury:*

i. James S.[8]
ii. William,[8] *m.* 1st, H. M. Van Ness; 2d, S. M. Hughes.
iii. Matthew,[8] *m.* E. Gilpin.
iv. Ann.[8]
v. Rutson,[8] Cotton Merchant; *d.* in New York, May 6, 1882.

Issue by his two marriages of William[8] *Maury:*

i. James.[9]
ii. Harriet Van Ness,[9] *m.* F. M. Ludlow.
iii. William.[9]
iv. Anne Fontaine.[9]
v. Rutson.[9]
vi. Matthew Fontaine.[9]
vii. Sarah Fanny.[9]
viii. Charles Williams.[9]
ix. Mytton.[9]
x. Walker.[9]
xi. Tobin.[9]

Issue of Matthew[8] and E. (Gilpin) *Maury:*

i. Mary Henrietta.[9]
ii. James Fontaine.[9]

Issue of Walker[7] and M. (Grymes) *Maury:*

i. James.[8]
ii. Mary Stith,[8] *m.* W. Hay.
iii. Ann Tunstall,[8] *m.* Isaac Hite.
iv. William Grymes,[8] *m.* A. Woolfolk.
v. Leonard Hill,[8] *m.* V. Campbell.
vi. Penelope,[8] *m.* R. Polk.

Issue of W. and Mary Stith[8] (Maury) *Hay*:

i. Mary.[9]
ii. Walker,[9] *m.* C. Maury.
iii. Isaac,[9] *m.* A. Baldwin.
iv. Penelope,[9] *m.* —— Eichelberger.

Issue of Isaac and Ann Tunstall[8] (Maury) *Hite*:

i. Ann Maury,[9] *m.* P. Williams.
ii. Mary,[9] *m.* S. Davison.
iii. Isaac,[9] *m.* L. Smith.
iv. Rebecca,[9] *m.* J. Lodor.
v. Walker,[9] *m.* —— Williams.
vi. Sarah,[9] *m.* Mark Bird.
vii. Bettie,[9] *m.* —— Green.
viii. Hugh,[9] *m.* A. Meade.
ix. Cornelius,[9] *m.* E. Smith.
x. Matilda,[9] *m.* A. Davison.

Issue of William G.[8] and A. (Woolfolk) *Maury*:

i. John Walker,[9] Mayor of Washington.
ii. Ellen,[9] *m.* Isabel Foyles; *d.* January, 1855.
iii. Fenella,[9] *m.* —— White.
iv. William Lewis,[9] attached to the Japan Exploring Expedition, United States Navy; Commander of the ship, Georgian, Confederate States Navy; *m.* M. A. Beckham; *d.* November 27, 1878; issue, five children.
v. Robert H.,[9] *m.* 1st, S. Wortham; 2d, —— Greenhow.
vi. Mary E.,[9] *m.* W. Hill.
vii. Jourdan W.,[9] *m.* S. McNier; *d.* January 19, 1883 in his 65th year.
viii. Ann Hite,[9] *m.* —— Magruder.
ix. Charles B.,[9] *m.* S. F. Maury.
x. James,[9] *m.* —— Ludwell.
xi. Lucy P. H.,[9] *d.* February 12, 1873.

Issue of Leonard Hill[8] and V. (Campbell) *Maury*:

i. Mary Dawson.[9]
ii. Virginia Pearce.[9]
iii. William Walker.[9]
iv. Matthew Hite.[9]
v. James L. Lee.[9]

vi. Thomas Fontaine.[9]
vii. John Lawrence.[9]
viii. Elizabeth Anne.[9]
ix. Alfred Pearce.[9]
x. America Strachan.[9]
xi. Harriet Georgianna.[9]
xii. Christopher Columbus.[9]
xiii. Sarah Susan Pearce.[9]
xiv. Joseph Woodson.[9]
xv. Eliza Francis.[9]
xvi. Catherine Mildred.[9]

Issue of R. and Penelope[8] (Maury) *Polk:*

i. Robert.[9]
ii. Susan,[9] *m.* —— Haverstick.
iii. Theophilus.[9]
iv. Mary Anne,[9] *m.* —— Brown.

Issue of Abraham[7] and Mildred (Thornton) *Maury:*

i. Nancy,[8] *m.* —— Fry.
ii. James Francis,[8] *m.* M. Thornton.
iii. Elizabeth B.,[8] *m.* James Vass.
iv. Abraham,[8] *m.* ——; issue, Abraham.[9]
v. Butler,[8] *m.* F. Sawyer.
vi. Willin G.,[8] *m.* W. Gregory.
vii. Catherine,[8] *m.* 1st, W. Hay: 2d, —— House.

Issue of —— and Nancy[8] (Maury) *Fry:*

i. Francis B.,[9] *m.* —— Ratcliff.

Issue of James Francis[8] and M. (Thornton) *Maury:*

i. Thomas F.,[9] *m.* A. R. Jenkins.
ii. James W.,[9] *m.* R. K. Harris.
iii. Gilbert La Fayette.[9]

Issue of James and Elizabeth B.[8] (Maury) *Vass:*

i. Sophia M.,[9] *m.* S. Fitzhugh.
ii. Roslyn Cumming.[9]
iii. Alexander Fridge.[9]
iv. Mary Mildred.[9]
v. Isabella.[9]
vi. Lachlan C.[9]

Issue of Butler[8] and F. (Sawyer) *Maury:*

i. George.[9]
ii. William.[9]
iii. Butler.[9]
iv. John Sifrein,[9] *m.* R. Reardon.
v. Jefferson.[9]
vi. Henry.[9]
vii. Mary Mildred.[9]

Issue of W. and Willia G.[8] *Gregory:*

i. Fanny Scott,[9] *m.* —— Conway, M. D.

Issue of W. and Catherine[8] (Maury) *Hay:*

i. Abrianna M.,[9] *m.* —— Crawford.
ii. T. William Gregory.[9]
iii. Elizabeth B.,[9] *m.* —— Preatte.
iv. Francis F.[9] *m.* —— Pierce.
v. Charles Edward.[9]

Issue of Fontaine[7] and E. (Brooke) *Maury:*

i. Eliza,[8] *m.* John M. Maury.
ii. Richard B.,[8] *m.* 1st, C. S. Hunton; 2d, E. Magruder.
iii. Albert.[8]
iv. Betty Brooke.[8]

Issue of Benjamin[7] and E. (Grant) *Maury:*

i. James W. F.[8]
ii. Judith N.,[8] *m.* Dudley Digges.
iii. Matthew W.,[8] *m.* S. Lightfoot.
iv. Ann Selina.[8]
v. Catherine A.,[8] *m.* —— Bagby.
vi. Eliza.[8]
vii. Peter.[8]
viii. Harriet L.[8]

Issue of John M. and Eliza[8] A. *Maury:*

i. William Lewis.[9]
ii. Dabney H.,[9] Major-General C. S. A., *m.* A. R. Mason.

Issue of Richard B.[8] *Maury:*

i. Sallie Fontaine,[9] *m.* C. B. Maury.
ii. John Minor.[9]
iii. Richard B.[9]

iv. Rev. Magruder,[9] *m.* Lelia A., daughter of Rev. C. W. Andrews, D. D. (she *d.* June 29, 1880, in her 40th year); *d.* May 8, 1877, in Philadelphia, Pa., in his 42d year.
v. Thompson.[9]

Issue of Dudley and Judith N.[8] (Maury) *Digges:*
i. Bettie Brooke.[9]
ii. Ann Whiting.[9]
iii. Lucy Fitzhugh.[9]
iv. Dudley.[9]
v. Washington.[9]

Issue of Matthew W.[8] and S. (Lightfoot) *Maury:*
i. William A. Wirt.[9]
ii. Thomas W.,[9] *m.* —— Amon.
iii. John S.,[9] *m.* —— Buckerstowe.
iv. Martha,[9] *m.* T. Potter.
v. Eliza M.,[9] *m.* W. Balthis.
vi. Reuben Edward.[9]
vii. Susan Frances.[9]

Issue of —— and Catherine A.[8] (Maury) *Bagby:*
i. Mary Eliza,[9] *m.* F. White.
ii. Mildred A.,[9] *m.* T. Alfred.
iii. Selina Maury,[9] *m.* —— Dawson.
iv. Benjamin S.,[9] *m.* —— Lancaster.
v. Shepley Niel.[9]
vi. George.[9]

Issue of Richard[7] and Diana (Minor) *Maury:*
i. Mary,[8] *m.* N. M. Ludlow.
ii. John Minor,[8] *m.* E. Maury.
iii. Matilda,[8] *m.* R. Guthrie.
iv. Walker.[8]
v. Elizabeth,[8] *m.* K. S. Holland.
vi. Richard L.[8]
vii. Matthew Fontaine;[8 i] *b.* January 16, 1806, in Spotsylvania county; "Philosopher of the Seas"; *m.* Anne, daughter

---

i Midshipman United States Navy, 1825; Lieutenant, 1837. Being disabled for active service by having a leg broken, he spent several years in Fredericksburg in study and in preparing a series of articles ("The Lucky Bag," by Harry Bluff,) for the *Southern Literary Mes-*

of Dabney and Elizabeth Herndon,[j] for many years president of the Virginia Bank at Fredericksburg, Va.

viii. Charles.[8]

ix. Catherine.[8]

---

senger, which wrought a revolution in the Navy Department and led to the establishment of the Naval Academy, the Memphis Navy-Yard, and the general warehousing system. He had also the special thanks of the State of Illinois for his papers on the enlargement of the Illinois and Michigan Canal. In 1842 he was made Superintendent of the Depot of Charts and Instruments in Washington, which, under his inspiration, became the National Observatory. Here he made his renowned current charts and sailing directions, and wrote his "Physical Geography of the Sea," pronounced by Humboldt a new science. Here he suggested the conference of maritime nations at Brussels, to secure co-operation in observation and researches at sea. In recognition of his eminent services in the cause of science the leading Powers of Europe showered honors and decorations on him. President Tyler wished to put him at the head of the Navy Department, and though but a young Lieutenant the position of Chief Hydrographer of the Southern Exploring Expedition was offered him He was the first to advocate the little ship and big gun theory, so verified by experience in the late war, and also the substitution of open batteries and earthworks for casemated forts. The French Emperor, upon his advice, determined that it was inexpedient to undertake the Nicaraugua Ship Canal. The Academies of Science of Paris, Berlin, Brussels and St. Petersburg conferred membership on him, as did Cambridge (England) the degree of LL.D. When Virginia seceded from the Union he offered her his services, and was made a Captain and a member of the Advisory Council, the first act of which body was the recommendation of R. E. Lee as Commander of the Army of Virginia.

When it was known in Europe that Captain Maury had left the United States Navy, France and Russia invited him to become their guest, with every provision for his comfort and studies. He replied that his first duty was to Virginia. He gave much attention to electrical torpedoes in the beginning of the war, and had the Confederary have had the means to carry out his plans it is probable that no Southern port might have been entered by the enemy. When in London, after the war, he instructed committees of the armies and navies of Continental Governments in this formidable mode of defence. In 1862 he was sent on a special mission to England, where he remained until 1865. He was then persuaded by Napoleon and Maximilian to make his home in Mexico, and was appointed Honorary Counsellor of State, a member of the Cabinet, and Imperial Commissioner of Emigration. Before the death of Maximilian he was sent on a special mission to

Issue of N. M. and Mary[8] (Maury) *Ludlow:*

i. Cornelia B.,[9] *m.* M. Field.
ii. Noah.,[9] *m.* E. Steelmon.
iii. Richard C.,[9] *m.* M. Aiken.
iv. Frank M.,[9] *m.* H. V. Maury.
v. Mary,[9] *m.* W. Arnold.
vi. William.[9]

Issue of John Minor[8] and E. (Maury) *Maury:*

i. William Lewis.[9]
ii. Dabney H.,[9] *b.* 1824; graduated from West Point Military Academy, 1846; served in the Mexican war; severely wounded at Cerro Gordo, April, 1847; Captain United States Army and Assistant Professor at West Point, 1847–50; resigned from the United States Army June 20,

---

Europe, where he remained until 1868, preparing his School Geographies. Being elected Professor of Physics at the Virginia Military Institute, he declined the charge of the Imperial Observatory at Paris, and returned to Virginia, where he devoted himself chiefly to the study of the resources of Virginia and to perfecting a combined system of crop reports and weather forecasts, for the benefit of the farmer, as his combined observations at sea had been for the benefit of the sailor. These weather forecasts, now so famous, were urged by Maury upon public consideration in 1854. He died at Lexington, Va., February 1, 1873, his last words being "All is well."

j The sister of a singularly meritorious brotherhood. Captain Wm. Lewis Herndon, the explorer of the Amazon river, heroically went down with the ill-fated steamer "Central America," of which he was the commander, September 12, 1857, in the Gulf Stream, after having seen every passenger transferred from the decks of the sinking ship and saved; Dr. Dabney Herndon died a martyr to duty in the yellow-fever visitation of Mobile, Ala.; Dr. John Minor Herndon, Judge of the Hustings Court of Fredericksburg and Secretary of the Commonwealth, 1865–'67—died September 19, 1871, in the 64th year of his age; Charles Herndon, a lawyer of ability and member of the Virginia Senate, died at Fredericksburg, Va., December 17, 1883, aged 61 years; Dr. Brodie Strachan Herndon, a learned and beloved physician of Savannah, Ga., survives. A nephew of these brothers, Dr. James Carmichael Herndon, died at the post of duty at Fernandina, Fla., of yellow-fever, October 18, 1877.

William Herndon, the ancestor (probably) of this family, patented large tracts of land in St. Stephen's parish, New Kent county, Va., in February, 1673 [1674].

1861, and entering the Confederate States Army, attained the rank of Major-General; *m.* A. R. Mason.

Issue of R. and Matilda[8] (Maury) *Guthrie:*

i. Eliza,[9] *m.* —— Thomas.
ii. John.[9]
iii. Matthew.[9]
iv. Robert.[9]

Issue of K. S. and Elizabeth[8] (Maury) *Holland:*

i. Dick Fontaine.[9]
ii. Diana Catherine.[9]
iii. Kempe Sanderson.[9]
iv. William James.[9]

Issue of Richard L.[8] and —— (———) *Maury:*

i. Matthew Fontaine.[9]
ii. Diana Elizabeth.[9]
iii. Margaret Clay.[9]
iv. Parthenia.[9]
v. Nancy Richard.[9]

Issue of Commodore Matthew F.[8] and Anne (Herndon) *Maury:*

i. Eliz'h Herndon,[9] *b.* June 24, 1835; *m.* Feb. 24, 1857, William A. Maury, LL.D., late Assistant Attorney-General of the United States, Professor of Law in Columbia College.
ii. Diana Fontaine,[9] *b.* June 25, 1837; *m.* April 29, 1858, Spotswood Wellford Corbin.
iii. Richard Launcelot,[9] *b.* October 9, 1840; *m.* ——, 1862, Susan Gatewood Crutchfield, of "Green Branch," Spotsylvania county. He enlisted as a private in the Confederate States Army, April 28, 1861; promoted Lieutenant in Virginia State troops, June, 1861; promoted Major, and assigned to the Twenty-fourth Virginia infantry; elected Major at the reorganization of the regiment, May, 1862; badly wounded at the battle of Seven Pines, May 31, 1862; promoted Lieutenant-Colonel, May, 1863; badly wounded through hips at the battle of Drewry's Bluff; promoted Colonel, May 16, 1864; permanently disabled, but rejoined the army on the evacuation of Richmond, and surrendered

at Appomattox Courthouse, April 9, 1865; now a prominent member of the Richmond, Virginia, bar.

iv. John Herndon[9], *b.* October 21, 1842; Lieutenant Confederate States Navy. Going out alone from camp, opposite Vicksburg, Mississippi, January 27, 1863, to reconnoitre the enemy, his horse returned without its rider, who was supposed to have been murdered by the ambushed foe. He lies in an unknown grave.

v. Mary Herndon[9k] *b.* November 13, 1844; *m.* May 10, 1877, James R. Werth.[l]

vi. Eliza Hall,[9] *b.* December 5, 1846; *m.* September, 1878, Thomas Withers, and *d.* April 6, 1881, at Kokomo, Colorado, without issue. She was the author of a paper on the State Debt.

vii. Matthew Fontaine,[9] *b.* January 9, 1849; *m.* December 18, 1877, Rose, daughter of Captain John A. Robinson, of New York; Civil Engineer.

viii. Lucy Minor,[9] *b.* May 9, 1851; *m.* June 28, 1877, Meverell Locke Van Doren, of "Blenheim," Albemarle county, Virginia.

Issue of William A. and Eliz'h Herndon[9] (Maury), *Maury*:

i. Nannie Belle,[10] *b.* January 27, 1858.

ii. Alice Woolfolk,[10] *b.* June 7, 1863.

Issue of Spotswood Wellford and Diana Fontaine[9] (Maury) *Corbin*:

i. Anne Herndon,[10] *b.* July 27, 1864.

---

k The four younger children of Commodore Maury were his constant companions and co-workers with him in the preparation and revision of his *Geographies, Astronomy*, *Torpedo Practice* and *Physical Survey of Virginia*. He affectionately acknowledged their material assistance in his prefaces to several of these works.

l A great-grandson of Rev. Christopher McRae (of the Protestant Episcopal Church, a native of Scotland, graduate of the University of Edinburgh and Rector of Littleton parish, Cumberland county, Virginia, 1773–1785; died December 22, 1808, in Powhatan county, aged seventy-five years); grandson of Alexander McRae (a prominent member of the Richmond bar and United States Consul at Paris, France), and son of John J. and Amanda Pamela (McRae) Werth, of Richmond, Va. For an account of "Parson" McRae see Bishop Meade's *Churches and Families of Virginia*, II, pages 35–38.

ii. John Maury,[10] *b.* November 16, 1867; *d.* ——, 1873.
iii. Matthew Maury,[10] *b.* November 16, 1873.

Issue of Colonel Richard L.[9] and Susan G. (Crutchfield) *Maury*:

i. Matthew Fontaine,[10] *b.* July 8, 1863.
ii. Richard Launcelot,[10] *b.* January 16, 1868; *d.* —— 1869.
iii. Ann Herndon,[10] *b.* December 13, 1872.

Issue of James R. and Mary Herndon[9] (Maury) *Werth*:

i. Elie Maury,[10] *b.* February 24, 1878.
ii. Amy McRae,[10] *b.* June 3, 1879.
iii. Matthew Fontaine,[10] *b.* July 22, 1882.
iv. James Robert,[10] *b.* January 3, 1884.

Issue of Matthew Fontaine[9] and Rose (Robinson) *Maury*:

i. Madelaine La Rue,[10] *b.* August 4, 1881.
ii. Herndon Janson,[10] *b.* December ——, 1883.
iii. Rose Margaret,[10] *b.* ——, 1885.

Issue of Meverell Locke and Lucy Minor[9] (Maury) *Van Doren*:

i. Matthew Maury,[10] *b.* April 17, 1878
ii. Jacob,[10] *b.* April 8, 1881.
iii. Meverell Briarly,[10] *b.* March 31, 1884.

Issue of Matthew[8] and M. (Fry) *Maury*:

i. Lawrence Pike.[9]
ii. Matthew Henry.[9]
iii. Elizabeth Anne.[9]
iv. Reuben Thornton.[9]
v. Joseph Fry.[9]
vi. John.[9]
vii. Mary Peachy.[9]

Issue of —— and Mildred[8] (Maury) *Fry*:

i. Hugh.[9]
ii. Frank,[9] *m.* —— Barksdale.

Issue of Francis Fontaine[8] and Matilda (Fry) *Maury*:

i. Reuben Thornton.[9]
ii. Matthew Fontaine,[9] *m.* Eliza Chipman.
iii. Sarah Anne,[9] *m.* Rev. E. F. Berkeley.

Issue of Reuben[8] and E. (Lewis) *Maury:*

i. Jesse Lewis,[9] *m.* Lucy Price.

Issue of T. and Catherine[8] (Maury) *Lightfoot:*

i. Martha Anne.[9]
ii. William Henry.[9]
iii. Elizabeth Walker.[9]
iv. John James.[9]
v. Maria Frances[9]

Issue of John[8] and —— (——) *Maury:*

i. James Matthew.[9]

Issue of D. and Mary[6] (Maury) *Claiborne:*

i. Matthew,[7] *m.* —— Claiborne. Issue: Fontaine.[8]
ii. Mary,[7] *b.* 1750; *m.* —— Butts.
iii. Hannah,[7] *b.* ——; *m.* —— Triplett.
iv. Dorothea,[7] *b.* ——; *m.* —— Tatum.

Issue of Matthew[7] and —— (Claiborne) *Claiborne:*

i. Fontaine.[8]

Issue of —— and Dorothea[7] (Claiborne) *Tatum:*

i. Mary Branch.[8]
ii. James Henry.[8]
iii. Theophilus.[8]
iv. Anne Maury,[8] *m.* James Boyd.

Issue of James[8] and Ann (Maury) *Boyd:*

i. Thomas Claiborne.[9]
ii. Mary.[9]
iii. James Henry.[9]

Issue of Abraham[6] and Susanna (Poindexter) *Maury:*

i. Matthew,[7] *b.* 1760; *m.* F. Tabb.
ii. Elizabeth,[7] *b.* 1762; *m.* W. Dowsing.
iii. Susan,[7] *b.* 1764; *m.* Joel Parrish.
iv. Abram P.,[7] *b.* 1766; *m.* M. Worsham.
v. Mary,[7] *b.* 1768; *m.* Metcalf de Graffenriedt.[m]

---

m Metcalf de Graffenreidt was probably a grandson of Christopher, Baron de Graffenreidt, who received from the Lord Proprietors of North Carolina, in 1709, a grant of 10,000 acres of land on the Neuse and Cape Fear rivers, at the rate of £10 sterling for every thousand

vi. Philip P.,[7] *b.* 1770; *m.* E. Cunningham.
vii. Martha,[7] *b.* 1772; *m.* Chapman White.

Issue of Matthew[7] and F. (Tabb) *Maury:*

i. Thomas.[8]
ii. Abram.[8]

Issue of W. and Elizabeth[7] (Maury) *Dowsing:*

i. Mary.[8]
ii. Edward,[8] *m.* R. Eubank.
iii. Matthew.[8]
iv. William,[8] *m.* C. Lewis.
v. Elizabeth,[8] *m.* M. Thomson.
vi. Susanna,[8] *m.* 1st, N. Bussy; 2d, R. Ware.
vii. Martha Maury,[8] *m.* Rev. A. Turner.
viii. Nancy,[8] *m.* Rev. T. B. Turner.
ix. Priscilla A.[8]
x. Abram Fontaine.[8]

Issue of Edward[8] and R. (Eubank) *Dowsing:*

i. Elizabeth.[9]
ii. William.[9]
iii. Everard.[9]
iv. Jeremiah.[9]

Issue of William[8] and C. (Lewis) *Dowsing:*

i. Elizabeth.[9]

---

acres, and five shillings quit-rent. A great number of Palatines and fifteen hundred Swiss followed the Baron and settled at the confluence of the Trent and the Neuse. The town was called New Berne, after Berne, in Switzerland, the birth-place of the Baron. But the settlers were so disheartened by the Indian ravages in September, 1711, in which more than sixty of them were massacred, that De Graffenreidt sold his landed interests to Thomas Pollock for £800 and removed to Virginia. Many of his followers were employed by Governor Spotswood in his iron-works, inaugurated at Germanna in 1714. The following grants of land are of record in the Virginia Land Registry Office: Christopher De Graffenreidt, "Gent.," of Prince George county, 1,845 acres in Brunswick county, February 27, 1734, Book No. 5, p. 462; Tscharner De Graffenreidt, 414 acres in Brunswick county, November 25, 1743, Book No. 20, p. 596. In the *Virginia Gazette* of October 31, 1739, a Mrs. De Graffenreidt announces an entertainment to be given at her house in Williamsburg, Va.

ii. William.[9]
iii. Jane Catherine.[9]
iv. Mary Howell.[9]
v. Martha Maury.[9]
vi. Emily Susanna.[9]
vii. Caroline Matilda.[9]
viii. Fielding Lewis.[9]
ix. Julia Anne.[9]
x. Priscilla Rebecca.[9]
xi. Amanda Kennon.[9]
xii. John Wesley.[9]
xiii. Edward.[9]
xiv. Charles Richard.[9]
xv. Virginia Ellen.[9]

Issue of Susanna[8] (Dowsing) and N. *Bussy* and R. *Ware:*

i. Eliz'h Dowsing[9] Bussy.
ii. William Dowsing[9] Bussy.
iii. Hezekiah[9] Bussy.
iv. Harriett[9] Bussy.
v. Nathan[9] Bussy.

---

vi. Priscilla C.[9] Ware.
vii. Josephine Anthony[9] Ware.

Issue of Rev. A. and Martha Maury[8] (Dowsing) *Turner:*

i. William,[9] *m.* Baker White.
ii. Eliza Dowsing.[9]
iii. John Wesley.[9]
iv. Mary Fletcher.[9]
v. Thomas Coke.[9]
vi. William Allen.[9]

Issue of Joel and Susan[7] (Maury) *Parrish:*

i. Caroline,[8] *m.* Hinchey Petway.
ii. Matthew Fontaine,[8] *m.* Priscilla North.
iii. Robert.[8]
iv. Joel,[8] *m.* Sophy Sanders.
v. Abram Maury,[8] *m.* Catherine Staggs.
vi. David Winston,[8] *m.* Mary Clarke.

Issue of Hinchey and Caroline[8] (Parrish) *Petway:*

i. John,[9] *m.* —— Vaulx.

ii. Thomas,[9] *m.* —— Smith.
iii. William,[9] *m.* —— Hobson.
iv. Franklin.[9]
v. Susan.[9]
vi. Ferdinand.[9]
vii. Martha,[9] *m.* —— Hume.
viii. Robert.[9]
ix. Hinchey.[9]

Issue of Matthew Fontaine[8] and Priscilla (North) *Parrish:*

i. Joel.[9]
ii. Caroline.[9]
iii. Rhoda.[9]
iv. Robert.[9]
v. Sarah[9]
vi. Elisha.[9]

Issue of Joel[8] and Sophy (Sandars) *Parrish:*

i. Sarah Anne.[9]
ii. Thaddeus.[9]
iii. Leonidas.[9]
iv. Frances.[9]
v. Joel.[9]
vi. Sophia.[9]

Issue of Abraham Maury[8] and Catherine (Staggs) *Parrish:*

i. Joel.[9]
ii. Abram.[9]

Issue of David Winston[8] and Mary (Clarke) *Parrish:*

i. Susan.[9]

Issue of Abram[7] and M. (Worsham) *Maury:*

i. Elizabeth,[8] *m.* 1st, John Reid; 2d, F. T. Reid.
ii. Matthew Fontaine.[8]
iii. Daniel Worsham.[8]
iv. Abram,[8] *m.* Mary Claiborne.
v. James Philip.[8]
vi. William Henry,[8] *m.* Jane W. Worsham.
vii. Martha,[8] *m.* Carey A. Harris.
viii. Zebulon M. Pike,[8] *m.* Virginia Ashley.

Issue of John and Elizabeth[8] (Maury) *Reid:*

i. Sophia Thorpe.[9]

ii. William Steptoe.[9]
iii. John.[9]
iv. Martha Elizabeth.[9]
v. Frances T.[9]

Issue of Abram[8] and Mary (Claiborne) *Maury:*

i. Martha Thomas.[9]
ii. Sarah C.[9]
iii. Mary Baker.[9]
iv. Elizabeth James.[9]
v. Josephine.[9]
vi. Abram Poindexter.[9]
vii. Septimir.[9]
viii. Octavia.[9]
ix. Ferdinand Claiborne.[9]

Issue of Wm. Henry[8] and Jane W. (Worsham) *Maury:*

i. Abram.[9]
ii. Lucy Jane.[9]
iii. Mary Daniel.[9]
iv. James Montgomery.[9]
v. Martha Elizabeth.[9]
vi. Carrie Booth.[9]

Issue of Carey A. and Martha[8] (Maury) *Harris:*

i. James Maury.[9]
ii. Mary Fontaine.[9]
iii. Carey Allen.[9]

Issue of Zebulon M. Pike[8] and Virginia (Ashley) *Maury:*

i. James Henry.[9]
ii. William H.[9]
iii. Mary Elizabeth, } twins.[9]
iv. Martha Worsham, }
v. Zebulon M. Pike.[9]

Issue of Metcalf and Mary[7] (Maury) *de Graffenreidt:*

i. Abram Maury,[8] *m.* 1st, Mary Hill; 2d, Maria White.
ii. Metcalf,[8] *m.* 1st, Dorothy Persel; 2d, Candace Pope; 3d, Lucy Gee.
iii. Sarah,[8] *m.* Lewis Garrett.
iv. Susan,[8] *m.* Beverley Reese.
v. Matthew Fontaine,[8] *m.* 1st, P. Stuart; 2d, M. White.

Issue of Abram Maury[8] *de Graffenreidt*.

i. Abram.[9]
ii. Mary.[9]
iii. Martha.[9]
iv. Fontaine.[9]

Issue of Metcalf[8] *de Graffenreidt*:

i. Catherine.[9]
ii. Metcalf.[9]

Issue of Lewis and Sarah[8] (de Graffenreidt) *Garrett*:

i. Phenice.[9]
ii. Abram Maury.[9]
iii. James.[9]
iv. Anne.[9]

Issue of Beverley and Susan[8] (de Graffenreidt) *Reese*:

i. Susan,[9] *m.* —— Puryear.
ii. Jourdan[9].
iii. Elizabeth,[9] *m.* —— Curran.

Issue of Philip P.[7] and E. (Cunningham) *Maury*:

i. William Fontaine.[8]
ii. James Harvey,[8] *m.* Lucinda Smith.
iii. Abram.[8]
iv. Philip Albert.[8]
v. John Michaux,[8] *m.* Caroline Sessions.
vi. Alexander C.,[8] *m.* M. G. Thornton.
vii. Elizabeth,[8] *m.* F. L. Owen.
viii. Matthew Quintus.[8]
ix. Robert Emmet.[8]

Issue of James Harvey[8] and Lucinda (Smith) *Maury*:

i. Mildred H.,[9] *m.* B. Humphreys.
ii. Elizabeth M.,[9] *m.* T. Harding.
iii. Anne Boursiquot.[9]
iv. Caroline,[9] *m.* A. Green.
v. Julian Philip.[9]
vi. Lucinda Smith.[9]
vii. Philip Alexander.[9]
viii. James Fontaine.[9]
ix. William Smith.[9]

Issue of John Michaux[8] and Caroline (Sessions) *Maury*:

i. Sarah Elizabeth.[9]
ii. Fannie Eggleston.[9]
iii. Delia Fontaine.[9]

Issue of F. L. and Elizabeth[8] (Maury) *Owen*:

i. Richard B.,[9] *m.* A. Gale.
ii. John Michaux.[9]
iii. Philip Albert.[9]
iv. Gannaway.[9]
v. George W.[9]
vi. Franklin A.[9]
vii. Elizabeth Caroline.[9]

Issue of Chapman[7] and Martha (Maury) *White*:

i. William Chapman,[8] *m.* M. Campbell.
ii. Abram Maury,[8] *m.* Susan Parrish.
iii. Moses,[8] *m.* Emily Voorhees.
iv. Lucinda,[8] *m.* Joseph Wallace.

Issue of William Chapman[8] and M. (Campbell) *White*:

i. Martha.[9]
ii. William.[9]
iii. Josiah.[9]
iv. Mary.[9]
v. Anne.[9]

Issue of Abram Maury[8] and Susan (Parrish) *White*:

i. Martha.[9]
ii. Virginia.[9]
iii. Petronella.[9]
iv. Robert.[9]
v. Abram.[9]

Issue of Joseph and Lucinda[8] (White) *Wallace*:

i. William.[9]
ii. Martha.[9]
iii. Mary.[9]
iv. Sarah Ross.[9]
v. Joseph.[9]

Issue of Daniel and Elizabeth[5] (Fontaine) *Torin*:

i. Abraham.[6]

ii. Samuel.[6]
iii. Mary.[6]

Issue of Rev. Peter[5] *Fontaine:*

i. Mary Anne,[6] *b.* 1718; *m.* Isaac Winston.
ii. Peter,[6] *b.* 1720; County-Lieutenant of Halifax county; *m.* E. Winston.

---

iii. Moses,[6] *b.* 1742; *m.* —— Ballard.
iv. Sarah,[6] *b.* 1744.
v. Eliz'h,[6] *b.* 1747; *m.* William Mills.
vi. Joseph,[6] *b.* 1748.
vii. Aaron,[6] *b.* 1754; *m.* thrice.
viii. Abraham,[6] *b.* April 9, 1756; *m.* Sarah Ballard.

Issue of Isaac and Mary Anne[6] (Fontaine) *Winston:*

i. Peter,[7] *b.* November 14, 1741; *d.* October 24, 1784; *m.* December 9, 1767, E. Povey, or Povall; *b.* August 21, 1751; *d.* August 1, 1782.
ii. Isaac,[7] *b.* 1745; *m.* 1st, —— Smith; 2d, Lucy, daughter of John Coles.
iii. Lucy.[7]
iv. Mary Anne.[7]
v. William.[7] [n]
vi. Joseph.[7]

Issue of Peter[7] and E. (Povey) *Winston:*

i. Isaac,[8] *b.* September 16, 1768; *m.* Miss Burton.
ii. Mary Anne,[8] *b.* August 29, 1770; *m.* Alexander Jones.
iii. Elizabeth, } twins;[8] *m.* Hezekiah Jones.
iv. Peter, } *b.* Oct. 8, 1772; *m.* twice, two sisters, Jones.
v. Susanna,[8] *b.* December 10, 1774; *m.* Anderson Grubbs.
vi. John Povall,[8] *b.* December, 1776; *m.* Susan, daughter of John Austin.
vii. —— Sarah,[8] *b.* May 25, 1778; *m.* John Mosby.
viii. William,[8] *b.* June 20, 1780; *m.* Martha Mosby.
ix. Anne,[8] *b.* July 23, 1782; *m.* Benjamin Mosby.

---

n Rev. William S. Fontaine, adds v. and vi. to the *Fontaine-Maury Chart.*

Issue of Alexander and Mary Anne[8] (Winston) *Jones:*

i. John Winston,[9] Speaker of the United States House of Representatives, *m.* Harriet Boisseau.
ii. Eliza,[9] *m.* John Mosby. Issue: John A.[10]
iii. Gustavus,[9] *m.* Eliz'h, daughter of William Winston, of "Half Sink," Henrico county, and moved to Paducah, Kentucky.

Issue of John Winston[9] and Harriet (Boisseau) *Jones:*

i. Mary,[10] *m.* George W. Townes, Governor of Georgia.
ii. James B.,[10] *m.* Ann Crawley, daughter of Peter Winston.
iii. Alexander.[10]

Issue of Benjamin and Anne[8] (Winston) *Mosby:*

i. Peter Winston.[9]
ii. Eliz'h,[9] *m.* Mann Satterwhite Valentine;[o] *d.* December 22, 1872, in her 72d year.
iii. John O.[9]
iv. Robert P.[9]
v. Mary Anne,[9] *m.* Thomas Delaware Quarles.
vi. Sarah Winston.[9]
vii. Benjamin.[9]
viii. Lucy.[9]
ix. Patrick Henry.[9]
x. William H.[9]
xi. Susanna Virginia.[9]

Issue of Mann S. and Eliz'h[9] (Mosby) *Valentine:*

i. Eliz'h Anne,[10] *m.* William F. Gray.
ii. Mann S.,[10] discoverer of "Valentine's Meat Juice;" possesses a highly important Archaeological collection; *m.* Anne M. Gray.
iii. Benjamin Batchelder.[10]

---

o A most estimable and successful merchant of Richmond, of aesthetic tastes. His children bear venerating testimony to the impulses which they inherited from him, and which he directed. He was also of Huguenot blood; and some interesting correspondence has been held by his sons with Colonel Valentan of the French army, who deduces from the same springs.

iv. William Winston,[10] *b.* 1828; artist, philologist and elocutionist; *d.* February 17, 1885, leaving unfinished an important contribution to philology, a portion of which had been printed.
v. Robert Mosby.[10]
vi. Mary Martha,[10] *m.* Major J. W. Woods.
vii. Sarah Benetta,[10] a frequent contributor to the press in prose and poetry.
viii. Virginia Louisa.[10]
ix. Edward Virginius,[10] Virginia's sculptor; *m.* Alice Churchill,[p] daughter of William Robinson, of "Benville," King and Queen county, Va., of the family of "Cleasby," Yorkshire, England, of which was John Robinson, Bishop of London, and John Robinson, Speaker of the House of Burgesses and Treasurer of Virginia. She *d.* August 23, 1883, childless, leaving a void in the life of her adoring husband apparently not to be filled.

Issue of Isaac[7] *Winston:*

i. Elizabeth,[8] *m.* C. Dabney.
ii. Isaac,[8] *m.* 1st, M. Thornton; 2d, S. F. Dade.
iii. William.[8]
iv. Mary Anne.[8]
v. Walter.[8]
vi. Lucy.[8]
vii. Walter Coles,[8] *m.* Lucinda Dade.
viii. Martha F.,[8] *m.* P. F. Armistead.
ix. Dorothea.[8]
x. Eliza.[8]
xi. Dolly,[8] *m.* —— Beckwith.
xii. William Alexander,[8] *m.* M. Wallace.
xiii. Felix.[8]

Issue of Isaac[8] *Winston:*

i. James Madison.[9]
ii. Susan.[9]

---

p A descendant of Colonel William Churchill, of Middlesex county, member of the Virginia Council, who died November, 1710. The Churchills have intermarried with the Armistead, Bassett, Fontaine, Carter, Dawson, Lewis, and many other estimable Virginia families.

Issue of Walter Coles[8] and Lucinda (Dade) *Winston:*

i. Mary Anne,[9] *m.* A. Thornton.
ii. Elizabeth,[9] *m.* —— Spears.
iii. Lucy Coles.[9]
iv. Susan.[9]
v. Ellen,[9] *m.* —— Catlett.
vi. Walter.[9]
vii. Isaac.[9]
viii. Sally.[9]
ix. Rosina,[9] *m.* —— Tankersley.

Issue of P. F.[8] and Martha F.[8] (Winston) *Armistead:*

i. William Bowles.[9]
ii. Peter Fontaine.[9]
iii. Patrick Henry,[9] *m.* —— Clanton.
iv. Isaac Coles.[9]
v. Eliza.[9]
vi. Virginia,[9] *m.* —— Lanier.
vii. George Washington.[9]
viii. Mary Anne.[9]
ix. Martha.[9]

Issue of —— and Dolly[8] (Winston) *Beckwith:*

i. Isaac.[9]
ii. William.[9]
iii. Elizabeth.[9]

Issue of William Alexander[8] and M. (Wallace) *Winston:*

i. Walter.[9]
ii. Martha.[9]
iii. Mary.[9]
iv. James.[9]
v. William.[9]
vi. Wallace.[9]
vii. Isaac.[9]
viii. Caroline.[9]
ix. Arthur.[9]
x. Lucien.[9]

Issue of Peter[6] and E. (Winston) *Fontaine:*

i. John,[7] b. 1750; *m.* Martha, daughter of Patrick Henry, the orator.

ii. William,[7] *b.* 1753; Colonel of the Virginia line in the Revolution; at Yorktown; *m.* Anne Morris.
iii. Edmund.[7]
iv Sarah,[7] *b.* 1755; *m.* Charles Rose.
v. James,[7] Major of a volunteer regiment of Cavalry in Kentucky, and mortally wounded in an engagement with the Indians there.
vi. Mary,[7] *m.* 1st, Bowles Armistead; 2d, Colonel —— Lewis.

Issue of John[7] and Martha (Henry) *Fontaine:*

i. Patrick Henry,[8] *m.* Nancy Miller.
ii. Charles B.[8] *m.* —— Carrington.
iii. Martha H.[8] *m.* N. W. Dandridge.
iv William Winston,[8] *m.* Martha Dandridge.
v. Rev. John J.,[8] *m.* Mary Redd; *d.* January 3, 1852, aged 64.

Issue of Patrick Henry[8] and Nancy (Miller) *Fontaine:*

i Edward,[9] *m.* A. Swisher.
ii. Charles D.,[9] *m.* S. Dandridge.
iii. Martha,[9] *m.* W. Perkins.
iv. Nancy,[9] *m.* J. Brooke.
v. Elizabeth,[9] *m* E. Winston.
vi. Mary B.[9] *m.* Jesse Perkins.

Issue of N. W. and Martha H.[8] (Fontaine) *Dandridge:*

i. Charles F.[9] *m.* —— McGehee.
ii. William F.[9] *m.* —— Stith.
iii. Anne,[9] *m.* W. Hereford.
iv. Martha,[9] *m.* R. Bolton.
v. Henry.[9]
vi. Nat West,[9] *m.* H. Wylie.
vii. Rosalie,[9] *m.* W. D. Bradford.

Issue of William Winston[8] and Martha (Dandridge) *Fontaine:*

i. Wm. Spotswood,[9] *m.* S. Aylett.
ii. Patrick Henry,[9] *m.* S. Cole.
iii. Sarah Anne,[9] *m.* E. B. Redd.

Issue of John J.[8] and Mary (Redd) *Fontaine:*

i. John R.,[9] *m.* M. Green.
ii. William G.[9]

iii. Mary,[9] *m.* J. Waller.
iv. Martha,[9] *m.* —— Anderson.
v. Madison R.[9]
vi. Charles.[9]
vii. Laura,[9] *m.* J. Waller.

Issue of William[7] and Anne (Morris) *Fontaine:*

i. Sarah,[8] *m.* A. F. Rose.
ii. Peter Fourreau.[8]
iii. Louisa.[8]
iv. William.[8]
v. John.[8]
vi. Charles.[8]
vii. James,[8] *m.* Juliet Morris; *d.* January 20, 1875, in his 77th year.
viii. Edmund,[8] *m.* L. Shackelford.
ix. Alexander.[8]

Issue of Charles and Sarah[7] (Fontaine) *Rose:*

i. John.[8]
ii. Peter.[8]
iii. Elizabeth.[8]
iv. Alex. Fontaine,[8] *m.* Sarah[8] Fontaine.

Issue of A. F. and Sarah[8] (Fontaine) *Rose:*

i. Alexander.[9]
ii. Fontaine.[9]
iii. Louisa,[9] *m.* —— Potts.
iv. Charles.[9]

Issue of Bowles and Mary[7] (Fontaine) *Armistead:*

i. Peter Fontaine,[8] *m.* Martha F. Winston.
ii. Mary,[8] *m.* 1st, C. Alexander; 2d, W. C. Selden.
iii. Elizabeth,[8] *m.* F. L. Lee.
iv. daughter,[8] *m.* —— Terrill.

Issue of James[8] and Juliet (Morris) *Fontaine:*

i. William Morris.[9]
ii. James.[9]
iii. Peter.[9]
iv. Charles.[9]
v. Nancy.[9]

vi. John, } Twins.[9]
vii. Susan Watson, }
viii. Maury.[9]

Issue of Mary[8] (Armistead) by her two marriages with C. *Alexander* and W. C. *Selden* :

i. Ellen[9] Alexander, *m.* —— Selden.
ii. C. Armistead[9] Alexander.
iii. Mary F.[9] Alexander, *m.* Rev. E. R. Lippitt.
iv. W. Fontaine[9] Alexander, *m.* L. Washington.

---

v. Cary[9] Selden.
vi. John[9] Selden.
vii. Elizabeth[9] Selden, *m.* —— Lloyd.

Issue of F. L. and Elizabeth[8] (Armistead) *Lee* :

i. Ellen,[9] *m.* ——.
ii. F. Lightfoot.[9]
iii. Mary,[9] *m.* —— Selden.
iv. daughter,[9] *m.* Rev. —— Knapp.

Issue of —— and ——[8] (Armistead) *Terrill* :

i. John.[9]

Issue of Moses[6] and —— (Ballard) *Fontaine* :

i. Peter.[7]
ii. Ballard.[7]
iii. William Fontaine.[7]
iv. Tabitha,[7] *m.* —— Thompson.
v. Eliza,[7] *m.* —— Beavers.

Issue of William and Elizabeth[6] (Fontaine) *Mills* :

i. William Fontaine.[7]
ii. Aaron.[7]
iii. Frances.[7]
iv. Sarah,[7] *m.* —— Oakley.

Issue of Aaron[6] *Fontaine* :

i. Mary,[7] *m.* —— Cosby. Issue : 7 children.
ii. Elizabeth,[7] *m.* —— Bullock. Issue : 3 children.
iii. Matilda,[7] *m.* —— Prather. " 7 "
iv. Martha,[7] *m.* —— Pope. " 6 "
v. Sarah,[7] *m.* —— Floyd. " 6 "

vi.	Maria,[7] *m.* —— Grymes.	Issue:	4	children.
vii.	America,[7] *m.* —— Vernon.	"	10	"
viii.	Barbara,[7] *m.* —— Saunders.	"	2	"
ix.	Anne,[7] *m.* —— Jacobs.	"	3	"
x.	Emeline,[7] *m.* —— Dillon.	"	1	child.
xi.	Peter,[7] *m.* ——.	"	3	children.
xii.	James T.,[7] *m.* ——.	"	8	"
xiii.	William Maury,[7] *m.* ——.	"	5	"
xiv.	Henry,[7] *m.* ——.	"	3	"
xv.	Aaron,[7] *m.* ——.	"	4	"

Issue of Abraham[6] and Sarah (Ballard) *Fontaine:*

i. Clement,[7] *m.* E. Evans.
ii. Edmund,[7] *m.* M. Dickenson.
iii. James.[7]
iv. Walter Lloyd,[7] *m.* 1st, M. F. Nicholas; 2d, G. Nicholas.
v. Catherine Maury.[7]
vi. Maria,[7]
vii. Eliza.[7]

Issue of Clement[7] and E. (Evans) *Fontaine:*

i. Abraham Walter.[8]
ii. William James.[8]

Issue of Edmund[7] and M. (Dickinson) *Fontaine:*

i. Virginia.[8]
ii. Edmund[8]

Issue of Walter Lloyd[7] *Fontaine:*

i. Margaret F.[8]
ii. Sarah B.[8]
iii. Walter S.[8]
iv. Anne S.[8]
v. Frances E.[8]
vi. Catherine M.[8]
vii. Clement.[8]
viii. Martha V.[8]

Issue of John G.[8] and Eliza (White) *Patrick:*

i. George.[9]
ii. Emma.[9]
iii. Sophia Eliza.[9]
iv. Edward John.[9]

Issue of John[8] and M. (Stewart) *Fontaine:*

i. Henrietta,[9] *m.* —— Flewellyn.
ii. Mary.[9]
iii. John.[9]
iv. Benjamin.[9]
v. Theophilus.[9]
vi. Frances.[9]
vii. George.[9]

Issue of John[5] and M. M. (Sabatiere) *Fontaine:*

i. Anne,[6] *b.* 1729; *m.* J. Fontaine.
ii. James,[6] *b.* 1731; *m.* L. Lemoine.
iii. John,[6] *b.* 1734.
iv. David,[6] *b.* 1739; *m.* M. M. Plowman.
v. Mary,[6] *b.* 1741.
vi. William,[6] *b.* 1742; *m.* M. Howell.
vii. Daniel, } Twins.[6]
viii. Moses, }

Issue of David[6] and M. M. (Plowman) *Fontaine:*

i. Sophia,[7] *b,* 1773; *m.* John Patrick.
ii. George D.,[7] *b.* 1774; *m.* E. Smith.
iii. James,[7] *b.* 1778; *m.* F. E. Shepherd.

Issue of John and Sophia[7] (Fontaine) *Patrick:*

i. John G.,[8] *m.* Eliza White.

Issue of James[7] and F. E. (Shepherd) *Fontaine:*

i. Frances Elizabeth.[8]
ii. Charles.[8]
iii. Sophia.[8]
iv. Lucy Sarah.[8]

Issue of William[6] and M. (Howell) *Fontaine:*

i. John,[7] *b.* 1770.
ii. William,[7] *b.* 1773; *m.* Issue, William;[8] *m.* Issue, William.[9]
iii. Anne,[7] *b.* 1780.

Issue of Rev. Francis[5] *Fontaine* by his two marriages with Mary *Glanisson* and —— *Brush:*

i. Francis,[6] *b.* 1721; removed to Newberne, N. C.; *m.* ——.
ii. Mary,[6] *b.* 1724.

iii. John,[6] *b.* 1726; removed to Newberne, N. C.; *m.* ——.
iv. Thomas,[6] *b.* 1730; *d.* young.

---

v. James Maury,[6] *b.* 1738.
vi. Judith,[6] *b.* 1740.

Issue of Francis[6] *Fontaine*:

i. Francis.[7]
ii. Mary.[7]
iii. Thomas,[7] *b.* 1752; *m.* Clarissa Benton.
iv. Benjamin,[7] *b.* 1754.

Issue of Thomas[7] and Clarissa (Benton) *Fontaine*:

i. Thomas.[8]
ii. John,[8] *m.* M. Stewart.
iii. Francis.[8]
iv. Peter.[8]
v. Benjamin B.,[8] *m.* S. Beall.
vi. Lucy,[8] *m.* —— Thompson.
vii. daughter,[8] *m.* Peacham.

Issue of Benjamin B.[8] and S. (Beall) *Fontaine*:

i. John Thomas,[9] *m.* 1st, A. Marrast; 2d, F. Butler.
ii. Mary E.,[9] *m.* C. Stewart.
iii. Milicent,[9] *m.* —— Queen.
iv. Benjamin Beall.[9]
v. Alfred Battle.[9]
vi. Robert Augustus.[9]

A PARTIAL LIST OF THE DESCENDANTS

OF

BARTHOLOMEW DUPUY,[a]

PRESENTING DATA OF THE DUPUY, TRABUE, AND OTHER FAMILY NAMES.

"Dupuy, or Du Puy, is a very ancient French name. It is composed of two words—'Du,' meaning '*of the*,' and 'Puy' (old French), meaning '*mountain*.'

"In the first crusade Hugues Du Puy, a French Knight, and his sons, Adolph, Romain and Raymond, accompanied Godefroy de Bouillon to Palestine.

"About the year 1113, Raymond Du Puy founded and was the first Grand Master of the military order of the Knights of St. John of Jerusalem, afterwards styled the Knights of Malta. This and a kindred order, the Knights Templar, organized a few years later, acquired great wealth and wielded great military power for several centuries.

"According to the custom of the age of chivalry, Raymond

---

a Two pictorial "trees" of the "Dupuy Family," "prepared with great care," severally, in 1852, by Mrs. Eliza M. Ratcliffe, Louisville, Ky., and in 1861 by Mrs. Martha J. Stovall, Memphis, Tenn., form the basis of this deduction. Although every effort has been made by the Editor towards accuracy, in data gathered during many years past and by every reference at his command, he is fearful that this compilation contains many errors; but as the whole matter is clearly presented, it is to be hoped that those immediately interested will endeavor due correction. He gratefully acknowledges essential aid rendered him in his somewhat difficult and embarrassing task by C. L. C. Dupuy, Esq., New Orleans, La.; W. M. Bridges, Esq., and Colonel W. C. Knight, Richmond, Va., and Dr. J. J. Dupuy, Davidson College, North Carolina.

Du Puy quartered his own arms—a red lion, with blue tongue and claws, rampant on a field of gold—with the arms of the Knights of St. John—a broad white cross of eight points on a field of red.

"In later years, the Dupuy family were among those who were identified with the reformed religion of France, and who were called Huguenots, a term of reproach, meaning *confederates* or *leaguers*.

"Bartholomew Dupuy, the immediate progenitor of the Virginia family, entered the army at the age of eighteen and served fourteen years.

"Becoming an officer of the guards of the King, Louis IV, he was frequently charged with the performance of duties of such importance that his orders bore the signature and seal of the King himself. The possession of one of these orders aided him subsequently in effecting his escape from France.

"Shortly before the revocation of the Edict of Nantes, which was immediately followed by the memorable persecutions which drove from France all Huguenots who were so fortunate as to escape the galleys or death, he had married the Countess Susanne Lavillon, also a Huguenot, and had retired to his country seat. Here he was soon waited upon by a priest, who announced that the Edict would soon be revoked, and that the King, from motives of esteem, desired him to abjure his creed and avoid the fate which awaited all heretics; and he was also informed that compliance would be rewarded by preferment at the hands of the King. Soon afterwards he was visited by a detachment of soldiery and the parish priest, who *demanded* his abjuration upon penalty of arrest and its well-known consequences. He was allowed a few hours in which to make known his decision.

"The Huguenots were powerless to defend themselves, and submission to persecution could accomplish no practical good. He, therefore, wisely availed himself of the short respite to make hurried arrangements for flight into Protestant Germany.

"In the dead of night, and mounted upon picked horses, he and his young wife commenced their perilous ride of eighteen days to the frontier; he attired in his best uniform and wearing the sword which had done him and his ancestors good service on many fields of battle, and she disguised as his attendant, or page, and clad in a suit which had been hastily made by the village tailor. They were provided with such money and valuables only as could be concealed upon their persons.

"Their flight was soon discovered, and dragoons were sent to capture them; but the troopers were not as well mounted, and were compelled to abandon the pursuit, not, however, until one or two of the best mounted had come so near as to oblige Dupuy to turn and make good use of his sword.

"As they approached the frontier they were frequently halted and interrogated by troops who had been stationed on the various roads to intercept fugitives. His uniform, however, was deemed sufficient passport, and, with occasional comments upon the beauty and feminine appearance of his page, permission was accorded to pass on. At the outposts, however, a very vigilant officer demanded his warrant for passing. Holding out with one hand a document so opened as to display the signature and seal of the King, and quickly drawing his sword with the other, he demanded of the astonished officer an apology for the interruption, and coolly required him to furnish him an escort to the boundary.

"The frontier was soon reached and the escort dismissed.

"His sword was long treasured as an heirloom by his descendants; but, during a raid of Federal troops near Petersburg, was lost in the burning of the residence of Mrs. Julian Ruffin, in whose charge it had been left by its last owner, Dr. John J. Dupuy, now of Davidson College, North Carolina.

"Dr. Dupuy served the 'Lost Cause' in the cavalry, and was therefore obliged to wear a sword of modern pattern. It was worn, however, in the Revolutionary War by Captain James Dupuy, of Nottoway county, a grandson of the old Huguenot, who, with his brothers, Captain John Dupuy and Lieutenant Peter Dupuy, served in the same regiment of Virginia infantry. It was of a pattern now obsolete; the blade was straight and three-sided throughout its length, like the modern bayonet; at the guard it was very stout, but it rapidly diminished in thickness for about eight inches, when it became comparatively slender. This construction combined perfect poise with lightness and great strength, and made the weapon very effective in the hands of a skilled swordsman.

"Bartholomew Dupuy and his wife resided about fourteen

years in Germany and about two years in England, whence, in the year 1700, they came to Virginia, and settled in King William parish, on James river, above Richmond, upon lands granted to Huguenot refugees, and which were once occupied by the Monacan Indians, a warlike tribe, which had withstood the power of Powhatan, but which disappeared before the whites.

"The old Huguenot and his faithful wife lived many years in their new home, and their memory is cherished with just pride by a posterity whose name is 'legion,' and who are found to-day not only in Virginia, but also in Kentucky, Tennessee, Mississippi, Alabama, Missouri, and other States of the Republic."

Issue of Bartholomew[1] and Susanne (Lavillon) *Dupuy*:[b]

i. Peter,[2] *m.* Judith ——, and settled in Virginia.
ii. John Bartholomew,[2] *m.* Miss La Garronde, and settled in Virginia.
iii. John James,[2] *m.* Susan Levillain.

Issue of Peter[2] and Judith (——) *Dupuy*:

i. Jean,[3] *b.* January, 1723.
ii. Elizabeth,[3] *m.* twice: 1st —— Hundley; 2d, Thomas Atkinson.
iii. Peter,[3] *b.* February 12, 1728 [1729], *m.* ——.
iv. Mary,[3] *b.* February 20, 1729 [1730], *m.* —— *Jackson.* Issue: i. James;[4] ii. Magdalene;[4] iii. Joel;[4] iv. Lucretia.[4]
v. Isaac,[3] *b.* February 7, 1732 [1733].
vi. Judith,[3] *b.* October 11, 1734.
vii. Patsy,[3] *m.* —— *Jackson.* Issue: i. Olly;[4] ii. Esther;[4] iii. Patience;[4] iv. Eddy;[4] v. Jordan.[4]
viii. James,[3] *m.* Prudence Wills.
ix. Phillippa,[3] *m.* John Peter Le Villain.

Issue of Elizabeth[3] (Dupuy) and —— *Hundley*:

i. Quintus C.,[4] *m.* twice: 1st, —— West; 2d, —— Tuck.
ii. Elizabeth,[4] *m.* John E. Trabue.
iii. Frances.[4]

---

b The names of Anthoyne Dupuy, page 22, and Francois Dupuy, pages 74 88, though probably relatives of Bartholomew Dupuy, the fact does not appear to have been preserved by tradition with his descendants.

Issue of Peter[3] and —— *Dupuy:*

i. William.[4]
ii. Robert.[4]
iii. John.[4]
iv. Stephen.[4]
v. Jesse,[4] *m.* M. A. Thompson, and had issue:
  i. James.[5]
  ii. Mary.[5]
  iii. John.[5]
  iv. Virginia.[5]
  v. William.[5]
  vi. Eliza Anne;[5] author of "Morton," "Conspirator," etc.
  vii. Oscar O.[5]
  viii. Alexander.[5]
  ix. Lucy N.,[5] *m.* —— Hatton.

Issue of James[3] and Prudence (Wills) *Dupuy:*

i. Lawrence.[4]
ii. James,[4] *m.* Miss Mann, and moved to Mississippi.
iii. Edmund,[4] *m.* —— Glasscock.
iv. Nancy,[4] *m.* John Dupuy, and moved to Alabama.
v. Eliza,[4] *m.* —— Wright, and moved to the Southwest.

Issue of John Peter and Phillippa[3] (Dupuy) *Le Villain:*

i. Samuel.[4]
ii. Elizabeth,[4] *m.* Matthew *Woodson*, Goochland county, Virginia, and had issue:
  i. Thomas,[5] *m.* —— *Saunders*, and moved to Kentucky about 1800. Issue:
    i. Mary Lavillain,[6] *m.* —— *Wellberger*, and had issue: i. Elizabeth,[7] *m.* Macy; ii. Ann Warner;[7] iii. Egbert;[7] iv. Catharine.[7]
    ii. Edwin.[6]
    iii. Child.[6]
    iv. Anthony Le Villain,[6] *m.* —— Chaplin, and had issue: i. Albert;[7] ii. Virginia;[7] iii. Thomas,[7] *m.* —— Clarkson, and had issue five children.
    v. Philip J.[6]
    vi. Jane,[6] *m.* —— *Ardinger*, and had issue:
      i. H. Woodson.[7]
      ii. Mary Jane.[7]

iii. Hugh Little.[7]
iv. Eugenia Margaret.[7]
v. Caroline Dupuy.[7]

Issue of John Bartholomew[2] and —— (La Garronde) *Dupuy:*

i. John,[3] Captain of Cavalry in the Revolution; *m.* Mary Watkins.
ii. Peter,[3] of Powhatan county, removed to Richmond in 1818; *m.* November 14, 1789, Margaret Martin.
iii. Magdalene,[3] *m.* Thomas Watkins, Pittsylvania county.
iv. James,[3] *m.* Mary Purnell.

Issue of John[4] and Mary (Watkins) *Dupuy:*

i. Joseph,[5] *m.* —— Thomas.
ii. Mary,[5] *m.* —— Walker.
iii. Elizabeth,[5] *m.* James Dupuy.
iv. Susanna,[5] *m.* Benjamin Watkins.
v. James L.,[5] *m.* Amanda Butler. Issue: Reuben,[6] *m.* —— Ruffin.
vi. Jane,[5] *m.* Nicholas Edmonds.
vii. Francis,[5] *m.* Miss Daniel. Issue: Joel,[6] *m.* Elizabeth Dupuy.
viii. Watkins,[5] *m.* —— Watson. Issue: John,[6] *m.* —— Hunter, and had issue: i. Hunter;[7] ii. Henry,[7] and iii. Watkins.[7]
ix. John,[5] *m.* —— Daniel, and had issue:
  i. Mary,[6] *m.* —— Holliday.
  ii. Nannie.[6]
  iii. Charles.[6]
  iv. Susan.[6]
  v. Beverley.[6]
x. William H.[5], *m.* Miss Ware.
xi. Henry[5], *m.* Miss Taylor, and had issue: i. Francis,[6]; ii. Mary,[6] *m.* —— Gilliam.
xii. Joel Watkins,[5] M. D., of Prince Edward county, *m.* Pauline Pocahontas Eldridge, of Brunswick county.

Issue of —— and Mary[5] (Dupuy) *Walker:*

i. John.[6]
ii. Susan A.[6] *m.* Henry Watkins.
iii. Wm. T.[6]

iv. Judith,[6] *m.* —— Watkins.
v. Mary D.[6]
vi. Sarah Ann,[6] *b.* April 15, 1818; *d.* August 8, 1864; *m.* Col. Joseph Dupuy.
vii. Elizabeth.[6]
viii. Francis J.[6]

Issue of Nicholas and Jane[5] (Dupuy) *Edmonds:*

i. Henry,[6] *m.* —— Barksdale.
ii. Sarah,[6] *m.* —— Scott.
iii. Mary,[6] *m.* Joseph Dupuy.
iv. Nicholas Dupuy.[6]
v. Nannie.[6]
vi. John.[6]
vii. Susan,[6] *m.* —— *Flournoy*, and had issue: i. Sallie;[7] ii. Stanhope,[7] and iii. Nicholas.[7]
viii. Jane.[6] *m.* Dr. Berkeley.
ix. Thomas,[6] *m.* Miss Martin, and had issue: i. Nicholas;[7] ii. Thomas;[7] iii, Jane;[7] iv. Frances;[7] v. William;[7] vi. Elizabeth.[7]

Issue of William H.[5] and —— (Ware) *Dupuy:*

i. John Ware,[6] *m.* Elizabeth Withers.
ii. Joel.[6]
iii. William H.[6]
iv. Susan P.,[6] *m.* ——Faulkner.
v. Mary,[6] *m.* —— *Richardson*, and had issue: i. Mary Isabella,[7] and ii. Agnes.[7]
vi. Agnes,[6] *m.* Benjamin L. *Redford* and had issue: i. Mary;[7] ii. Morton;[7] iii. Lee.[7]

Issue of John Ware[6] and Elizabeth (Withers) *Dupuy:*

i. William E.,[7] M. D., *m.* Cornelia Leffler, and had issue: Louis Rogers.[8]
ii. Leonella C,[7] *m.* John Faulds, of Scotland.

Issue of Dr. Joel W.[5] and Pauline P. (Eldridge) *Dupuy:*

i. Martha Elizabeth,[6] *m.* Joel W. *Daniel*, Farmville, Virginia. Issue: i. Joel;[7] ii. Lina;[7] iii. Robert;[7] iv. Lavillon.[7]
ii. Joseph Thomas,[6] M. D., *m.* Mollie Madison, Cartersville, Virginia. Issue: i. Flood;[7] ii. Joseph;[7] iii. Susan;[7] iv. Paulina;[7] v. Mary.[7]

iii. Powhatan Eldridge,[6] *m.* Marietta Breeden. He is a leading druggist of Richmond, Virginia.

iv. John Howell,[6] Lieutenant and Adjutant Twenty-third Virginia regiment, C. S. A.; killed at the Battle of the Wilderness.

v. Paulina Pocahontas,[6] *m.* Rev. Lewis B. *Johnston*, Augusta county, Virginia. Issue: i. Carter;[7] ii. Lewis;[7] iii. ——.[7]

vi. Henry Rolfe,[6] *m.* Nannie Grayson Walton, New Canton, Virginia. Issue: i. Mary P.;[7] ii. Nannie C.;[7] iii. Rolfe Walton;[7] iv. Howell Eldridge.[7]

vii. Ella Nash,[6] unmarried.

viii. Alice Townes,[6] *m.* William C. Kean, Goochland county, Virginia. Issue: two children.

ix. Joel W.,[6] *m.* ——; lives in Mississippi. Issue: two children.

Issue of Peter[3] and Margaret (Martin) *Dupuy:*

i. Martha Branch,[4] *b.* October, 1790; *d.* June 25, 1819; *m.* November 14, 1810, Wm. McKinney, *b.* September 6, 1781; *d.* November 16, 1832.

ii. Anthony Martin,[4] *b.* December 21, 1791; *d.* December 19, 1869, unmarried.

iii. Thomas,[4] *b.* April 24, 1793; *d.* July 4, 1795.

iv. Sarah,[4] *b.* April 15, 1795; *d.* September 11, 1795.

v. Louisa Margaret,[4] *b.* August 14, 1796; *d.* July 26, 1873.

vi. Linnæus,[4] *b.* April 28, 1798; *d.* August 22, 1849; *m.* April 28, 1831, Celine Cugneau Tate, *b.* April 23, 1798; *d.* November 10, 1851.

vii. Sarah Holman,[4] *b.* January 26, 1800; *d.* August 14, 1864; *m.* November 21, 1816, Stephen Dupuy Watkins, *b.* January 27, 1788; *d.* July 13, 1862.

viii. Jane Guerrant,[4] *b.* September 12, 1801; *d.* October 13, 1853; *m.* July 4, 1826, Thomas McKinney, *b.* March 12, 1794; *d.* September 20, 1867.

ix. Newton,[4] *b.* November 18, 1803; *d.* February 21, 1827.

x. James Barret,[4] *b.* May 31, 1805; *d.* March 29, 1878. An honored merchant of Richmond for 32 years, long of the firm of Dupuy & McKinney; at one time Grand Secretary of the Grand Lodge of A., F. and A. Masons of Virginia.

xi. Mary Elethia,[4]	twins; *b* June 8, 1807.	Never married; *d.* Aug. 4, 1817.
xii. Harriet Amasia,[4]		*d.* April 9, 1872; *m.* April 21, 1825, Ptolemy Lefebvre Watkins, *b.* May 18, 1793; *d.* April 5, 1857.

xiii. Virginia Ann,[4] *b.* February 15, 1809; *d.* February 9, 1834; *m.* June 10, 1830, Watson Michie, *b.* February 15, 1809; *d.* February 9, 1834.

xiv. Amelia Elizabeth,[4] *b.* June 10, 1811; *d.* November, 1885; *m.* January 26, 1846, John Hamilton Patterson, *b.* July 4, 1800; *d.* November 12, 1873.

xv. Adelaide Lawrence,[4] *b.* August 5, 1814; *m.* June 13, 1854, Thomas Sale Campbell, *b.* August 5, 1814.

Issue of William and Martha Branch[4] (Dupuy) *McKinney:*

i. Robert Jennings,[5] *b.* October 6, 1811; *d.* September 11, 1833.

ii. Martha Louise,[5] *b.* January 28, 1813; *d.* May 27, 1845; *m.* March 8, 1831, David Bridges, *b.* December 23, 1810.

iii. Peter Dupuy,[5] *b.* June 6, 1815; *d.* August 5, 1875; *m.* May 15, 1856, Sarah Ann Lyle, *b.* October 13, 1824; *d.* January 22, 1885.

Issue of David and Martha Louisa[5] (McKinney) *Bridges:*

i. Kate Louisa,[6] *b.* February —, ——; *m.* October 10, 1841, James Philip Roy, *b.* April 30, 1828; *d.* October 24, 1876.

ii. Martha Caskie,[6] *b.* November —, ——; *d.* October, 1883.

iii. William McKinney,[6] *b.* May 5, 1835; *m.* April 13, 1871, Lucy Cary Cocke.

iv. Julia Cabell,[6] *b.* September 4. 1837; *d.* October 10, 1837.

v. Florence,[6] *b.* October 23, 1838; *d.* February 25, 1839.

vi. David,[6] *b.* October 2, 1841; *d.* May 18, 1863, of disease contracted as a member of "F" Company, Twenty-first Virginia regiment, in the Confederate States Army.

vii. Clifford Cabell,[6] *b.* March 26, 1845; *m.* November 24, 1870, Lizzie Ragan Macgill.

Issue of James Philip and Kate Louisa[6] (Bridges) *Roy:*

i. Lizzie Perkins,[7] *b.* May 19, 1856.

ii. Kate Louisa,[7] *b.* September 25, 1857.

iii. Susan Carter,[7] *b.* October 6, 1859.
iv. James Philip,[7] *b.* September 24, 1861.

Issue of William McKinney,[6] and Lucy Cary (Cocke) *Bridges:*

i. Philip St. George,[7] *b.* March 3, 1872.
ii. Lucy Cary,[7] *b.* August 28, 1873.
iii. Maggie Fergusson,[7] *b.* March 13, 1875; *d.* June 15, 1875.
iv. Courtney Bowdoin,[7] *b.* August 23, 1876.
v. William Kennon,[7] *b.* January 30, 1878.
vi. Evelyn Condie,[7] *b.* July 7, 1880.
vii. David Quarrier,[7] *b.* February 14, 1883.

Issue of Clifford Cabell[6] and Lizzie Ragan (Macgill) *Bridges:*

i. Kate Condie,[7] *b.* September 11, 1871; *d.* July 27, 1875.
ii. Mary Macgill,[7] *b.* April 29, 1873; *d.* June 18, 1873.
iii. Lizzie Macgill,[7] *b.* September 10, 1874.
iv. Ida Hairston,[7] *b.* September 25, 1876; *d.* April 9, 1878.
v. Lelia Carroll,[7] *b.* July 23, 1878.
vi. Condie Roy,[7] *b.* July 17, 1880.
vii. Mollie Macgill,[7] *b.* May 18, 1882.
viii. Charles Macgill,[7] *b.* November 27, 1884.

Issue of Peter Dupuy[5] and Sarah Anne (Lyle) *McKinney:*

i. Helen Le Vert,[6] *b.* February 28 1858.
ii. William Barrett,[6] *b.* May 13, 1859
iii. Lelia Bland,[6] *b.* September 20, 1861; *d.* July 4, 1862.
iv. Charles Lyle,[6] *b.* February 2, 1866.

Issue of Linnæus[4] and Celine C. (Tate) *Dupuy:*

i. Charles Lewis Cooper,[5] *b.* February 8, 1832; *m.* October 20, 1869, Anna Wood Dupuy; *b.* May 16, 1839. Issue: Louisa Abbott,[6] *b.* October 27, 1872.
ii. Marguerite Eloise,[6] *b.* Aug. 21, 1836; *d.* July 18, 1837.

Issue of Stephen Dupuy and Sarah Holman[4] (Dupuy) *Watkins:*

i. Mary Louisa,[5] *b.* March 22, 1819; *d.* October 8, 1820.
ii. Thomas Linnæus,[5] *b.* October 20, 1821; *d.* September 24, 1823.
iii. Washington Lafayette,[5] *b.* January 10, 1824; *m.* twice; 1st,

June 10, 1851, Maria Sophia Hall (*b.* June 4, 1833; *d.* September 21, 1864); 2d, October 9, 1866, Lizzie Stringfellow, *b.* September 9, 1845.

iv. Anna Margaret,[5] *b.* May 16, 1826; *d.* May 22, 1866; *m.* September 25, 1861, Richard Sterling Taliaferro, *b.* June 12, 1807.

v. Marcellus Dupuy,[5] *b.* November 30, 1828; *d.* October 22, 1846.

vi. Ella Amelia,[5] *b.* December 19, 1831; *d.* September, 1833.

Issue of Washington Lafayette[5] and Maria Sophia (Hall) *Watkins:*

i. Thomas Gholson,[6] *b.* June 17, 1852.

ii. John Dupuy,[6] *b.* July 13, 1854.

iii. Anna Martin,[6] *b.* July 20, 1856; *d.* December 17, 1857.

iv. Harriet Hall,[6] *b.* March 20, 1858; *d.* July 18, 1859.

v. Sallie Harrison,[6] *b.* August 7, 1860.

vi. Alverda Hall,[6] *b.* May 19, 1862; *d.* May 16, 1864.

vii. Maria Hall,[6] *b.* May 3, 1864; *d.* May 17, 1865.

Issue of Thomas and Jane Guerrant[4] (Dupuy) *McKinney:*

i. Margaret Susan,[5] *b.* March 30, 1827.

ii. Charles Eugene,[5] *b.* June 23, 1828; *d.* November 16, 1848.

iii. Thomas Hampden,[5] *b.* May 24, 1830; *m.* April 23, 1867, Emma Arsenath Thomas, *b.* December 6, 1842.

iv. Sarah Jane,[5] *b.* September 22, 1832; *d.* September 5, 1834.

v. Robert Martin,[5] *b.* June 25, 1837; Colonel C. S. A.; killed in battle April 16, 1862.

vi. Linnæus Barrett,[5] *b.* June 29, 1827; killed in battle March 31, 1865.

vii. Ellen Dupuy,[5] *b.* March 24, 1842; *m.* November 5, 1872, John Thomas Berry, *b.* December 4, 1839.

Issue of Thomas Hampden[5] and Emma Arsenath (Thomas) *McKinney:*

i. Maggie Belle,[6] *b.* March 15, 1868.

ii. Ro. Linnæus,[6] *b.* February 2, 1870.

iii. Kate Dupuy,[6] *b.* May 10, 1872.

Issue of John Thomas and Ellen Dupuy[5] (McKinney) *Berry:*

i. Margaret Olivia,[6] *b.* April 13, 1874.

ii. Thos. Dorsey,[6] *b.* February 22, 1876.
iii. Wm. Elbert,[6] *b.* November 24, 1877.

Issue of Ptolemy Lefebvre and Harriet Amasia[4] (Dupuy) *Watkins:*

i. Mary Elethia,[5] *b.* January 10, 1826.
ii. Thos. Dupuy,[5] *b.* December 9, 1827; killed in battle April 7, 1865.
iii. Margaret Louisa,[5] *b.* July 17, 1830; *d.* October 28, 1856.
iv. Powhatan Virginius,[5] *b.* March 17, 1832; *d.* July 1, 1835.
v. Adelaide Amelia,[5] *b.* March 16, 1835; *m.* twice; January 18, 1853, Rev. Williamson Milner Fergusson (*b.* September 22, 1822; *d.* August 2, 1864); 2d, May 24, 1876, Peter Hunter, *b.* September 6, 1804.
vi. Charlotte Harris,[5] *b.* January 6, 1839; *d.* March 28, 1843.
vii. Peter Dupuy,[5] *b.* December 12, 1840; *d.* August 16, 1862.
viii. James Martin,[5] *b.* June 23, 1842; *d.* June 6, 1843.
ix. Linnæus Dupuy,[5] *b.* April 12, 1844; *d.* May 31, 1864, of wounds received in battle.
x. Harriet Virginia,[5] *b.* February 10, 1846; *m.* February 16, 1875, John Thomas *Thornton*, *b.* March 9, 1848. Issue: Thomas Jefferson,[6] *b.* December 18, 1875; *d.* July 23, 1877.

Issue of Rev. Williamson Milner and Adelaide Amelia[5] (Watkins) *Fergusson:*

i. Mary Elethia,[6] *b.* August 10, 1854; *m.* May 5, 1873, George Washington Swain, *b.* June 16, 1846.
ii. Harriet Louisa,[6] *b.* June 24, 1855; *d.* December 27, 1855.
iii. Samuel James,[6] *b.* September 10, 1856.
iv. Agnes Virginia,[6] *b.* September 1, 1858.
v. Elizabeth Noel,[6] *b.* October 4, 1862.

Issue of Wm. Watson and Virginia Ann[4] (Dupuy) *Michie:*

i. Cornelia Virginia,[5] *b.* March 22, 1831; *m.* January 19, 1849, Robert Bruce *Watkins*, *b.* August 13, 1822. Issue:
    i. Robert Bruce,[6] *b.* November 21, 1849.
    ii. Virginia Dupuy,[6] *b.* September 3, 1851; *d.* October 3, 1851.
    iii. Edward Waverly,[6] *b.* August 19, 1852; *d.* October 22, 1858.

iv. Evangeline St. Clair,[6] *b.* March 13, 1855.
v. Amelia Louisa,[6] *b.* March 29, 1857.
vi. Florence Nightingale,[6] *b.* May 21, 1859; *d.* November 19, 1862.
vii. Virginia Judith,[6] *b.* October 9, 1861.
viii. Anna Adelaide,[6] *b.* March 1, 1864.
ix. Corinne Lawrence,[6] *b.* April 11, 1867.
x. Charlotte Ellen,[6] *b.* March 20, 1870.
xi. Raymond Lavillon,[6] *b.* March 11, 1872.

Issue of Thomas and Magdalene[3] (Dupuy) *Watkins:*

i. John,[4] *m.* —— Wilson.
ii. Benjamin,[4] *m.* Susan,[4] daughter of John[3] Dupuy.

Issue of John[4] and —— (Wilson) *Watkins:*

i. Polly,[5] *m.* —— Clay.
ii. Ptolemy,[5] *m.* H. Dupuy.
iii. Stephen,[5] *m.* Susan Dupuy.
iv. Joel,[5] *m.* ——.
v. Peter.[5]
vi. Magdalene.[5]
vii. Thomas.[5]

Issue of Benjamin[4] and Susan (Dupuy) *Watkins:*

i. Stephen.[5]
ii. Benjamin,[5] *m.* Miss Peyton.
iii. William L.[5]
iv. Thomas[5] *m.* Eliza Gunn.
v. Henry Anderson,[5] *m.* Susan Watkins.
vi. Agnes,[5] *m.* —— Jones.
vii. Anne,[5] *m.* —— *Williams.* Issue: i. Watkins;[6] ii. Robert.[6]
viii. Mary,[5] *m.* —— Daniel.
ix. Caroline,[5] *m.* —— *Martin.* Issue: Anne.[6]
x. Jane,[5] *m.* Scott.
xi. John,[5] *m.* —— Martin.
xii. Susanna,[5] *m.* —— *Mayber.* Issue: Anne Dupuy.[6]

Issue of James[3] and Mary (Purnell) *Dupuy:*

i. Elizabeth,[4] *m.* —— *Osborne.* Issue: Catherine,[5] *m.* —— Johns.
ii. John Purnell,[4] resided in Nottoway county, near Burkeville.

iii. Colonel Joseph,[4] *m.* twice: 1st, —— Edmunds; 2d, —— Walker.
iv. Elvira,[4] *m.* Colonel R. B. Eggleston, of Amelia county. Issue: ——.
v. William J.,[4] M. D., *m.* Jane, sister of Edmund Ruffin, the distinguished agriculturist.
vi. Nancy,[4] *m.* thrice: 1st, —— Jeffries; 2d, —— Morris; 3d, —— Wootton.
vii. Asa,[4] *m.* E. Howe; she *d.* December 26, 1883; resided in Prince Edward county; farmer; presiding justice of the county.
viii. Mary Purnell,[4] *m.* twice: 1st, L. Dickinson; 2d, —— Jeter.
ix. James H.,[4] *m.* Elizabeth G. Dupuy.

Issue of Joseph[4] *Dupuy:*

i. Asa.[5]
ii. Louisa.[5]
iii. William P.,[5] *m.* —— Booker.
iv. Joseph.[5]
v. James.[5]
vi. Jennie.[5]
vii. Mary P.[5]
viii. Elvira.[5]

Issue of —— and Elvira[4] (Dupuy) *Eggleston:*

i. James Asa.[5]
ii. George M.[5]
iii. John W.,[5] *m.* —— Morton.
iv. Cornelia.[5]
v. Mary J.,[5] *m.* —— Shore.
vi. Joseph D.,[5] *m.* —— Booker.

Issue of William J.[4] and Jane (Ruffin) *Dupuy:*

i. Alexander.[5]
ii. George Ruffin,[5] *m.* Sydney Thompson; *d.* ——.
iii. William (1st).[5]
iv. Rebecca Cocke,[5] *m.* Freeman Eppes.
v. Montgomery,[5] *m.* L. C. Coleman.
vi. Mary Jane,[5] *m.* John Marshall, Mobile, Ala.
vii. Indianna.[5]
viii. William (2d),[5] *m.* Mary Bebee.

ix. Anna,[5] *m.* Charles Dupuy.

x. John James,[5] M. D., *m.* twice: 1st, —— Ruffin; 2d, —— Sampson; now resides at Davidson College, North Carolina.

Issue of Asa[4] and E. (Howe) *Dupuy:*

i. Mary Purnell,[5] *m.* Richard W. Watkins, a successful lawyer.

ii. Annie L.[5]

iii. Elizabeth.[5]

iv. Maria L.,[5] *m.* Captain Abner Anderson, Editor and Proprietor Danville, Virginia, *Register*, and now of the Richmond *Whig*.

v. Lavallette.[5]

vi. Emily H.[5]

Issue of Mary[4] and —— (Dupuy) *Dickinson:*

i. Mary Anne,[5] *m.* John A. *Bland.* Issue: i. Martha Rebecca,[6] *m.* Charles W. Fitzgerald; ii. Robert;[6] iii. Cornelia,[6] *m.* John H. Knight; iv. Mary.[6]

ii. Thomas H.,[5] moved to California, and *d.*

iii. Robert,[5] M. D., moved to Alabama in 1838, and *d.*

iv. Asa Dupuy,[5] graduated from Hampden Sydney College in 1836; Circuit Court Judge, Prince Edward county; member of House of Delegates and of Senate of Virginia; *b.* 1817; *d.* July 19, 1884; *m.* twice: 1st, —— Michaux; 2d, —— Irving.

v. Elizabeth Guerrant,[5] *d.* September 1, 1849; *m.* May, 1840, Colonel William Carter Knight.[c]

---

c William Carter, son of John Howell and Sallie E. (Carter) Knight, a direct descendant in the third generation of George Walton, signer of the Declaration of Independence; graduated in law from William and Mary College; member of Virginia Senate 1857–'60; has been prominently connected with the agricultural and manufacturing interests of Virginia (having been successively Secretary and President of the State Agricultural Society), and is now the editor of the *Southern Planter and Farmer*. The name Knight is of early seating in Virginia. Peter Knight patented land in New Norfolk county, March 18, 1638. Peter Knight, probably the same, was the Burgess from Northumberland county in March, 1658. There are grants of land of record in the State Registry, aggregating more than 25,000 acres in Norfolk, Isle of Wight, James City, and Gloucester counties, to Peter, Joseph, Edward, John, William, and Guy Knight, during the period 1638, 1675.

vi. William Purnell,[5] *m.* twice: 1st, —— Barksdale; 2d, —— Venable.

vii. Sarah Jane.[5]

Issue of James H.[4] and Elizabeth (Dupuy) *Dupuy:*

i. Emma Wirt,[5] *m.* E. P. Gayce.

ii. Francis J., } twins,[5] { *m.* Rev. —— Smith.

iii. Sallie Lyle, } twins,[5] { *m.* —— Pease.

iv. Cornelia Susan.[5]

v. John James,[5] *m.* Miss Baskerville.

vi. Asa Purnell,[5] *m.* —— Williams.

vii. Margaret L.,[5] *m.* Richard Thompson.

viii. Mary Ellen,[5] *m.* twice, 1st, J. T. Trueheart; 2d, Jerome Berryman, of Missouri.

ix. Virginia,[5] *m.* M. P. Cayce, of Missouri.

x. Ann Eliza,[5] *m.* Charles Welling, of Missouri.

Issue of Judge Asa Dupuy[5] and —— (Michaux[d]) *Dickinson:*

i. Robert M.,[6] lawyer; resides in Prince Edward county; *m.* —— Cralle.

ii. John Purnell,[6] *d.* January 2, 1886. Issue by second marriage, six children.

Issue of Colonel William Carter and Elizabeth Guerrant[5] (Dickinson) *Knight:*

i. Carter Dupuy,[6] *d.* young.

ii. Robert P.,[6] member of First Company Richmond Howitzers, served throughout the war, 1861–5; *m.* Miss —— Clay, of Chesterfield county, and has six children.

iii. Jennie Wickliffe,[6] *m.* twice: 1st, Captain Henry Delaplaine *Danforth*, Confederate States Army and private "F."

---

d A descendant of Abraham Michaux, from Sedan, France, p. 75, whose will is of record in Henrico county court, July, 1717. Legatees—wife, Susanna (*née* Rochette); sons: Jacob, John, Paul, Abraham; daughters: Anne, Jane, Magdalene, Susanna, Olive (Jude), Elizabeth, Amanda, "Easter," Mary. The Michaux family in its connections include, with others, the estimable names of Abbott, Anderson, Archer, Branch, Calhoun, Carrington, Caulfield, Chase, Cocke, Cunningham, Daniel, Flournoy, Gaines, Hill, Hughes, Kilpatrick, King, Legrand, Lockett, Martin, Mason, Matthews, McNutt, Moorman, Morgan, Morton, Nance, Quin, Reid, Rice, Robard, Scott, Spencer, Venable, Watkins, Wherry, Williams, Wood and Woodson.

Company, Twenty-first Virginia volunteers, Confederate States Army, Secretary Mutual Assurance Society of Richmond.[e] (Issue: John B.) 2d, Colonel Charles T. O'Ferrall, Confederate States Army, and Member of Congress.

iv. Emmet Carter,[6] *m.* Josephine Mayo; tobacconist, residing in Toronto, Canada.

Issue of John James[2] and Susan (LeVillain) *Dupuy:*

i. Elizabeth,[3] *m.* Thos. Atkinson. Issue: i. John;[4] ii. Nancy;[4] iii. Patsy;[4] moved to Kentucky.

ii. Olymphia,[3] *b.* November 12, 1729; *m.* John James Trabue; *d.* in Kentucky, aged 93 years.

iii. Anne.[3]

iv. Bartholomew,[3] *m.* Mary Mottley and moved to Kentucky.

v. Rev. John,[3] *m.* Elizabeth Minter and moved to Kentucky.

vi. James,[3] *m.* Anne Stark and moved to Kentucky.

Issue of John (James) and Olymphia[3] (Dupuy) *Trabue:*[f]

i. Daniel,[4] *b.* March 31, 1760; *d.* 1840; *m.* Mary Haskins.

ii. John Trabue,[4] *b.* March 17, 1737 [1738]; *d.* in Logan's Fort, Kentucky, in 1788; *m.* —— Pearce.

iii. Aaron,[4] *m.* Olymphia Wilson. Issue: Lucy, Luvin, Mary, Nancy.

iv. Stephen,[4] *m.* Jane Haskins.

v. Susan,[4] *m.* Thomas Major.

vi. Edward,[4] *m.* 1st, L. M. "Patsy" Haskins; 2d, Jane Clay.

vii. Judith,[4] *m.* John Major.

viii. Magdalene,[4] *m.* Edward Clay; descendants live in Alabama.

ix. Mary,[4] *m.* Lewis Sublett.

x. James,[4] *m.* Miss Porter.

xi. Elizabeth,[4] *b.* September 4, 1740; *m.* Fenelon Wilson.

xii. William,[4] *m.* Mary Haskins.

xiii. Jane,[4] *m.* Joseph *Minter;* lived in Woodford county, Kentucky. Issue: Anthony Kerr.

xiv. Martha,[4] *m.* Josiah Wooldridge.

xv. Nancy,[4] *m.* Joseph *Watkins.* Issue: i. Jacob; ii. Lucy, *m.* J. Smith.

---

e The oldest Insurance Company in Virginia, established in 1794.

f See Note erroneously placed *ante* p. 22, as to Anthony Trabue.

Issue of Daniel[4] and Mary (Haskins) *Trabue:*

i. Judith,[5] *m.* S. *Scott.* Issue: Judith S.,[6] *m.* —— Brown.
ii. Sallie,[5] *m.* G. *Anderson.* Issue: Martha,[6] *m.* —— Penix.
iii. Eliza,[5] *m.* —— Barrett.
iv. Sallie,[5] *m.* —— *Terry.* Issue: i. Betty;[6] ii. George;[6] iii. Mary.[6]
v. Martha.[5]
vi. James,[5] *m.* Eliza Stiles. Lives in Louisville, Kentucky. Issue: i. Richard;[6] ii. Corina;[6] iii. Sarah,[6] *m.* —— Barksdale; iv. James.[6]
vii. Polly,[5] *m.* Lewis *Sublett.* Lives in Green county, Kentucky. Issue: i. Sallie;[6] ii. Mary;[6] iii. Judith;[6] iv. Mary;[6] v. Robert;[6] vi. William,[6] *m.* ——; vii. Daniel,[6] *m.* ——.
viii. John,[5] was murdered at the age of twelve years by the notorious Harpers, in Kentucky.
ix. Daniel,[5] *m.* Mary Paxton. Lives in Texas. Issue: i. Robert;[6] ii. Ann;[6] iii. Ellen,[6] *m.* —— Smith; iv. Presley;[6] v. William,[6] *m.* ——; vi. George,[6] *m.* ——.
x. Presley,[5] died young.
xi. Robert T.,[5] *m.* Lucy Waggoner; *d.* in Illinois. Issue: i. Eliza;[6] ii. Robert,[6] *m.* M. Witherspoon; iii. Sallie,[6] (*m.* George *Patterson.* Lives in Memphis. Issue: i. Robert.[7] ii. Annie,[7] *m.* William B. Mitchell; iii. Oliver G.;[7] iv. Holmes;[7] v. John;[7] vi. Reuben;[7] vii. Thomas.[7]) iv. Polly,[6] *m.* Joseph Lester; v. John;[6] vi. Martha;[6] vii. Olymphia,[6] *m.* —— Hall.

Issue of Stephen[4] and Jane (Haskins) *Trabue:*

i. William T.,[5] *m.* E. Caldwell.
ii. Chastaine,[5] *m.* Elizabeth Trabue. Issue: i. Judith;[6] ii. Marianne;[6] iii. Stephen;[6] iv. Isaac;[6] v. William.[6]
iii. Haskins D.[5]
iv. Rebecca.[5]
v. Elizabeth.[5]
vi. Edward,[5] *m.* ——.
vii. Francis.[5]

Issue of Thomas and Susan[4] (Trabue) *Major:*

i. Betsy,[5] *m.* G. *Gunnel.* Issue: Thomas.[6]
ii. John,[5] *m.* ——.

iii. Oliver,[5] *m.* Nancy Gunnel. Issue: i. Alva[6]; ii. Olivia[6]; iii. Laura;[6] iv. Susan,[6] *m.* Thomas *Gregory*. Issue: i. Joseph;[7] ii. Martha;[7] iii. Nancy.[7] v. Margaret;[6] vi. Thomas;[6] vii. Elizabeth;[6] viii. Ellinor.[6]

Issue of Edward[4] *Trabue* by his two marriages with L. M. Haskins and Jane Clay:

i. Susan,[5] *m.* —— Clayton.
ii. Matilda,[5] *m.* —— Sutton.
iii. Cynthia,[5] *m.* —— Johns.
iv. George,[5] *m.* Mrs. Buford. Issue: Joseph, Benjamin, Judith.
v. Betsy,[5] *m.* K. *Hatcher*. Issue: Robert, Sallie, Jeremiah, Edward, Henry.
vi. Jane,[5] *m.* —— Lewellen, and had issue.
vii. John E.,[5] *m.* Elizabeth Atkinson. Issue: i. Sylvia,[6] *m.* —— Latimer; ii. Thomas E.;[6] iii. Arabella,[6] *m.* —— Stuart; iv. Susan,[6] *m.* —— *Turner*. Issue: John E.[7] v. Jane E.,[6] *m.* —— *Foster*. Issue: Robert.[7]
viii. Patsy,[5] *m.* Aaron *Trabue*. Issue: i. Nancy;[6] ii. Rebecca;[6] iii. Mysander;[6] iv. Edward;[6] v. Margaret.[6]
ix. Charles C.,[5] *m.* Agnes Woods. Issue: i. Joseph;[6] ii. Robert;[6] iii. Anthony E. D.;[6] iv. Charles C.;[6] v. Sarah,[6] *m.* —— Stephens; vi. George;[6] vii. Martha,[6] *m.* George *Thompson*. Issue: i. Agnes;[7] ii. Bessie;[7] iii. Charles;[7] iv. Mattie;[7] v. Fannie;[7] vi. John A.;[7] vii. Jennie;[7] viii. Kate.[7]
x. Nancy,[5] *m.* Asa *Pitman*. Issue: i. Jefferson;[6] ii. Elizabeth;[6] iii. Martha Jane;[6] iv. Charles;[6] v. Williamson,[6] *m.* —— Davis, issue; vi. Asa Anna;[6] vii. Edward,[6] *m.* —— *Thompson*. Issue: George[7]

Issue of John and Judith[4] (Trabue) *Major:*

i. William,[5] *m.* —— Shipp.
ii. John,[5] *m.* Eliza Wilkins.
iii. Benj.[5]
iv. Joseph,[5] *m.* —— Catlett.
v. George Buford.[5]
vi. Elizabeth,[5] *m.* —— *Davenport*. Issue: i. William;[6] ii. Chester;[6] iii. Benj.;[6] iv. Jackson.[6]
vii. Chester,[5] *m.* —— Davenport.

Issue of Edward and Magdalene[4] (Trabue) *Clay:*

i. Sarah.[5]
ii. John.[5]
iii. Edward.[5]
iv. Samuel.[5]
v. Phœbe.[5]
vi. Martha.[5]
vii. Mary.[5]
viii. James.[5]
ix. Judith.[5]
x. Francis.[5]

Issue of Lewis and Mary[4] (Trabue) *Sublett:*

i. Francis,[5] *m.* —— Vaughan.
ii. James,[5] *m.* ——. Issue: i. Francis;[6] ii. James;[6] iii. Matthew;[6] iv. Taylor.[6]
iii. William,[5] *m.* —— Samuel.
iv. John.[5]
v. Lewis,[5] *m.* —— Coleman. Issue: i. John;[6] ii. Lewis;[6] iii. Joel;[6] iv. William,[6] *m.* G. G. Brown, and had issue: Kate.[7]
vi. Thomas,[5] *m.* twice: 1st, J. Bogan; 2d, J. O'Neil. Issue: i. Mary;[6] ii. John;[6] iii. Alice;[6] iv. Kate.[6]
vii. Mary,[5] *m.* —— *Huggins.* Issue: i. Susan;[6] ii Sarah;[6] iii. William;[6] iv. Margaret;[6] v. Andrew;[6] vi. James.[6]
viii. Thomas,[5] *m.* Kate Morton. Issue: i. Mary;[6] ii. John;[6] iii. Alice;[6] iv. Kate.[6]

Issue of James[4] and —— (Porter) *Trabue:*

i. Judith,[5] *m.* —— Ewing.
ii. Edward.[5]
iii. Betsy,[5] *m.* Chastaine *Trabue.* Issue: Isaac,[6] Judith,[6] William,[6] Stephen,[6] Joseph,[6] Marianne,[6] Harriet[6] (*m.* Nesbitt), Elizabeth.[6]
iv. Robert.[5]
v. James,[5] *m.* 1st, Judith Wooldridge; 2d, Lucy Cosby.

Issue of Fenelon and Elizabeth[4] (Trabue) *Wilson:*

i. Olymphia,[5] *m.* Aaron Trabue (or Haskins[g]) *Trabue.* Issue:

---

g The two "trees" of Mrs. Ratcliffe and Mrs. Stovall differ thus.

i. Joseph;[6] ii. John W.;[6] iii. Stephen;[6] iv. Rebecca;[6] v. Eliza J.;[6] vi. Mary O.;[6] vii. William;[6] viii. Benjamin;[6] ix. Edward;[6] x. Hudgins W.;[6] xi. Fenelon,[6] *m.* Martha Parks; xii. Olymphia.[6]

ii. Rev. John S.,[5] Pastor of Walnut Street Baptist Church, Louisville, Kentucky, one of the most zealous of ministers; *d.* 1835; *m.* Martha Waggoner. Issue: i. Josephine;[6] ii. Luther;[6] iii. Sallie;[6] iv. Hodges J.;[6] v. Lelia,[6] *m.* A. J. Heth; vi. Hester,[6] *m.* Benjamin Herring; vii. Emma,[6] *m.* J. H. Halbert; viii. Mary,[6] *m.* J. H. Bagby.

iii. Lelia Anne.[5]

Issue of William[4] and Mary (Haskins) *Trabue:*

i. Phœbe,[5] *m.* Rev. Isaac *Hodgen.* Issue: i. Isaac H.[6] *m.* —— Ritter; ii. Walter;[6] iii. Sallie,[6] *m.* —— Cole; iv. Betsy,[6] *m.* 1st, William Caldwell; 2d, Samuel Scott; v. Harriett;[6] vi. Mary;[6] vii. Robert.[6]

ii. Nancy,[5] *m.* William *Caldwell.* Issue: i. George Alfred;[6] ii. Elizabeth,[6] (*m.* William *Trabue.* Issue: i. M. Alfred;[7] ii. L. Alice;[7] iii. Lucy Ellen;[7] iv. Matilda;[7] v. Edward H.;[7] vi. Nancy,[7] *m.* —— Shearer.) iii. Isaac,[6] *m.* —— Smith. (Issue: Palmer.[7]) iv. Letitia,[6] (*m.* —— *Rochester.* Issue: i. Alfred;[7] ii. William Isaac;[7] iii. Junius C.;[7] iv. Augusta;[7] v. Anna.[7]) v. Phœbe,[6] (*m.* —— *Helm.* Issue: i. George A.;[7] ii. Anne Rebecca;[7] iii. Augusta.[7]) vi. Anne Jane,[6] *m.* J. Dudley *Winston,* of Nashville. Issue: i. J. Dudley;[7] ii. Judith Dudley;[7] iii. William Caldwell;[7] iv. Geo. Alfred;[7] v. Mary Overton;[7] vi. Augusta;[7] vii. Anne,[7] (*m.* S. C. Pitts. Issue: M. Denny;[8] A. Winston;[8]) viii. Jane Elam;[7] ix. Ida Rochester;[7] x. Jane C.[7]

iii. Junius.[5]

Issue of Joseph and Jane[4] (Trabue) *Minter:*

i. Anthony,[5] *m.* E. Kerr.

ii. Tabitha,[5] *m.* —— *Pitman.* Issue: Angeline,[6] *m.* Thomas Gregory.

iii. Jane,[5] *m.* Benjamin Watkins.

iv. Jeremiah,[5] *m.* S. McDowell.

v. Patsey,[5] *m.* Peter Gregory.

vi. Benjamin.[5]

vii. Joseph,[5] *m.* E. Cosby.

viii. James,[5] *m.* ——.
ix. Betsy,[5] *m.* James Major.
x. William,[5] *m.* Elizabeth C. Waggoner.
xi. Sallie,[5] *m.* —— *Cosby.* Issue: i. William,[6] *m.* —— Porter; ii. Lucy,[6] *m.* James Trabue; iii. Betty,[6] *m.* —— Huff; iv. Mary;[6] v. Joseph.[6]
xii. John,[5] *m.* Elizabeth Scarce.

Issue of Benjamin and Jane[5] (Minter) *Watkins:*

i. Rebecca,[6] *m.* William Yates.
ii. Tabitha,[6] *m.* John *Gill.* Issue: i. Philip;[7] ii. Ellen;[7] iii. James;[7] iv. Sarah;[7] v. John;[7] vi. Elizabeth;[7] vii. Alice.[7]
iii. Susan,[6] *m* John *Hardin.* Issue: i. Adelia;[7] ii. Walter;[7] iii. ——.[7]
iv. Jane,[5] *m.* Philip Gill.
v. Elizabeth,[6] *m.* Isaac *Carter.* Issue: i. Benjamin;[7] ii. Susan;[7] iii. Ellen.[7]
vi. Anne Maria.[6]
vii. Martha,[6] *m.* —— *Lake.* Issue: Mary J.,[7] *m.* ——Albright.
viii. James,[6] *m.* Martha Scarce. Issue: i. Benjamin;[7] ii. Parker;[7] iii. Anne;[7] iv. Jennie;[7] v. Amelia;[7] vi. Susan;[7] vii. Laban;[7] viii. Alice;[7] ix. Laura;[7] x. Edwin.[7]
ix. Benjamin,[6] *m.* Elvira Adkins.
x. Mary,[6] *m.* John *Handy.* Issue: i. George;[7] ii. Mary;[7] iii. Martha;[7] iv. William;[7] v. Walter.[7]
xi. Walter L.,[6] *m.* Mary Holloway. Issue: i. Catherine;[7] ii. George;[7] iii. John;[7] iv. Martha;[7] v. Lizzie;[7] vi. Jewell;[7] vii. Caroline;[7] viii. Judson;[7] ix. Joseph.[7]
xii. Caroline,[6] *m.* Parker *Harden.* Issue: i. Charles;[7] ii. Watkins;[7] iii. Benjamin.[7]
xiii. Margaret,[6] *m.* twice: 1st, Milton Bynam; 2d. A. D. Blythe. Issue: i. Alvin,[7] ii. Robert P.;[7] iii. Mary F.;[7] iv. Susan;[7] v. Samuel J.[7]

Issue of Jeremiah[5] and S. (McDowell) *Minter:*

i. Ann M.,[6] *m.* —— *Slaybuck.* Issue: i. A. W.,[7] *m.* —— Waddell; ii. Charles E.,[7] *m.* —— Newman; iii. Preston;[7] iv. Minnie,[7] *m.* —— Bond.
ii. Magdalene,[6] *m.* —— Kidd.
iii. Mary S.,[6] *m.* —— Hife.

iv. Marshall.[6]
v. Sarah Jane.[6]
vi. Ellen.[6]
vii. Bertholde.[6]
viii. Susan.[6]

Issue of Peter and Patsy[5] (Minter) *Gregory*:

i. Edwin,[6] *m.* Anne Lane. Issue: i. Carrie;[7] ii. Lou;[7] iii. Charles.[7]
ii. Joseph M.[6]
iii. Pauline.[6]
iv. Thomas.[6]
v. Lou.[6]
vi. Mary,[6] *m.* Wm. *Clarkson.* Issue: i. William C.;[7] ii. George;[7] iii. Matty;[7] iv. Minter.[7]

Issue of Joseph[5] and E. (Cosby) *Minter*:

i. Martha,[6] *m.* —— Rolland.
ii. William.[6]
iii. Benjamin.[6]
iv. Caroline.[6]
v. John.[6]
vi. Joseph.[6]

Issue of James and Betsy[5] (Minter) *Major*:

i. Thomas.[6]
ii. Benjamin,[6] *m.* Sallie Leftwich. Issue: i. Sallie;[7] ii. Benjamin;[7] iii. Lelia;[7] iv. Emma.[7]
iii. Joseph,[6] *m.* Jane Boone. Issue: i. Elizabeth;[7] ii. Joseph;[7] iii. Alfred;[7] iv. Catherine;[7] v. Boone;[7] vi. Mary;[7] vii. Agnes;[7] viii. Susan.[7]
iv. James,[6] *m.* Kate Allen. Issue: i. Mary;[7] ii. John;[7] iii. Harriet;[7] iv. Benjamin;[7] v. James.[7]
v. Jane,[6] *m.* Albert *Branham.* Issue: i. John T.;[7] ii. Ellen;[7] iii. Sallie;[7] iv. Laura;[7] v. Mary;[7] vi. Olivia;[7] vii. Albert;[7] viii. Alvin.[7]
vi. William,[6] *m.* A. McCarton. Issue: i. Ida;[7] ii. George;[7] iii. Florence;[7] iv. Eleanor.[7]

Issue of William[5] and Elizabeth C. (Waggoner) *Minter*:

i. William Garnett.[6]
ii. Martha J.,[6] *b.* 1811; compiled a "Dupuy Tree"; *m.* Wiliam H. *Stovall.* Issue: i. Elizabeth,[7] *m.* J. M. Gregory;

ii. James K. B.;^{7} iii. George A.,^{7} *m.* L. Williams; iv. William H.^{7}

iii. Lemira,^{6} *m.* R. A. *Parker.* Issue: i. S. Elizabeth,^{7} *m.* J. D. Beattie; ii. Thomas;^{7} iii. William Garnett;^{7} iv. Robert A.,^{7} *m.* S. Flowers; v. Walter,^{7} *m.* —— Burr; vi. Lou Kay,^{7} *m.* —— Henry; vii. Mary,^{7} *d.* September, 1865; viii. Lemira,^{7} *m.* —— Clapp; ix. Arthur,^{7} *m.* —— Berry; x. Minter,^{7} *m.* —— Pillow.

iv. Rose,^{6} *m.* twice; 1st, William *Eagle.* (Issue: William^{7}); 2d, J. W. Fowler.

v. Eliza J.^{6}

vi. Sarah A.,^{6} *m.* Dr. R. H. *Lewis.* Lives in Texas. Issue: i. Rosa;^{7} ii. Mary,^{7} *m.* —— Holman; iii. Charles,^{7} *m.* —— Elenan; iv. Lemira,^{7} *m.* —— Frank; v. Joseph;^{7} vi. Roberta,^{7} *m.* —— Hall; vii. William;^{7} viii. Bailie Peyton;^{7} ix. Robert H.^{7}

vii. Louisa,^{6} *m.* G. B. *Goodwin.* Issue: i. John E.;^{7} ii. George;^{7} iii. Annie;^{7} iv. Louisa;^{7} v. Albert F.;^{7} vi. William;^{7} vii. Arthur;^{7} viii. Mary;^{7} ix. Martha;^{7} x. Lemira^{7}

viii. Mary,^{6} *m.* W. S. *Rainey.* Issue: i. Sallie;^{7} ii. Mary L.;^{7} iii. Walter;^{7} iv. Horace;^{7} v. W. S.;^{7} vi. William Garnett;^{7} vii. and viii. twins—George,^{7} and Jessie G.;^{7} ix. Joseph M.;^{7} x. Isaac Nelson.^{7}

Issue of John^{5} and Elizabeth (Scarce) *Minter:*

i. Benjamin Franklin.^{6}

ii. Henrietta,^{6} *m.* —— *Owens.* Issue: i. Catherine;^{7} ii. Anne.^{7}

iii. Jeptha,^{6} *m.* Lavinia Minor. Issue: John Mills.^{7}

iv. George.^{6}

v. George,^{6} *m. twice:* 1st, C. Dicky; 2d, L. Ware. Issue: i. William;^{7} ii. Sarah,^{7} *m.* —— *House* (issue, Zella T.^{8}); iii. James F.;^{7} iv. Eugenia C.;^{7} v. Leonida A.;^{7} vi. Thomas S.;^{7} vii. Anna S.^{7}

vi. Jane,^{6} *m.* —— *Lowry.* Issue: i. John;^{7} ii. Jane;^{7} iii. Elizabeth.^{7}

vii. Martha,^{6} *m.* —— *Key.* Issue: i. Minter P.;^{7} ii. Wellington A.;^{7} iii. Walter;^{7} iv. John F.;^{7} v. Fannie;^{7} vi. Martha A.;^{7} vii. Mary E.;^{7} viii. Maggie;^{7} ix. Annetta.^{7}

viii. Margaret,^{6} *m.* —— *Terry.* Issue: Catherine.^{7}

Issue of Josiah and Martha^{4} (Trabue) *Wooldridge:*

i. Seth.^{5}

ii. Daniel,[5] *m.* ——

iii. Samuel.[5]

iv. Patsy,[5] *m.* —— Cheatham.

v. Polly,[5] *m.* Joseph White.

vi. Claiborne,[5] *m.* ——

vii. Stephen.[5]

viii. Josiah[5].

ix. Judith,[5] *m.* J. Trabue.

x. Levi.[5]

Issue of Joseph and Polly[5] (Wooldridge) *White :*

i. Oscar,[6] *m.* —— McMullin. Issue: Oscar.[7]

ii. Elizabeth,[6] *m.* Egbert Wooldridge.

iii. Amanda,[6] *m.* James Gregory.

iv. Sarah,[6] *m.* J. H. Hickman.

Issue of Egbert and Elizabeth[6] (White) *Wooldridge :*

i. Oscar.[7]

ii. Charles.[7]

iii. Egbert.[7]

iv. William.[7]

v. Albert.[7]

vi. Margaret.[7]

vii. Harriet,[7] *m.* J. G. Simpson.

viii. Mary,[7] *m.* T. J. Latham.

Issue of J. H. and Sarah[6] (White) *Hickman :*

i. Louisa.[7]

ii. Sarah.[7]

iii. Fannie.[7]

iv. Harrison,[7] *m.* Sarah Brooks.

v. Linwood.[7]

Issue of James and Amanda[6] (White) *Gregory :*

i. Lou.[7]

ii. Mary.[7]

iii. Elizabeth.[7]

iv. Edgar.[7]

v. Fanny.[7]

vi. Charles.[7]

vii. Hortense.[7]

Issue of Bartholomew[3] and Mary (Mottley) *Dupuy :*

i. Achsa,[4] *m.* Benjamin Davis. Both died with the cholera in 1822.

ii. Susan.[4]
iii. Joel,[4] *m.* Lucy Craig.
iv. Betsy,[4] *m.* —— Fogg.
v. John.[4]
vi. Judith,[4] *m.* —— Samuel.
vii. Sallie,[4] *m.* Poindexter Thomason.
viii. James.[4]
ix. Nancy,[4] *m.* A. McClure.
x. Martha,[4] *m.* Colonel Abram Owen, who was killed at the battle of Tippecanoe in 1844.
xi. Joseph,[4] *m.* Nancy Peay (or Dupuy).

Issue of —— and Betsy[4] (Dupuy) *Fogg*:
i. Mary,[5] *m.* Rev. Joseph Taylor.
ii. John.[5]
iii. Elizabeth.[5]
iv. Benjamin.[5]
v. Joel.[5]
vi. Dione.[5]
vii. Lucy.[5]
viii. Joseph.[5]

Issue of —— and Judith[4] (Dupuy) *Samuel*:
i. Washington,[5] *m.* —— Grey. Issue: i. Eleanor;[6] ii. Benjamin;[6] iii. Edmond.[6]
ii. Mary,[5] *m.* —— *Suggett.* Issue: i. Lucy;[6] ii. Judith;[6] iii. Benjamin;[6] iv. Samuel.[6]

Issue of —— and Sallie[4] (Dupuy) *Thomason*:
i. Elias,[5] *m.* —— Snead.
ii. John,[5] *m.* —— Coleman.
iii. Dupuy.[5]
iv. Nelson.[5]
v. Joel,[5] *m.* —— *Kelley.* Issue: i. William;[6] ii. Sarah;[6] iii. Harriet.[6]
vi. William,[5] *m.* —— Leonard. Issue: i. Nelson;[6] ii. Charles;[6] iii. Cornelius;[6] iv. Laura;[6] v. John;[6] vi. Martin;[6] vii. Rankin,[6] *m.* Sarah ——.
vii. Joseph,[5] *m.* Martha Bartlett, and had issue: i. Henrietta;[6] ii, John;[6] iii. Joseph;[6] iv. Georgiana;[6] v. Martha,[6] (*m.* H. *Buckley.* Issue: Reuben.[7]) vi. Mary,[6] (*m.* Thomas *Hayden.* Issue: i. Joel;[7] ii. Martha;[7] iii. John;[7]) vii. Sallie,[6] *m.* *Rodman.* Issue: i. John;[7] ii. James;[7] iii. Martha.[7]

Issue of A. and Nancy[4] (Dupuy) *McClure:*

i. Abram.[5]
ii. Mary,[5] *m.* —— Campbell.
iii. Samuel.[5]
iv. Alexander,[5] *m.* —— Webb.
v. William.[5]
vi. Bartlett,[5] *m.* Miss Ashby. Issue: four children. The family moved to Texas, where Mrs. McClure killed three Comanche Indians in defence of herself and children, in the absence of her husband.
vii. Achsa,[5] *m.* —— Bacy (or Bosey).

Issue of Colonel Abram and Martha[4] (Dupuy) *Owen:*

i. James,[5] *d.* in Texas.
ii. Clark,[5] *m.* Laura Wells. Issue: i. Jane;[6] ii. Abram;[6] iii. Martha;[6] iv. Laura;[6] v. James.[6]
iii. Harriet,[5] *m.* Thomas Smith.
iv. Nancy,[5] *m.* —— Woolfolk.
v. Elizabeth,[5] *m.* Daniel Brannon.
vi. Lucy,[5] *m.* William Smith.
vii. Susan,[5] *m.* Henry Allen.

Issue of Thomas and Harriet[5] (Owen) *Smith:*

i. William.[6]
ii. Betty.[6]
iii. James.[6]
iv. Joseph.[6]
v. Clark Owen.[6]
vi. Nicholas.[6]
vii. Thomas D.[6]
viii. Harriet,[6] *m.* W. *Rowland.* Issue: Thomas.[7]
ix. Abram,[6] *m,* —— Hunter. Issue: i. Robert;[7] ii. Harriet;[7] iii. Janney;[7] iv. Martha;[7] v. Thomas;[7] vi. Abram;[7] vii. Owen.[7]
x. Martha Ann,[6] *m. G. W. Rowland.* Issue: i. and ii. Thos. Smith[7] and George[7] (twins); iii. Martha;[7] iv. Bettie.[7]

Issue of —— and Nancy[5] (Owen) *Woolfolk:*

i Robert.[6]
ii. George.[6]
iii. James.[6]
iv. Martha,[6] *m.* —— Winston.

Issue of Daniel and Elizabeth[5] (Owen) *Brannon*:

i. Clarke.[6]
ii. Catherine.[6]
iii. Elizabeth.[6]
iv. Webster.[6]
v. Georgiana,[6] *m.* S. Summers.
vi. John S.,[6] *m.* twice: 1st, C. Craig; 2d, M. Craig. Issue: i. Daniel;[7] ii. Grosvenor.[7]
vii. James,[6] *m.* Miss McRoberts. Issue: i. Laura;[7] ii. Daniel;[7] iii. Isaac.[7]
viii. Marianna,[6] *m.* —— *Hilliard.* Issue: i. Edwin;[7] ii. Isaac.[7]
ix. Abram,[6] *m.* twice: 1st, S. Roberts; 2d, E. Roberts. Issue: i. James;[7] ii. Laura;[7] iii. Bettie;[7] iv. Lucy James,[7] *m.* William Smith; v. Susan;[7] vi. Anne.[7]
x. Josephine,[6] *m.* E. Simmons.

Issue of William and Lucy[5] (Owen) *Smith*:

i. Susan.[6]
ii. Anne.[6]
iii. Martha.[6]
iv. James.[6]

Issue of Henry and Susan[5] (Owen) *Allen*:

i. David.[6]
ii. Elizabeth.[6]
iii. Henry.[6]
iv. Martin.[6]
v. Lucy.[6]
vi. James.[6]
vii. Abram.[6]

Issue of Joseph[4] and Nancy (Peay or Dupuy) *Dupuy*:

i. Bartlett.[5]
ii. Perry,[5] emigrated to Texas.
iii. Martha,[5] *m.* Edward *Branham.* Issue: i. Thomas;[6] ii. Joseph.[6]
iv. Anne,[5] *m.* —— *Brinker.* Issue: Mary,[6] *m.* —— Prior.
v. Mildred,[5] *m.* —— *Smith.* Issue: Zachary.[6]
vi. Cola,[5] *m* Dr. *Drane.* Issue: i. Edward;[6] ii. George G.;[6] iii. Martha,[6] *m.* —— Lane; iv. Agnes,[6] *m.* R. Logan; v. Joseph,[6] *m.* —— McGill.

vii. Austin,[5] *m.* Lucy Jane Thomas. Issue: i. Lucy Jane;[6] ii. Joseph;[6] iii. Rowland;[6] iv. Fannie;[6] v. Austin;[6] vi. Bartlett;[6] vii. Mary.[6]

Issue of Rev. John[3] and Elizabeth (Minter) *Dupuy:*

i. John,[4]
ii. Jane,[4]
iii. Tabitha,[4]
} Perished with cold in the Rocky Mountains.

iv. Lucy,[4] *m.* Rev. William Boggs, of Scotland.
v. Samuel,[4] *m.* Mary Ann Fawcett.
vi. Minter,[4] *m.* Mary Heifley.
vii. Elizabeth,[4] *m.* Samuel Rowzie.
viii. Benjamin F.[4] *m.* Mary Fawcett.
ix. Anne,[4] *m.* John Evans.
x. Martha,[4] *m.* Thomas Elley.

Issue of Samuel[4] and Mary Anne (Fawcett) *Dupuy:*

i. Josephine,[5] *d.* in infancy.
ii. John,[5] *d.* in infancy.
iii. Joseph Fawcett,[5] *d.* in infancy.
iv. Elizabeth Minter,[5] *m.* H. D. Ratcliffe, of Louisiana.
v. Samuel,[5] *d.* in Laracca, Texas.
vi. Emily.[5]
vii. Amanda,[5] *m.* C. A. Gosa.
viii. Louis Edward,[5] of St. Louis, Missouri.
ix. Mary Anne,[5] *m.* G. W. *Gosa.* Issue: i. Lewis;[6] ii. Georgiana;[6] iii. Franklin.[6]
x. Webster.[5]
xi. Maria Louisa,[5] *m.* Daniel Brannan.

Issue of C. A. and Amanda[5] (Dupuy) *Gosa:*

i. Louis.[6]
ii. Aaron.[6]
iii. S. Dupuy.[6]
iv. Elizabeth.[6]
v. George.[6]
vi. Emma.[6]
vii. Marianne.[6]

Issue of Daniel and Maria Louisa[5] (Dupuy) *Brannan:*

i. Louis E.[6]
ii. Ann Fawcett.[6]

iii. Elizabeth.[6]
iv Samuel Dupuy.[6]
v. Ellen.[6]
vi. Sallie.[6]

Issue of Minter and Mary[4] (Heifley) *Dupuy*:

i. Catharine.[5]
ii. William.[5]
iii. John.[5]
iv. Ferdinand.[5]
v. Benjamin.[5]
vi. Elizabeth.[5]
vii. Joseph.[5]

Issue of Samuel and Elizabeth[4] (Dupuy) *Rowzie*:

i. Merritt.[5]
ii. Samuel,[5] *m.* —— Whiteside.
iii. William,[5] *m.* —— Robert and lives in Philadelphia.
iv. Western,[5] *m.* A. Webster Watson.
v. Maria,[5] *m.* Louis Western.
vi. Eliza,[5] *m.* twice: 1st, —— Lewis; 2d, —— *Watkins*, and had by last, John.[6]
vii. Mary,[5] *m.* R. Owen.

Issue of William[5] and —— (Robert) *Dupuy*:

i. Robert.[6]
ii. Mary,[6] *m.* —— *Smith* and had issue, Western Rowzie.[7]

Issue of Louis and Maria[5] (Dupuy) *Western*:

i. John.[6]
ii. Robert.[6]
iii. William.[6]
iv. Louis Western.[6]
v. Eliza.[6]
vi. Lucy Jane.[6]

Issue of Benjamin F.[4] and Mary (Fawcett) *Dupuy*:

i. Benjamin Rush.[5]
ii. Mary Eliza.[5]
iii. Joseph F.[5]
iv. Augusta,[5] *m.* Rev. W. Dodge, of Illinois.
v. Julia Cecilia,[5] *m.* —— Caldwell, of Indiana.

Issue of Rev. W. and Augusta[5] (Dupuy) *Dodge*:

i. Henry Varick.[6]
ii. Helen M.[6]
iii. Jane Varick.[6]
iv. Mary Alice.[6]
v. B. F. Dupuy.[6]

Issue of —— and Julia Cecilia[5] (Dupuy) *Caldwell*:

i. Dupuy.[6]
ii. Mary Fawcett.[6]
iii. Franklin Dupuy.[6]
iv. Joseph Moffatt.[6]

Issue of John[5] and Anne (Dupuy) *Evans*:

i. Robert.[6]
ii. Alexander.[6]
iii. Ferdinand.[6]
iv. Susan.[6]
v. John,[6] *m.* ——, and had issue: i. Lilla;[7] ii. Mary;[7] iii. William;[7] iv. Alice;[7] v. Annie.[7]

Issue of Thomas and Martha[4] (Dupuy) *Elley*:

i. Henry.[5]
ii. Beverley.[5]
iii. George,[5] *m.* thrice: 1st, E. Allen; 2d, P. Holloway; 3d, A. Gist.
iv. Martha,[5] *m.* W. Robinson.
v. Eliza,[5] *m.* twice: 1st, M. Long; 2d, —— Walker. Issue: i. Ella;[6] ii. Thomas;[6] iii. John;[6] iv. Patrick Henry.[6]
vi. Mary Anne,[5] *m.* A. *Cosby*, and had issue: i. Caroline,[6] *m.* —— Tucker; ii. Mary;[6] iii. Henry;[6] iv. William;[6] v. George;[6] vi. Robert.[6]

Issue of James[3] and Anne (Starke) *Dupuy*:

i. Anne.[4]
ii. Jane,[4] *m.* —— Fields.
iii. Sallie,[4] *m.* —— Waddey.
iv. William,[4] *m.* Maria Newton.
v. Eliza Bomar,[4] *m.* Dr. *Shannon*, of Illinois. Issue: Albert,[5] *m.* S. J. Ready, and had issue, Thomas.[6]
vi. Susan,[4] *m.* —— *Richardson*. Issue: Nathaniel.[5]
vii. Starke,[4] *m.* Anne Webber.

viii. Lemuel W.,[4] *m.* twice: 1st, Lucinda Ann Smith; 2d, Mary Jane Stevenson.

ix. Ebenezer,[4] *m.* twice: 1st, —— Hickerson; 2d, —— Chinn.

x. James,[4] *m.* —— Maxwell.

xi. Ellen,[4] *m.* —— *Shannon.* Issue: Albert.[5]

Issue of Starke[4] and Anne (Webber) *Dupuy:*

i. Philip, } Twins.[5]
ii. Austin, }

iii. Eliza,[5] *m.* —— Ross.

iv. Starke,[5] *m.* —— Webber.

v. Rhodes,[5] *m.* Mary Gwyank.

vi. Whitfield,[5] *m.* —— Wall.

vii. Anne,[5] *m.* —— *Ross,* and had issue: i. Martha;[6] ii. Sarah;[6] iii. Thaddeus;[6] iv. Thomas.[6]

Issue of Lemuel W.[4] *Dupuy:*

i. James Robertson,[5] *m.* February 24, 1863, Florence Mary Low, and had issue: i. Robert Gay;[6] ii. Andrew Low.[6]

Issue of Ebenezer[4] *Dupuy:*

i. Albert.[5]

ii. Huldah.[5]

iii. Bettie.[5]

iv. James.[5]

v. John.[5]

Issue of James[4] and —— (Maxwell) *Dupuy:*

i. Nathaniel,[5] *m.* —— Bate.

ii. Napoleon.[5]

iii. Jane,[5] *m.* —— Davidson.

A PARTIAL LIST OF THE DESCENDANTS

OF

REV. JAMES MARYE.[a]

Rev. James Marye, a native of Rouen, Normandy, France, the second son of a wealthy and worthy parentage, was educated for and entered the priesthood of the Roman Catholic Church, but scruples as to the correctness of the tenets and practices of that faith, led him, in 1726, to flee to England, abjure it and to be ordained in the Protestant Episcopal Church. This act occasioned a breach between himself and his immediate relatives in France, who consisted of a widowed mother, an elder brother, Peter, and a younger, William, an officer in the French army. and as he could not conscientiously accede to their commands to return and re-enter the priesthood, communication with them ceased. In October, 1728, Mr. Marye married in London Miss Letitia Maria Ann Staige, the daughter of a deceased clergyman of the Established Church, and the sister of Rev. Theodosius Staige.[b] In September, 1729, Mr. Marye with his wife embarked for Virginia. His first child was born on the

---

a Prepared chiefly from data kindly supplied by Hon. J. L. Marye, Fredericksburg, Virginia.

b Rev. Theodosius Staige came, with an unmarried sister, to Virginia, and was the rector of St. George's parish, Spotsylvania county, some time prior to November, 1728. A daughter married Samuel Thompson, Orange county, and they had issue, among others possibly, a son, William Staige. The name Staige is a favored Christian name in the Davis and other families of Virginia. A distinguished instance was the late Professor John Staige Davis, M. D., of the University of Virginia.

passage across the Atlantic. He appears to have been called to the charge of the parish of St. James' Northam, Goochland county, soon after his arrival in Virginia, as "Mr. Marie, of St. James'" officiated at a christening at Manakin-town May 20th, 1730.[c] He continued in this first useful and extended ministry, supplying several churches, until called to a second,[d] that of St. George's parish, Spotsylvania, into which, upon the petition of its vestry to Governor Gooch, he was inducted in October, 1735. Here he acceptably and faithfully labored until his death in 1767, when he was succeeded by his son, Rev. James Marye, Jr. Two chapels were built by the efforts of Rev. James Marye, Sr. The farm, "Fayetteville," eight miles distant from Fredericksburg, which he purchased, and upon which he resided until his death,[e] and upon which he was buried, remains in the possession of his descendants.

Issue of Rev. James[1] and Letitia Maria Ann (Staige) *Marye:*

i. Lucy Mary,[2] *b.* 10th October, 1729, on the Atlantic Ocean; *m.* twice; 1st, Rev. Mungo Marshall; 2d, James Marsden, M. D.

ii. Rev. James,[2] *b.* 8th September, 1731; educated in England; Minister of St. Thomas' parish, Orange county, from 1761 to 1767 when he succeeded his father in St. George's parish, and served there until his death in 1780; "buried at Fayetteville;" *m.* twice; 1st, Letitia Courtney; 2d, Elizabeth, *née* Osborne, widow of —— Grayson, Loudoun county.

iii. William,[2] *b.* 6th April, 1733; graduated M. D. in Edinburgh; served as surgeon for three years on an East Indiaman; *d.* unmarried at Gravesend, England, on the eve of embarking for Virginia.

iv. Susanna,[2] *b.* 17th June, 1735; *m.* Dr. Henry *Heath*, and had issue, James.[3]

---

c See *Ante* p. 84.

d Leaving "the Huguenot settlement at Manikin town." *Meade's Old Churches and Families of Virginia*, II, p. 69.

e This is the family tradition; but in the State Land Office is recorded a grant to him of 400 acres in Spotsylvania county, 15th March, 1744. Book 23, p. 801.

v. Peter,[2] *b.* 20th February, 1737; graduate William and Mary College, Virginia; Member of House of Burgesses from Spotsylvania county, 1769; *m.* 6th December, 1773, Eleanor, daughter of Colonel William and Anne (Coleman) Green,[f] of Culpeper county, and settled on Hazel river, in that county, one mile from State Mills.

---

f William Green was the son of Robert Green, *b.* 1695 (son of William Green, a member of the Body Guard of King William III, of England), who migrated to Virginia about 1717, with his uncle, William Duff, a Quaker, and settled in what is now King George county. They became partners of Joist Hite and Robert McKay, who had warrants (1731) for locating 140,000 acres of land. Hence the firm of Hite, McKay, Green and Duff. In 1736, Lord Fairfax entered a *caveat* against Hite, alleging that these lands were within the Northern Neck, and hence his property. This led to the suit of Hite & Co. against Fairfax, which was not decided until 1786, when all the parties to it were dead. The representatives of Hite & Co. recovered a large sum of money and extensive tracts of land. Robert Green, who was the heir of his uncle, William Duff, *m.* Eleanor Dunn, of Scotland, and settled in Culpeper county. They had issue:

i. Colonel William, of the text, who left issue eight children: William; Francis Wyatt, *m.* Lucy Strother and removed to Kentucky; Eleanor, of the text; Anne, *m.* John Poindexter, Louisa county; Eliabeth, *m.* Henry Camp; Nancy, *m.* George Thomas; Mildred, *m.* —— Stringer; Susanna, *d.* unmarried; Lucy, *m.* James Madesette, Shenandoah county.

ii. Colonel Robert, *m.* Patty Ball, of Northumberland county. Issue, five children.

iii. Duff, *m.* twice: 1st, Miss Thomas; 2d, Anne, daughter of Major Henry Willis, of Fredericksburg, Virginia.

iv. John, Colonel in the Revolution, distinguished at Brandywine, Monmouth and Guilford; *m.* Susanna Blackwell. They were the parents of William, and grandparents of Judge John William Green, of the Supreme Court of Appeals of Virginia, *who* was the father of the late eminent Hon. William Green, LL.D., and of seven other highly worthy sons.

v. Nicholas.

vi. James.

vii. Moses.

See *Memoir of William Green, LL.D.*, by Rev. Philip Slaughter, D. D., Richmond, 1883.

Issue of Rev. Mungo and Lucy Mary[2] (Marye) *Marshall:*

i. James,[3] educated in Europe; *d.* unmarried.
ii. Lucy,[3] *m* John Daniel, Orange county; *d. s. p.*
iii. William,[3] graduated M. D. at Edinburgh, Scotland; practiced in Virginia; *d. s. p.*.
iv. Susanna,[3] *m.* Alexander Gordon, a native of Scotland.

Issue by his two marriages of Rev. James[2] Marye:

i. James,[3] *m.* Mildred, daughter of Lawrence Slaughter, Culpeper county.
ii. Lucy,[3] *m.* James Weir.

---

iii. Elizabeth,[3] *m.* Rev. —— Dunn.
iv. Nancy,[3] *m.* Yeoman Smith, who *d.* 1848.
v. Letitia,[3] *m.* Thomas B. Adams, merchant, Fredericksburg, Virginia.

Issue of James[3] and Mildred (Slaughter) *Marye:*

i. Robert V.,[4] *b.* 1798; removed to Shreveport, Louisiana; *m.* ——.
ii. John Lawrence,[4] *b.* ——; *d.* —, 1868; lawyer of Fredericksburg, Virginia; member of the Virginia Convention of 1860–'61, which passed the ordinance of secession; *m.* Anne Maria, daughter of Dr. Robert Burton, Buckingham county. He purchased in 1825 the "Brompton" premises, which, as "Marye's Heights," are historically famous through the events of the late war between the States. Upon the first range of hills, distant about three-fourths of a mile west of Fredericksburg, Mr. Marye built, in 1838, the large brick mansion, in which he resided until his death. An extensive lawn slopes from it to the public road which is bounded by the noted "stone fence," which afforded a breastwork for the Confederate infantry, who, supported by artillery posted on "Marye's Heights," signally repulsed the repeated desperate assaults of Burnside's army, December 12th, 1862. The mansion still bears the marks of the serious damage then inflicted by shot, shell, and minie-ball.[g]

---

g Marye's Heights was the scene recently of a somewhat interesting event. The press chronicled the marriage there, December 17, 1885, of

iii. Catherine Matilda,[4] *b.* ——; *m.* —— Beatty, Spotsylvania county, and removed to Caddo parish, Louisiana. Issue.

iv. Mildred Slaughter,[4] *b.* ——; *m.* twice; 1st, —— Blackwell; 2d, —— Cunliffe; removed to Caddo parish, Louisiana.

v. Elizabeth Letitia,[4] *b.* ——; *m.* —— Cunliffe and removed to Noxan county, Mississippi.

vi. Frances Anne,[4] *b.*——.

Issue of John Lawrence[4] and Anne Maria (Burton) *Marye:*

i. James Braxton,[5] *b.* ——; educated at the University of Virginia; graduated M. D. from the University of Pennsylvania in 1839, and has pursued that calling; *m.* Jane Christian, daughter of William Starke Jett, of Westmoreland county, Virginia. Issue: i. William N.;[6] ii. Robert;[6] iii. James B.;[6] iv. Anne M.;[6] v. Mary.[6]

ii. Robert Burton,[5] *b.* ——, 1819; educated at the University of Virginia; lawyer and farmer in Orange county, Virginia; Major and Quartermaster Confederate States Army, 1861–'65; *m.* twice: 1st, Mary, daughter of Major Ambrose Madison, of Orange county, Virginia, a nephew of President James Madison; 2d, Mrs. Jane Tunstall *née* Waller, of Norfolk, Virginia; *d.* 25th May, 1881, at Chattanooga, Tennessee. Issue by 1st *m.:* i. Alfred J.;[6] ii. Ambrose M.;[6] by 2d. *m.:* iii. Littleton W. T.;[6] iv. Margaret.[6]

iii. John Lawrence,[5] *b.* ——; was educated at the Academy in Fredericksburg and Concord Academy, Caroline county, Virginia; graduated A. B. and B. L. University of Virginia; has been a practicing lawyer in Fredericksburg, Virginia, since 1845; *m.* Mildred Stone, daughter of Dr. William Browne, of Fredericksburg; member of the Virginia Legislature, 1863–'65; of State Constitutional Convention in 1867; Lieutenant-Governor of Virginia

---

a romantic couple from New Jersey—one D. Emmons, an ex-Federal soldier, and Miss E. Eldridge. The groom declaring that having failed to take "The Heights" under Burnside, he was determined that the goal so desperately contended for then should now, in days of bounteous peace and good-will, witness the consummation of his greatest bliss.

1870–'73. Issue: i. Emily S.;[6] ii. William B.;[6] iii. Maria B.;[6] iv. Raleigh Travers;[6] v. John L.[6]

iv. Morton,[5] *b.* ——; *m* Homoisel, daughter of Robert Voss, of Rappahannock county, Virginia; entered Confederate States Army as Captain of the "Alexandria Rifles" in 1861; promoted Colonel Seventeenth Virginia Infantry in 1862; lost a leg at the Second Battle of Manassas; clerk of the Circuit and Corporation Courts of Alexandria, Virginia, 1870–1883; elected Auditor of Virginia in 1883, which position he still holds. Issue: i. Burton;[6] ii. Mary;[6] iii. Edward A.;[6] iv. Robert V.;[6] v. Morton;[6] vi. Mary Thornton,[6] *m.* February 15, 1884, J. S. B. Thómpson.

v. Lawrence Slaughter,[5] *b.* ——; educated at the University of Virginia; *m.* Maria W., daughter of John P. Wilson, of "Bonbrook," Cumberland county, Virginia; entered Confederate States Army as Lieutenant of the Hampden Artillery in 1861; served as Major on the staff of General W. W. Loring and that of General John C. Pemberton; has practiced law at Richmond, Memphis, Tenn., and at Lynchburg, where he has resided for the past eight years. He has for some months past also edited the Lynchburg *Virginian.* Has no issue.

vi. Edward Avenmore,[5] *b.* ——; never married; served in the Confederate States Army, first as Lieutenant of the Braxton Artillery; promoted Captain, and whilst thus serving in the siege of Petersburg, *d.* ——, 1864, from disease contracted in the trenches.

vii. Anne Maria,[5] *b.* ——; *m.* Robert Dabney, of Powhatan county (who served in the Confederate States Army as Lieutenant of the Powhatan Troop; was member of the Virginia Legislature 1863–'4; Professor of Mental Science in the University of the South at Sewanee, Tennessee, from 1872 until his death in 1877). Issue: i. William Pope;[6] ii. Marye;[6] iii. Lucy K.;[6] iv. Cary S.;[6] v. Evelyn;[6] vi. Anne M.;[6] vii. Robert.[6]

viii. Evelyn,[5] *b.* ——; unmarried.

ix. Charles Bonnycastle,[5] *b.* ——; served in the Braxton Artillery, Confederate States Army, from 1862 until the end of the war; unmarried.

x. Alexander Stuart,[5] *b.* ——; served in the Braxton Artillery, 1861–'5; unmarried; educated as a teacher and pursues that calling.

Issue of Yeoman and Nancy[3] (Marye) *Smith:*

i. Samuel,[4] *b.* ——; graduate B. A. and B. L. University of Virginia; removed to Hinds county, Mississippi; lawyer; *m.* ——.

ii. Elizabeth,[4] *b.* ——; *m.* George Dabney, Spotsylvania county, now Probate Judge of Hinds county, Mississippi.

iii. Letitia,[4] *b.* ——. Lives in Fredericksburg, Virginia.

iv. William Marye,[4] M. D., *b.* ——. Lives in Fredericksburg, Virginia.

v. Julia Bell,[4] *b.* ——; *m.* R. W. Marriott, Baltimore, Maryland.

vi. Mary Osborne,[4] *b.* ——; *m.* J. L. Stansberry, Fredericksburg, Virginia.

Issue of Peter[2] and Eleanor (Green) *Marye:*

i. William Staige,[3] *b.* at Colonel William Green's, near Culpeper Courthouse, 15th February, 1775; educated at William and Mary College; wrote a collection of sacred songs; *m.* 6th May, 1802, Mary (*b.* 25th April, 1785; *d.* 26th December, 1852), daughter Peter Ruffner, Shenandoah county; settled at "Hillside," Shenandoah county; *d.* 28th September, 1837. Buried with his wife in the Ruffner burying ground, Shenandoah county.

ii. James Theodosius,[3] M. D., *b.* ——; *m.* at the age of 50 Miss Bush, Orange county. Both dead.

iii. Mildred,[3] *b.* ——; *m.* Marshall Gordon, Culpeper county.

iv. Susanna,[3] *b.* ——; *d.* unmarried.

v. Lucy,[3] *b.* ——; *m.* James Madesette, Shenandoah county.

Issue of William Staige[3] and Mary (Ruffner) *Marye:*

i. Elizabeth,[4] *b.* 17th June, 1803; *m.* Joseph R. Sibert, Shenandoah county. Issue.

ii. Eleanor,[4] *b.* 21st October, 1804; *m.* John Sibert, and had issue; *d.* ——, 1853, at Woodstock, Virginia.

iii. Peter,[4] *b.* 24th January, 1807; *d.* 6th April, 1831.

iv. William Staige,[4] *b.* 22d July, 1808; *d.* 3d February, 1812.

v. Diana,[4] *b.* 20th October, 1809; *m.* Major Joel Ruffner, Kanawha county, West Virginia; *d.* October, 1881. Issue: 16 children.

vi. Frederick Augustus,[4] *b.* 2d May, 1811; *m.* Letitia Booton, Page county, Virginia; removed to Cooper county, Missouri. Issue.

vii. John Green Ruffner,[4] *b.* 12th February, 1813; *d.* 11th August, 1828.

viii. James Theodosius,[4] *b.* 19th December, 1814; *m.* 1839, in Port Gibson, Mississippi, Mary Passmore Hoopes; *b.* ——, 1818, in Westchester, Pennsylvania, of Quaker parents.

ix. Anne Maria,[4] *b.* 13th October, 1816; *d.* 11th February, 1817.

x. George Thomas,[4] *b.* 23d November, 1817; *m.* 13th July, 1839, Helen, daughter of William A. Tucker, of Baltimore, Maryland; removed to San Francisco, California, in 1849; merchant, contractor and banker; public spirited and highly successful citizen; *d.* December, 1882.

xi. Abram Sowers,[4] *b.* 2d April, 1819; *d.* 24th June, 1827.

xii. Lewis Conner,[4] *b.* 15th March, 1821; *d.* 13th September, 1847, of yellow fever, in New Orleans, Louisiana.

xiii. Mary Anne,[4] *b.* 10th June, 1823; *m.* Joshua Ruffner, Luray, Page county, Virginia.

xiv. Simon Bolivar,[4] *b.* 7th June, 1825; graduated B. A. and B. L. William and Mary College; read law with Judge Yerger; went to Yucatan in 1848 and served as an officer in the revolution there; returned in 1849; went to California, elected first State attorney; removed to Oregon in 1852, from thence to Washington, D. C., where he remained a year, then removed to Memphis, Tennessee, and lived there two years. Finally settled as a practicing lawyer in Bolivar county, Mississippi; *m.* Sarah Chapman, of Portland, Oregon.

xv. Willis Young,[4] *b.* 12th June, 1827; removed to California and engaged in gold mining.

Issue of James Theodosius[4] and Mary Passmore (Hoopes) *Marye:*

i. Anne Eliza.[5]
ii. Theodosius Staige.[5]
iii. Florence Vane.[5]
iv. Orrick Walton.[5]
v. Madie May.[5]

Issue of George Thomas[4] and Helen (Tucker) *Marye:*

i. William A.,[5] *b.* ——; Major United States Army.
ii. George Thomas,[5] *b.* ——; banker, San Francisco, California.
iii. Ada,[5] *b.* ——; *m.* Joseph C. Baily, surgeon, United States Army; *d.* ——, 1882.

CHASTAIN—COCKE.

DESCENDANTS OF

JAMES P. and M. M. (CHASTAIN) COCKE.[a]

It is held by tradition in the well-known Cocke family of the southern and western parts of the United States that its *propositus* in Virginia was Richard[1] Cocke,[b] who emigrated from Leeds, Yorkshire, England, some time prior to 1636, and settled in Henrico county, of which he was the representative in the House of Burgesses, 1644–1654, and some time County-Lieutenant. In virtue of the latter position he was designated Lieutenant-Colonel. His seat, "Malvern Hills," obtained celebrity during the late war between the States as the scene of a sanguinary contest. He *m.* —— and left issue:

---

a The editor gratefully acknowledges his indebtedness to Mrs. Fannie Allan Cocke, Wickliffe, Ballard county, Kentucky, and Thomas M. Cleemann, Esq., Philadelphia, Pennsylvania, for material data contributed by them towards this deduction.

b Richard Cocke, "Gentleman," patented 3,000 acres near the lands of John Pearce, Thomas Hallam and Thomas Harris, in Henrico county; 6th March, 1636, Book No. 1, page 413; 10th March, 1639, 2,000 acres, page 407; 6th December, 1652, 2,842 acres, No. 3, page 133; Richard Cocke, 100 acres on "Chickahomine" river, 24th August, 1664, No. 5, page 12; Richard Cocke, Senior, and John Beauchamp, 2,974 acres on the south side of Chickahominy river, 21st June, 1664, No. 5, page 399; which, after the death of Colonel Cocke, was confirmed to his three sons by Beauchamp. For various contributions towards a Cocke Genealogy, see the Richmond *Standard*, April 3–10, 1880, *et seq.*, to which refer for other descendants of Colonel Richard Cocke than those enumerated here.

i. Thomas,[2] of "Pickthorne Farm," Henrico county, *d.* 1697; *m.* Margaret ——.

ii. Richard,[2] of "Old Man's Creek," Charles City county, *d.* 1706; *m.* Elizabeth ——.

iii. William,[2 c] *d.* February, 1693 [1694]; *m.* Sarah ——.

Issue of Thomas[2] and Margaret (——) *Cocke:*

i. Captain Thomas,[3] appointed sheriff of Henrico county, 1699; *d.* 1707; *m.* ——.

ii. Stephen,[3] sold "Malvern Hills," in 1704 to his nephew, Thomas Cocke; *m.* twice: 1st, Elizabeth ——; 2d, between 1699, 1702, Martha ——.

iii. John,[3] *d.* 1697.

iv. James,[3] *d.* 1697; *m.* Elizabeth Pleasants.[d]

v. William.[3]

vi. Agnes,[3] *m.* —— Harwood.

vii. Temperance,[3] *m.* —— Harwood.

Issue of Captain Thomas[3] and —— (——) *Cocke:*

i. Thomas,[4] of "Malvern Hills."

ii. James Powell,[4] *b.* about 1690; vestryman Henrico parish, 1730–'47; *d.* 1747; *m.* Martha Anderson (?).

iii. Henry.[4]

iv. Brazure,[4] sold "Malvern Hills" to his brother, James Powell Cocke, in 1729.

v. Mary.[4]

vi. Elizabeth.[4]

Issue of James Powell[4] and Martha (Anderson ?) *Cocke:*

i. James Powell,[5] of "Malvern Hills," *m.* Mary Magdalene (*b* ——, 1727), daughter of Dr. Stephen and Martha Chastain, of Manakin-town, Virginia.

ii. Daughter.[5]

---

c In his will he mentions his "mother, Mrs. Mary Clarke."

d Daughter of John Pleasants, of the Society of Friends, who emigrated from Norwich, England, in 1665, in his 25th year; settled at "Curles," James river, Henrico county, and married Jane Tucker. Their descendants embrace, among other estimable names, those of Anderson, Armstrong, Atkinson, Bates, Brooke, Carrington, Carter, Coleman, Eustace, Ladd, Mosby, Mayo, Price, Randolph, Robinson, Rogers, Slaughter, Storrs, Turner and Woodson.

Issue of James Powell[5] and Mary Magdalene (Chastain) *Cocke:*

i Chastain,[6] *b.* 14th March, 1743; *d.* 19th March, 1795; *m.* Martha Field (*b.* 21st December, 1752; *d.* 27th February, 1816), daughter of John and Elizabeth (Royall—her mother a Field) Archer. He was the progenitor of the branch of Cockes of "Clover Pasture," Powhatan county.

ii. James Powell,[6] *b.* ——; died 13th January, 1829; *m.* twice: 1st, 29th November, 1767, Elizabeth Archer (*d.* 1773 without issue); 2d, September, 1777, Lucy Smith (*b.* October, 1756; *d.* 27th February, 1816). Lived at "Malvern Hills."

iii. Stephen,[6] *m.* Jane Segar Eggleston, of Amelia county, sister of Major Joseph Eggleston of the Revolution.

iv. Martha,[6] *m.* William Cannon, of Buckingham county. Issue: "Two sons, who emigrated to the West."

v. Elizabeth Chastain,[6] *m.* Henry *Anderson*, of Amelia county. Issue: Four sons and three daughters.

Issue of Chastain[6] and Martha Field (Archer) *Cocke:*

i. James,[7] *b.* 12th January, 1770; *d.* 17th August, 1825; *m.* Mary Lewis (*b.* November, 1775; *d.* 10th June, 1853) of Williamsburg, Virginia.

ii. William Archer,[7] *b.* 22d December, 1771; *d.* 13th January, 1844; *m.* Catherine Murray Winston (Ronald)[e] (*b.* 18th October, 1771; *d.* 2d March, 1840).

iii. Chastain,[7] *b.* 30th January, 1775; *d.* 1797, at sea.

iv. Bowler,[7] *b.* 15th August, 1777; *d.* 18th August, 1777.

v. Elizabeth Royall,[7] *b.* 14th April, 1778; *d.* 7th September, 1820; *m.* Joseph Royall.[f]

vi. John Field,[7] *b.* 9th April, 1784; *d.* 26th January, 1857; Captain of Cavalry in the war of 1812; *m.* 5th May, 1818, at "Comoton," Powhatan county, Anne Waller Ronald (*b.* 17th February, 1792; *d.* 24th June, 1834).

vii. Mary Magdalene Chastain,[7] *b.* 29th October, 1786; *d.* 23d February, 1802.

---

e Thus communicated; Why so, or what the surname may have been, is only conjecturable.

f "A descendant of a noble Scotch family."

viii. Richard Herbert, M. D.,[7] *b.* 31st August, 1788; *d.* 29th August, 1814; *m.* Eliza, daughter of Colonel Abram Green, Amelia county. No issue.

ix. Joseph Archer,[7] *b.* 15th October, 1790; *d.* 17th October, 1811.

x. Stephen Cannon,[7] *b.* 3d March, 1794; *d.* 7th March, 1795.

Issue of James[7] and Mary (Lewis) *Cocke:*

i. Martha,[8] lives in the family of her sister, Mrs. E. Aubyn Green.

ii. Chastain,[8] *d.* in infancy.

iii. Chastain,[8] *d.* in infancy.

iv. James.[8]

v. John Lewis.[8]

vi. Elizabeth Aubyn,[8] *m.* Armistead Green of "Farm Hill," Amelia county; *d.* ——.

vii. Susan Anne,[8] *d.* in infancy.

viii. Mary Chastain,[8] *d.* in infancy.

ix. Omeron,[8] *d.* in infancy.

x. James Everett.[8]

xi. Frances,[8] }
xii. Richard,[8] } twins; *d.* in infancy.

xiii. Mary Susan,[8] *m.* James Granville, son of Rev. James and Henrietta (Garland) *Boyd*, of Nelson county, an officer in the Confederate States Army, who was killed in battle, leaving issue: James Granville[9] Boyd.

xiv. Richard Herbert[8] *d.* in infancy.

Issue of Armistead and Eliza Aubyn[8] (Cocke) *Green:*

i. Rosalie,[9] *m.* Dr. Richard F., son of Richard and Mary (Harrison, of "Brandon,") *Taylor*, Prince George county, and had issue:

  i. Armistead Green,[10] M. D., *m.* Pattie Harvie, of Amelia county.

  ii. Evelyn Harrison.[10]

  iii. George Keith,[10] *m.* Courtney Harvie of Amelia county.

  iv. Richard Field.[10]

  v. James Aubyn.[10]

  vi. Mary Byrd.[10]

  vii. Rosalie Green.[10]

  viii. Anne Willing.[10]

Issue of William Archer[7] and Catherine Murray (Winston-Ronald) *Cocke:*

i. William Archer,[8] *b.* 20th May, 1796; *d.* 29th August, 1821; *m.* 1st December, 1819, Catherine Murray (*b.* 10th November, 1798; *d.* 25th October, 1878).

ii. Chastain,[8] (1st), *b.* 26th January, 1798; *d.* 1st October, 1798.

iii. Martha Judith,[8] *b.* 26th September, 1799; *d.* 24th February, 1859; *m.* 20th September, 1820, at "Comoton," Powhatan county, Everard Francis Eggleston (*b.* 6th July, 1798; *d.* 6th January, 1857).

iv. Rebecca Bentley,[8] *b.* 5th February, 1801; *d.* August, 1803.

v. Chastain,[8] (2d), *b.* 2d October, 1802; *d.* 26th April, 1860; *m.* twice: 1st, 31st January, 1825, Sallie Meade Eggleston (*b.* 29th January, 1802; *d.* 12th November, 1830); 2d, Mary Eggleston (*b.* 21st January, 1816; *d.* 8th March, 1873).

vi. Mary Magdalene Chastain,[8] *b.* 2d February, 1807; *d.* 17th May, 1880; *m.* James Ligon Saunders (*d.* 5th November, 1871).

Issue of William Archer[8] and Catherine (Murray) *Cocke:*

i. William Alexander,[9] *b.* 17th January, 1821; *d.* 16th September, 1822.

ii. William Archer,[9] *b.* 10th May, 1822; Author of valuable works on Constitutional Law, etc.; Attorney-General of Florida; *m.* 5th April, 1853, Kate Parkhill (*b.* 26th August, 1826). No issue.

Issue of Everard Francis and Martha Judith[8] (Cocke) *Eggleston:*

i. Judith Eggleston,[9] *b.* 24th October, 1821; *d.* 29th October, 1821.

ii. Catherine,[9] *b.* July 1823; *d.* July, 1823.

iii. Joseph,[9] *b.* 27th December, 1827; *d.* 27th September, 1846.

iv. William Archer,[9] *b.* 20th March, 1831; unmarried; served throughout the war in the Confederate States Army.

v. Martha Judith,[9] *b.* 4th February 1835; *m.* 18th April, 1860, at "Egglestetton," Amelia county, William Old, Jr., of Powhatan county, who resigned as editor of the Richmond *Examiner* to enter the Confederate States Army. No issue.

Issue by his two marriages with Sallie Meade Eggleston and Mary Eggleston, of Chastain[8] *Cocke:*

i. Chastain,[9] *b.* ——; *d.* 21st April, 1828.
ii. Josephine,[9] *b.* ——, 1830; *d.* 6th January, 1855; *m.* George William Hobson (nephew of Thomas Deane), of Richmond, Virginia, who was killed in battle, July, 1864.

---

iii. Mary Catherine,[9] *b.* 4th August, 1838; *d.* 12th June, 1840.
iv. Chastain,[9] *b.* 9th February, 1840; in the Confederate States Army; lives in Coffeeville, Mississippi.
v. Bettie Chaffin,[9] *b.* 21st March, 1842; *m.* 6th December, 1877, Luther Ransom; lives in Columbia, South Carolina.
vi. Catherine Archer,[9] *b.* 9th November, 1843; *d.* 6th August, 1848.
vii. Edward Eggleston,[9] *b.* 2d May, 1845; *d.* 24th July, 1869.
viii. Mary Eggleston,[9] *b.* 7th May, 1847; *m.* 28th February, 1871, Robert Edward Wynn; lives in Coffeeville, Mississippi.
ix. Helen Martha,[9] *b.* 15th September, 1849; lives in Columbia, South Carolina.
x. Sallie Meade,[9] *b.* 10th August, 1855; *m.* William Thomas, brother of Robert Edward Wynn; lives in Coffeeville, Mississippi.

Issue of Luther and Bettie Chaffin[9] (Cocke) *Ransom:*

i. Ronald Augustine,[10] *b.* 21st January, 1882.
ii. Mary Eggleston,[10] *b.* ——.

Issue of Robert Edward and Mary Eggleston[9] (Cocke) *Wynn:*

i. Bessie Eggleston,[10] *b.* 30th July, 1873; *d.* 19th May, 1877.
ii. Mary Eppes,[10] *b.* 28th January, 1875; *d.* 11th August, 1882.
iii. Norah Meade,[10] *b.* 23d August, 1877.

Issue of William Thomas and Sallie Meade[9] (Cocke) *Wynn:*

i. Judith Maria,[10] *b.* 1st October, 1876.
ii. Helen Archer,[10] *b.* 15th August, 1877.
iii. Mary Eggleston, } twins,[10] *b.* 1st June, 1882; both *d.* in June,
iv. Emma Clouston, } 1882.

Issue of James Ligon and Mary Magdalene Chastain[8] (Cocke) *Saunders:*

i. William James,[9] *b.* 9th December, 1846; served in the Powhatan Artillery, Confederate States Army, throughout the war; *m.* in Ballard county, Kentucky, Pattie Richardson (*b.* 13th January, 1850; *d.* 2d April, 1883), he living in Alabama. Issue:
   i. James Ligon,[10] *b.* 29th October, 1873; *d.* 4th August, 1874.
   ii. Mary William,[10] *b.* 23d April, 1875.
   iii. Frederick Courtney,[10] *b.* 19th July, 1878.

Issue of Joseph and Elizabeth Royall[7] (Cocke) *Royall:*

i. Joseph Albert,[8] *m.* Mary Bolling Weisiger, Manchester, Virginia. Issue:
   i. Elizabeth Cocke,[9] *d.* young.
   ii. Aubyn Archer,[9] burned to death.
   iii. Mary Alice.[9]
   iv. Sarah Seignora,[9] *m.* George Webb, son of Commodore Webb, of Norfolk, Virginia; *d.* without issue.
   v. Elizabeth Cocke,[9] *m.* John Wallace Powell, of Richmond, Virginia.
   vi. William Segar Archer,[9] *m.* Eliza J. Christian, of Richmond, Virginia. Both dead.
   vii. John Albert,[9] *d.* in infancy.
   viii. Richard Kendall;[9] Confederate States Army; killed at the battle of Ball's Bluff.

Issue of John Wallace and Elizabeth Cocke[9] (Royall) *Powell:*

i. Georgie Webb,[10] *m.* Dr. Lachlan Tyler, son of John Tyler, President of the United States.
ii. John Munford Gregory,[10] *d.* in infancy.
iii. Bessie Wallace.[10]
iv. Mary Archer,[10] *m.* Ashton Todd, son of Rev. —— Todd, of the Protestant Episcopal Church, Maryland.
v. Thos. Wallace.[10]
vi. William Price.[10]

Issue of William Segar[9] and Eliza J. (Christian) *Royall:*

i. Mary Aubyn.[10]

ii. John Powell.[10]
iii. Georgie Wyllie Powell.[10]
iv. William Archer.[10]

Issue of John Field[7] and Anne Waller (Ronald) *Cocke:*

i. Richard Ivanhoe,[8] *b.* 13th August, 1820; *d.* 30th August, 1873; Commonwealth's Attorney of Fluvanna county for years; Member of House of Delegates of Virginia and of Virginia Convention, 1850–'51; entered Confederate States Army as Lieutenant Powhatan Artillery, but had to resign because of feeble health; *m.* at the residence of her mother, corner of Second and Franklin streets, Richmond, Fannie Allan (*b.* 26th May, 1827), daughter of Charles and Margaret K. (Nimmo) Ellis.
ii. Rowena Glowina,[8] *b.* 1st January, 1823; *d.* 17th March, 1861; *m.* Joseph Wade Royall (*d.* 1866).
iii. William Ronald,[8] *b.* 18th August, 1824; *d.* 24th March, 1875; unable to serve in the Confederate States Army, he was detailed to raise provisions for it; after the war, Judge of Fluvanna county until his death; *m.* at "Red Hills," Fluvanna county, Bettie Ragland Boston[g] (*b.* 15th October, 1830).
iv. Amelia Archer,[8] *b.* 27th October, 1826; *d.* 4th January, 1849.

Issue of Richard Ivanhoe[8] and Fannie Allan (Ellis) *Cocke:*

i. John Field,[9] *b.* 7th February, 1849; *m.* 29th October, 1873, in Blandville, Ballard county, Kentucky, Laura A. Hite, (*b.* 28th July, 1853; *d.* 8th January, 1886).
ii. Son,[9] *b.* and *d.* at "Clover Pasture," Powhatan county, Virginia, September, 1862.

Issue of John Field[9] and Laura A. (Hite) *Cocke:*

i. Anna Allan,[10] *b.* 23d July, 1874; *d.* 6th August, 1874.
ii. Richard Ivanhoe,[10] *b.* 31st July, 1877; } Twins. { *d.* 17th April, 1878.
iii. George Washington,[10] *b.* 31st July, 1877; } Twins. { *d.* 1st May, 1878.
iv. Infant,[10] *b.* and *d.* September ——.

---

g A descendant of John and Anne (Beaufort) Ragland, from Glamorganshire, Wales, who settled in that portion of New Kent county which was subsequently Hanover county, in 1705.

Issue of Joseph Wade and Rowena Glowina[8] (Cocke) *Royall*:

i. Ann Elizabeth,[9] *b.* 29th February, 1857; *d.* 7th May, 1877.
ii. Rowena Glowina,[9] *b.* 12th September, 1859.

Issue of William Ronald[8] and Bettie Ragland (Boston) *Cocke*:

i. Amelia Archer,[9] *b.* 12th June, 1851; *m.* 28th October, 1884, William Forbes Churchill, of England.
ii. Bettie Boston,[9] *b.* 22d February, 1853.
iii. William Ronald,[9] *b.* 6th February, 1855.
iv. Clarence Chastain,[9] *b.* 26th September, 1857.
v. Margaret Boston,[9] *b.* 26th October, 1859.
vi. Rowena Glowina,[9] *b.* 4th July, 1861; *m.* 22d August, 1883, Dabney Minor *Trice*, of Albemarle county. Issue: Robert Nelson[10] Trice.
vii. Grace Dudley,[9] *b.* 28th November, 1863.
viii. Blanche Beverley,[9] *b.* 28th July, 1865.
ix. Eloise,[9] *b.* 21st June, 1867.
x. Richard Ivanhoe,[9] *b.* 31st December, 1870.
xi. Ann Waller,[9] *b.* 28th December, 1873.

Issue of James Powell[6] and Lucy (Smith) *Cocke*:

i. James Powell,[7] *b.* 10th October, 1779; *d.* 27th December, 1811; *m.* Martha Ann Lewis (*d.* 4th June, 1856, without issue).
ii. Smith,[7] *b.* 2d August, 1792; *d.* —, 1835, without issue.
iii. Chastain,[7] *b.* 1st February, 1795; *d.* 16th December, 1838, unmarried.
iv. Mary,[7] *b.* 21st October, 1796; *m.* 18th April, 1816, Charles Warner Lewis Carter, M. D. (*b.* August, 1773; *d.* 7th November, 1867), son of Edward and Mary Randolph (Lewis) Carter.
v. Martha,[7] *b.* 14th June, 1799; *d.* 12th July, 1874; *m.* 1st February, 1825, Valentine Wood *Southall*,[h] his second

---

h Son of Major Stephen and Martha (Wood) Southall; grandson of Turner and Elizabeth (Barret) Southall, and great-grandson of Dacey and Martha (daughter of Nathaniel Vandervall) Southall, who settled in Henrico county about 1750. See *Standard*, October 9, 1880, for "The Southall Family." Martha, wife of Major Stephen Southall, was the daughter of Valentine and Lucy (Henry, daughter of Colonel John,

wife (*b.* 1793; *d.* 22d August, 1861), of Charlottesville, Virginia; distinguished lawyer; Speaker of the House of Delegates of Virginia and member of the Virginia Convention of 1850–'1 and 1861; *m.* 1st, Mary Anne, daughter of Alexander *Garrett*, and had issue. William Garrett,[8] *d.* in infancy.

Issue of Charles Warner Lewis and Mary[7] (Cocke) *Carter*:

i. Mary Lewis,[8] *b.* 13th January, 1817; *m.* 22d September, 1836, John Coles Singleton, of South Carolina (*d.* 20th September, 1852).

ii. Lucy Smith,[8] *b.* 29th July, 1819; *m.* 15th October, 1840, Peter Carr Minor (*b.* 21st March, 1816; *d.* 30th October, 1879).

iii. Charles Everett,[8] *b.* 5th February, 1821; *d.* 5th November, 1847, in the city of Mexico.

iv. Martha Champe,[8] *b.* 5th April, 1830; *m.* 6th November, 1850, Moses Green[i] Peyton, Major Confederate States Army.

Issue of John Coles and Mary Lewis[8] (Carter) *Singleton*:

i. Mary Carter,[9] *m.* Rev. Robert W. *Barnwell*, of South Carolina. Issue: i. John Singleton;[10] ii. Robert.[10]

ii. Rebecca Coles,[9] *m.* Hon. Alexander C. *Haskell*, of South Carolina. Issue: Rebecca Singleton[10] Haskell.

iii. Richard Randolph,[9] *m.* Annie Broome. Issue: i. Eliza;[10] ii. Maria;[10] iii. Lucy Champe;[10] iv. Chas. Carter;[10] v. Kate;[10] vi. Rebecca Coles.[10]

iv. Charles Carter,[9] *m.* ——.

v. John Coles,[9] *m.* Harriet B. ——. Issue: i. John;[10] ii. Mary Carter;[10] iii. Harriett;[10] iv. Lucy.[10]

vi. Lucy E.,[9] *m.* David Hemphill, of South Carolina.

Issue of Peter Carr and Lucy Smith[8] (Carter) *Minor*:

i. Frank Hugh,[9] *b.* 29th November, 1842; *d.* 11th October, 1870. In the Confederate States Army.

ii. Charles Carter,[9] *b.* 18th August, 1844.

---

and sister of Patrick Henry the orator) Wood. See "The Henry Family," *Standard*, May 29, 1880.

i Moses Green was Adjutant-General of Virginia during the war of 1812.

Issue of Major Moses Green and Martha Champe[8] (Carter) *Peyton*.

i. Bernard,[9] A. M. of the University of Virginia; medalist of the Jefferson Literary Society; practiced law in Richmond, Virginia, for several years, and was associate editor with William Lawrence Royall, of *The Commonwealth*; general counsellor of the Georgia Pacific Railroad; with brilliant prospects before him, he was killed in a railroad accident near Atlanta, Georgia, 14th December, 1885.
ii. Charles Carter,[9] *m.* Elizabeth Kendrick.
iii. Champe Carter.[9]
iv. Mary Carter.[9]
v. Julia Amanda.[9]
vi. Imogene.[9]

Issue of Valentine Wood and Martha[7] (Cocke) *Southall*:

i. William Henry,[8] *b.* 14th August, 1826; *m.* 10th January, 1849, Bettie Allen.
ii. James Cocke,[8] LL.D., *b.* 2d September, 1828; *m.* 10th November, 1869, Eliza F. Sharp (*b.* 28th May, 1836); author and scientist; editor of Richmond *Examiner*, and joint editor with Rev. William T. Richardson, D. D., of the *Central Presbyterian*.
iii. Stephen Valentine,[8] *b.* 27th April, 1830; prominent lawyer of Charlottesville, Virginia; *m.* 8th February, 1866, Emily Gordon Voss.
iv. Lucy Smith,[8] *b.* 12th April, 1833; *m.* November, 1856, Charles Sharp, of Norfolk, Virginia (*b.* 1828).
v. Mary Martha,[8] *b.* 19th November, 1834; *m.* twice: 1st, April, 1858, Colonel John Thompson Brown, lawyer; Colonel Confederate States Artillery; (killed at the battle of the Wilderness, May, 1864); 2d, 5th July, 1876, Charles Scott *Venable*,[j] Colonel Confederate States Army, on the staff of General R. E. Lee; Professor of Mathematics, University of Virginia, from 1866; Chairman of its Faculty 1870–'73. Issue: Charles, *b.* 1877.

---

j See the *Standard*, November 27, December 4, 1880, for "The Venable Family."

vi. Florence Carter,[8] *b.* 29th September, 1836; *d.* 20th January, 1854.

Issue of William Henry[8] and Bettie (Allen) *Southall:*

i. Joseph Allen,[9] *b.* 5th April, 1854.
ii. Lizzie Lyle,[9] *b.* 12th August, 1858; *m.* 20th April, 1881, Ludolph Wilhelm *Gunther*, Jr., of Baltimore, Maryland. Issue: Maude Cecil,[10] *b.* February, 1882.
iii. Valentine,[9] *b.* 16th June, 1863.
iv. William,[9] *b.* 25th November, 1864.
v. Thompson Brown,[9] *b.* December 1866.

Issue of Dr. James Cocke[8] and Eliza F. (Sharp) *Southall:*

i. James Powell Cocke,[9] *b.* 4th April 1871.
ii. Evelyn Henry,[9] *b.* 10th April, 1873.

Issue of Stephen Valentine[8] and Emily Gordon (Voss) *Southall:*

i. Mary Stuart,[9] *b.* December, 1866.
ii. Martha Cocke,[9] *b.* November, 1867.
iii. Emily,[9] *b.* April, 1869.
iv. Valentine,[9] *b.* May, 1871.

Issue of Charles and Lucy Smith[8] (Southall) *Sharp:*

i. Florence Southall,[9] *b.* September, 1857.
ii. William Willoughby Southall,[9] *b.* October, 1861.

Issue of Stephen[6] and Jane Segar (Eggleston) *Cocke:*

i. Joseph Eggleston,[7] *m.* Anne Mosby. No issue.
ii. James Powell,[7] *m.* Caroline Lewis.
iii. Charles,[7] *m.* Sarah W. Taylor.
iv. Judith,[7] *m.* Peterfield Archer.
v. Mary C.,[7] *m.* Richard Archer.
vi. Martha,[7] *m.* W. T. Eggleston.
vii Nancy,[7] *d.* young.
viii. Jane Segar,[7] *m.* James Hobson.

INDEX.

COMMUNICATION FROM

Governor Francis Nicholson

OF VIRGINIA,

TO THE BRITISH LORDS OF TRADE,

Concerning the Huguenot Settlement,

WITH "LIST OF YE REFUGEES,"

AUGUST 12TH, 1700.

COMMUNICATION FROM

Governor Francis Nicholson

OF VIRGINIA.

VIRGINIA, JAMES CITY, August 12, 1700.[86]

P. R. O.
Am. & W. Ind. } May it please Yo'r Lordp.:
No. 638.

[Extract.]

The 24th of the last month, I had the good Fortune of receiving his Ma'y's Royal Commands of March ye 18th, 1$\frac{699}{700}$, sent me by yo'r Lord'p, concerning the Marquis de la Muce, Mons'r de Sailly, and other French Protestant Refugees; and I beg leave to assure yo'r Lord'p, that as I have, so I will endeavor to obey them (they were on board the ship Mary and Ann, of London, George Haws, Commander, who had about 13 weeks passage, and the 23d of the last month arrived at the mouth of this River), and upon receipt of them, I immediately went down to Kickotan, to give directions in order to their coming hither, some of wh. came on Sunday in the evening, the rest the next day. I wrote to Colo. Byrd and Colo. Harrison to meet them here, w'ch they did, and we concluded that there was

---

[86] Kindly communicated to the editor by W. Noel Sainsbury, Esq., of the Public Record Office, London, England. The list of the refugees subjoined presents some names not given in the lists included in *Documents relating to the Huguenot Emigration to Virginia, Collections of the Virginia Historical Society, New Series*, Vol. V.

no settling them in Norfolk nor thereabouts, because esteemed an unhealthfull place, and no vacant land, except some that is in dispute now betwixt us and No. Carolina: So we thought it would be best for them to go to a place about twenty miles above the Falls of James River, commonly called the Manikin Town. There is a great deal of good Land and unpatented, where they may at present be all together, w'ch we thought would be best for his Ma'ty's Service and Interests, and that they would be astrengthing to the Frontiers, and would quickly make a settlement, not only for themselves, but to receive others when his majesty shall be graciously pleased to send them. They may be prejudicial to his Ma'ty's interest and Service, vizt., by living long together, and using their own language and customs, and by going upon such manufactures, and handicraft Trades, as we are furnished with from England; but according to duty, I shall endeavour to regulate these affairs, and when, please God, the Council meets, I shall lay before them the matters relating to these Refugees. On Tuesday I mustered them, and No. 1 is a copy of the List of them. Colo. Byrd went before them in order to meet them at the Falls of this River, where he formerly lived, to dispose of them thereabouts, till they can gett housses or sheds in the place for their Reception, and he promised to go along with the Marquis and Mons'r de Sailly to show them the Land. The people at present seem to be very well affected towards them, and to commiserate their condition, and some who have seen them have given them money, viz: Colo. Harrison, 5£; Mr. Commissary Blair, the like Sum. The Reverend Mr. Stephen Touaie, thereabouts; Mr. Benjamin Harrison, 5£; Mr. Attorney General Fowler, something, as likewise Mr. William Edwards, Merchant of this place. I am apt to think that Several Gentlemen and others will be charitable to them. They went from hence yesterday.

If his majesty be graciously pleased to send over more, I humbly propose that Mr. Micajah Perry, merchant of London, may be spoken with about their passage hither, and that they may have their passage on board the Ships which come to the upper parts of James River, w'ch is the nighest place to their settlement, and that there may not above 40 or 50 come in any one Ship: So they may be better accommodated in all respects, for I have observed that when Ships that come into these parts, are crowded with people, 'tis very prejudicial to their health; some getting sicknesses, w'ch not seldom prove catching, some dy on board, and others soon after they come on shore.

Your Lord'ps' dutifull and faithfull humble servant.

FFRS. NICHOLSON.

[Endorsement]. The Gov'r of Virginia.
2 Aug., 1700.
R. 21 Octob.
Accounts of proceedings there, &c.

LIST OF YE REFUGEES.

Pierre Delomè, et sa femme.
Marguerite Sene, et sa fille.
Magdalaine Mertle, Jean Vidau.
Tertulien Sehult, et sa femme et deux enfants.
Pierre Lauret, Jean Roger.
Pierre Chastain, sa femme et cinq enfants.
Philippe Duvivier.
Pierre Nace, sa femme et Leur deux filles.
François Clere, Symon Sardin.
Soubragon, et Jacques Nicolay.
Pierre du Loy, Abraham Nicod.
Pierre Mallet, Françoise Coupet.
Jean Oger, sa femme et trois enfants.
Jean Saye, Elizabet Angeliere.
Jean et Claude Mallefant, avec leur mere.
Isaac Chabanas, sou fils, et Catharine Bomard.
Estienne Chastain, Adam Vignes.
Jean Menager et Jean Lesnard.
Estienne Badoüet, Pierre Morriset.
Jedron Chamboux, et sa femme.
Jean Farry et Jerome Dumas.
Joseph Bourgoian, David Bernard.
Jean Chevas, et sa femme.
Jean Tardieu, Jean Moreau.

Jaques Roy, et sa femme.
Abraham Sablet, et des deux enfants.
Quintin Chastatain et Michael Roux.
Jean Quictet, sa femme et trois enfants.
Henry Cabanis, sa femme et un enfant.
Jaques Sayte, Jean Boisson.
François Bosse, Jean Fouchie.
Françoise Sassin, Andre Cochet.
Jean Gaury, sa femme et un enfant.
Pierre Gaury, sa femme et un enfant.
Jaques Hulyre, sa femme et quatre enfants.
Pierre Perrut, et sa femme.
Isaac Panetier, Jean Parransos, sa seur.
Elie Tremson, sa femme, Elizabet Tignac.
Antoine Trouillard, Jean Bourru et Jean Bouchet.
Jaques Voyes, Elizabet Mingot.
Catharine Godwal, Pierre la Courru.
Jean et Michell Cautepie, sa femme et deux enfants.
Jaques Broret, sa femme et deux enfants.
Abraham Moulin et sa femme.
François Billot, Pierre Comte (?).
Etienne Guevin, Réné Massoneau.
François du Tartre, Isaac Verry.
Jean Parmentier, David Thonitier et sa femme.
Moyse Lewreau, Pierre Tillou.
Marie Levesque, Jean Constantin.
Claud Bardon, sa femme.
Jean Imbert et sa femme.
Elizabet Fleury, Loys du Pyn.
Jaques Richard, et sa femme.
Adam et Marie Prevost.
Jaques Viras, et sa femme.
Jaques Brousse, sou enfant.
Pierre Cornu, Louiss Bon.
Isaac Fordet, Jean Pepré.
Jean Gaillard et son fils.
Anthonie Matton, et sa femme.
Jean Lucadou, et sa femme.
Louiss Orange, sa femme et un enfant.
Daniel Taure, et deux enfants.

Pierre Cupper, Daniel Roy, Magdelain Gigou.
Pierre Grelet, Jean Jovany, sa femme, deux enfants.
Pierre Ferrier, sa femme, un enfant.
La vefve faure et quatre enfants.
Isaac Arnaud, et sa femme.
Pierre Chatanier, sa femme et son pere.
Jean Fonasse, Jaques Bibbeau, Jean March.
Catharine Billot, Marie et Symon Jourdon.
Abraham Menot, Timothy Moul, sa femme, un enfant.
Jean Savin, sa femme, un enfant.
Jean Sargeaton, sa femme, un enfant.
Claude Philipe et sa femme.
Gabriel Sturter, Pierre de Corne.
Helen Trubyer.

59 femmes ou filles.	
38 enfants.	
108 hommes.	Messrs. De la Muce
————	et de Sailly fout en
205 personnes.	tout 207 personnes.

VIRGINIA: James Town, July 31, 1700.
This is a true Copy.

OLIVIER DE LA MUCE.
CH. DE SAILLY.

Received of ye hon'ble Marquis de la Muce and Chas. de la Sailly, ye summe of nine hundred, fourty-five pounds in full for ye passage of two hundred and five people aboord ye ship Mary Ann, bound for Virginia, I say receiv'd this 19th April, 1700.

£945. GEO. HAWES.

Witness:
ALEXANDER CLEERE.

VIRGINIA: James City, July 31, 1700.
This is a true Copy.

OLIVIER DE LA MUCE.
CH DE SAILLY.

This is a true copy, the original being in the Custody of—

(Signed,) FFRS. NICHOLSON.

www.ingramcontent.com/pod-product-compliance
Lightning Source LLC
Chambersburg PA
CBHW031119020426
42333CB00012B/148
* 9 7 8 1 6 3 9 1 4 1 4 8 7 *